P9-CFL-206

"Chicken Soup for the Soul has the unique ability to change people's consciousness and make a difference in each of our lives. It certainly touched this ocean lover's soul."

Wyland
ocean artist

"The first two *Chicken Soup* books have enriched my life in a powerful fashion. It's hard to imagine, but *A 3rd Serving* tastes even better than the first two. Go ahead, indulge yourself."

Pat Williams
general manager, Orlando Magic

"Chicken Soup for the Soul is also a treat for the mind and a lift for the heart."

Norman Lear
television producer

"A 3rd Serving of Chicken Soup for the Soul is a veritable gold mine of insight and inspiration."

Thea Alexander
author, *2150 A.D.*

"A 3rd Serving of Chicken Soup for the Soul may or may not cure your cold, but it will surely open your heart. These inspiring stories are just what the doctor ordered to reduce your stress, lift your spirits and connect you to healing wisdom and the power of optimism."

Joan Borysenko, Ph.D.
author, *Minding the Body, Mending the Mind* and *Fire in the Soul*

"This is another outstanding collection of powerful, heartwarming stories, full of ideas and inspiration for life and work. *A 3rd Serving* is easily the best book in the *Chicken Soup* series."

Brian Tracy
author, *The Psychology of Achievement*

"Congratulations, chefs! Your latest dose of *Chicken Soup* has all my favorite ingredients: wit, wisdom, insight and inspiration—all blended perfectly. I want *another* helping, and another, and . . ."

Bob Moawad
chairman and CEO, Edge Learning Institute

A 3rd Serving of
CHICKEN SOUP
FOR THE SOUL

More
101 Stories To
Open The Heart And
Rekindle The Spirit

Jack Canfield
and
Mark Victor Hansen

Health Communications, Inc.
Deerfield Beach, Florida

We would like to acknowledge the following publishers and individuals for permission to reprint the following material. (Note: The stories that were penned anonymously, that are public domain or were written by Jack Canfield or Mark Victor Hansen are not included in this listing.)

We have also taken a risk with several of the stories. After an exhaustive search, we were unable to find the authors or copyright holders of the following stories which we have included in the book:

Whoever Finds This, I Love You! by Author Unknown

It's How You Play the Game That Counts by Danny Warrick

Make a Wish by LeAnne Reaves

Roles—and How We Play Them by Marie Curling

God's Jobs by Dan Sutton

If you are, or if you know, the authors or copyright holders, please contact us and we will properly credit you and reimburse you for your contribution.

(Continued on page 348)

Library of Congress Cataloging-in-Publication Data

Cataloging-in-Publication data is available from the Library of Congress.

© 1996 by Jack Canfield and Mark Victor Hansen
ISBN 1-55874-379-0 (trade paper) — ISBN 1-55874-380-4 (hard cover)

All rights reserved. Printed in the United States of America. No part of this publication may be reproduced, stored in a retrieval system or transmitted in any form or by any means, electronic, mechanical, photocopying, recording or otherwise without the written permission of the publisher.

Publisher: Health Communications, Inc.
3201 S.W. 15th Street
Deerfield Beach, FL 33442-8190

Cover re-design by Andrea Perrine Brower

Stories are Beings. You invite them to live with you. They'll teach you what they know in return for being a good host. When they're ready to move on, they'll let you know. Then you pass them on to someone else.

A Cree storyteller

With love we dedicate this book
to the over 5 million people who have
read and shared the *Chicken Soup for the Soul*
books with their families, friends, business partners,
employees, students and congregations; and
the over 5,000 readers who have sent us stories, poems
and quotes for possible inclusion in
A 3rd Helping of Chicken Soup for the Soul.
Although we couldn't use everything you sent in,
we were deeply touched by your heartfelt
intention to share yourselves and your
stories with us and our readers.
Love to you!

IN THE BLEACHERS   By Steve Moore

"I'm worried about Carl."

IN THE BLEACHERS ©1995 Steve Moore. Reprinted with permission of Universal Press Syndicate. All rights reserved.

Contents

5. A MATTER OF PERSPECTIVE

6. A MATTER OF ATTITUDE

7. OVERCOMING OBSTACLES

Acknowledgments

This third volume of *Chicken Soup for the Soul* has taken over a year to write, compile and edit. It continues to be a true labor of love for all of us, and we would like to thank the following people for their contributions, without which this book could never have been created:

Peter Vegso and Gary Seidler at Health Communications, for continuing to see the vision and for putting their full support behind us and the books.

Our wives, Georgia and Patty, and our children, Christopher, Oran, Kyle, Melanie and Elisabeth, who continue to support us with their love, emotional support, editing and story writing. We especially appreciate your support when it looks like it will never come together, but with your belief and encouragement, it always does.

Patty Aubery, who once again spent countless hours typing and retyping the manuscript as well as supervising the final production phase of the book. Patty—we couldn't have done it without you!

Nancy Mitchell, who read every story that was submitted and who spent countless hours and exhibited Herculean resourcefulness in handling the maze of permissions that had to be researched and obtained to make this book a reality.

Kim Wiele, who always gives us her important literary feedback and suggestions for improvement.

Angie Hoover, who typed many of the stories and handled most of Jack's office work in the final days of completing this book.

Heather McNamara, who helped with the editing and typing as well as the final stages of the permissions process.

Kelly Apone, who typed and edited many of the stories.

Larry and Linda Price, Laverne Lee, and Michele Nuzzo, who, in addition to keeping Jack's Foundation for Self-Esteem operating smoothly, got the Soup Kitchens for the Soul project up and running and successfully distributed over 15,000 *Chicken Soup for the Soul* books to prisoners, the homeless, welfare recipients, youths at risk and other people in need across North America.

Lisa Williams, for continuously taking care of Mark's business so he could be dedicated to the task of finishing this book.

Trudy at Office Works, Wanda Pate and Alyce Shuken, who typed the first draft of the book in record time and with very few errors. Thanks a lot!

Christine Belleris and Matthew Diener, our editors at Health Communications, for their generous efforts in bringing this book to its high state of excellence.

Dottie Walters, who continued to believe in us and constantly introduced us to people who might have a story.

The over 5,000 people who submitted stories, poems and other pieces for consideration; you all know who you are. While most of the pieces were wonderful, some just didn't fit into the overall structure of this book. However, many will be used in future volumes of *Chicken Soup for the Soul*. We will be publishing such books as *Chicken Soup for the Surviving Soul, Chicken Soup for the Grieving Soul, Chicken Soup for the Soul for Parents, Chicken Soup for the Teenage Soul,* and *Chicken Soup for the Woman's Soul.*

We also want to thank the following people who read the first *very rough* draft of over 200 stories, helped us make the final selections and made invaluable comments on how to improve the book: Steve Andreas, Kelly Apone, Gerry Beane, Michael and Madonna Billauer, Marsha Blake, Rick Canfield, Taylor and Mary Canfield, Dominic and Linda Cirincione, Kate Driesen, Jim Dyer, Thales Finchum, Judy Haldeman, Patty Hansen, Jennifer Hawthorne, Kimberly Kirberger, Randi Larsen, Sandy and Phil Limina, Donna Loesch, Michele Martin, Hanoch and Meladee McCarty, Ernie Mendes, Linda Mitchell, Christan Hummel, Cindy Palajac, Dave Rabb, Martin Rutte, Marci Shimoff, Susan Sousa, Carolyn Strickland, Diana von Welanetz Wentworth, Dottie Walters, Lilly Walters, Harold Clive Wells (Jack's co-author on *100 Ways to Enhance Self-Concept in the Classroom*), Kathy Wiele, Niki Wiele, Martha Wigglesworth and Maureen Wilcinski.

And the following people who contributed in other important ways: Tricia Serfas; John Hotz at Economics Press for always helping when we needed him; Brian Cavanaugh, who was the source of many of the quotations we used; Trevor Dickinson, for all the quotes he sent to us; Pam Finger, whose newsletter is a constant source of inspiration to us; Jillian Manus, for the information on writers who faced rejection and persevered to become famous; Bob Proctor, for sending us so many stories to consider; Ruth Stotter, for her wonderful collection of quotes on stories and storytelling; Dena Sherman at the BookStar in Torrance, California, for always being there when we had a research question and for helping us track down some of the permissions we needed; and Arielle Ford and Kim Weiss, our publicists, who keep us on radio and television so we can get the word out.

Because of the immensity of this project we are sure we have left out the names of some very important people who helped us along the way. You know who you are. Please know that we apologize for the oversight and that we really do appreciate all of you from the bottom of our hearts for your caring and your efforts. We are truly grateful for the many hands that made this book possible. We love you all!

Introduction

God created man because he loves stories.
Elie Wiesel

From our hearts to yours, we are delighted to offer you *A 3rd Helping of Chicken Soup for the Soul.* This book contains over 100 stories that we know will inspire and motivate you to love more unconditionally, live more passionately and pursue your heartfelt dreams with more conviction. This book will sustain you in times of challenge, frustration and failure, and comfort you in times of confusion, pain and loss. It will truly become a lifelong companion, offering continual insight and wisdom on many areas of your life.

We believe you are about to experience a truly remarkable book. Our first three books, *Chicken Soup for the Soul, A 2nd Helping of Chicken Soup for the Soul* and the *Chicken Soup for the Soul Cookbook,* have deeply touched the lives of over 6 million readers worldwide. In the hundreds of letters that we receive every week, we read of the miracles of transformation that have been occurring for individuals and organizations that have been reading and using the books. They report that the love, hope, encouragement

and inspiration they have found in these stories has profoundly impacted their lives.

> *A story may illuminate our relationship to others,*
> *encourage compassion, create a sense of wonder, or*
> *sanction the concept "We are all in this together." A*
> *story can make us ponder why we are here. . . . A story*
> *may shock us into recognizing a new truth, provide a*
> *new perspective, a new way to perceive the universe.*
>
> Ruth Stotter

After reading the reports of how our first book power-
fully touched so many lives, we are now more convinced
than ever that stories are one of the most potent ways to
transform our lives. They speak directly to the subconscious mind. They lay down blueprints for living. They
offer solutions to our everyday problems and they
model behavior that works. They remind us of our grand
nature and our infinite possibilities. They awaken us
from our habitual day-to-day lives, invite us to dream,
and inspire us to do more and be more than we might
have originally thought possible. They remind us of
what is most important and they model for us the
expression of our highest ideals.

How to Read This Book

This book can be read all at once in one sitting—many
people have done that with good results. We, however,
recommend that you slow down and take your time,
savoring each story like a glass of fine wine—in little sips
that will give you the time to reflect upon the meanings
and implications for your life of each story. If you take the

time, you will find that each story will deeply nourish your heart, mind and soul in a different way.

> *A Zuni once asked an anthropologist, who was carefully writing down a story, "When I tell you these stories, do you see it, or do you just write it down?"*
>
> Dennis Tedlock

> *The word "story" comes from "storehouse." So a story is a store or a storehouse. Things are actually stored in the story, and what tends to be stored there is its meaning.*
>
> Michael Meade

Each and every story in this book contains possible meanings for your life. Take the time to reflect upon and discern that deeper meaning for your life.

> *We really don't learn anything from our experience. We only learn from reflecting on our experience.*
>
> Robert Sinclair

Many of the stories, when we first found them, or when they were first submitted to us, had predigested morals and prescriptions for living at the end of them. For the most part, we have removed the moralizing and preaching from the stories so that they stand alone and allow you to take your own meanings from them.

> *A disciple once complained, "You tell us stories, but you never reveal their meaning to us."*
> *The master replied, "How would you like it if someone offered you fruit and chewed it up for you before giving it to you?"*
>
> Source Unknown

Share These Stories with Others

Stories can teach, correct errors, lighten the heart and the darkness, provide psychic shelter, assist transformation and heal wounds.

Clarissa Pinkola Estes

What a gift a story is!

Diane MacInnes

Some of the stories you read will move you to share them with a loved one or a friend. When a story really touches you to the depths of your soul, close your eyes ever so briefly and ask yourself, "Who needs to hear this story right now?" Someone you care about may come to mind. Take the time to go to that person or call, and share the story. You will get something even deeper for yourself from sharing the story with someone you care about.

Consider sharing these stories at work, at church, synagogue or temple, and at home with your family.

Stories are stepping stones on the path to spiritual enlightenment.

Ruth Stotter

After sharing a story, discuss how it affected you and why you were drawn to share it with the other person or people. And most important, let these stories inspire you to share your own stories.

Reading about, telling and listening to each others' stories can be very transformational. Stories are powerful vehicles that release our unconscious energies to heal, to integrate, to express and to grow. Hundreds of readers have told us about how the first two books of *Chicken Soup* stories opened a floodgate of emotions and facilitated deep family and group sharings. Family members started recalling and relating important experiences in their lives and began to bring those to the dinner table, the family meeting, the classroom, the support group, the church fellowship and even the workplace.

> *To Navajos, a person's worth is determined by the stories and songs she or he knows, because it is by this knowledge that an individual is linked to the history of the entire group.*
>
> Luci Tapahonso

Ministers, rabbis, psychologists, counselors, trainers and support group leaders have been starting and ending their sermons, meetings and counseling sessions with stories from the book. We encourage you to do this too. People are hungry for this nurturance for the soul. It takes so little time and it can have such long-term impact.

We also encourage you to begin telling *your* stories to those around you. People may need to hear your story. As several stories in this book will point out, your story might even save a life.

> *Stories are love gifts.*
>
> Lewis Carroll

Many people have inspired us with their stories over the years, and we are grateful to them. We hope that in some small way, we will be part of inspiring you to love and to live more fully. If we achieve that, then we have been successful.

Finally, we would love to hear about your reactions to

this book. Please write to us and tell us how these stories affect you. Also, we invite you to become part of this wonderful "network of upliftment" by sending us your stories.

Stories are like fairy gold. The more you give away the more you have.

Polly McGuire

Please send us any stories, poems and cartoons you think we should include in future volumes of *Chicken Soup for the Soul*. See page 333 for our address. We look forward to hearing from you. Until then . . . may you enjoy reading *A 3rd Serving of Chicken Soup for the Soul* as much as we have enjoyed compiling, editing and writing it.

Jack Canfield and Mark Victor Hansen

1

ON LOVE

Love conquers all.

Virgil

A Secret Promise Kept

The appointment I was on my way to was very important; I was very late and very lost. With my male ego in check, I began to look for a place to ask directions, preferably a gas station. Since I had been crisscrossing the city, my gas gauge was perilously low and time was of the essence.

I spotted the amber glow of light outside the local fire station. What better place to ask directions?

I quickly stepped from my car and crossed the street to the station. All three overhead doors were open and I could see red fire engines with their doors ajar, chrome shining, waiting in anticipation for the bell to ring.

As I stepped inside, the aroma of the station assaulted me. It was the smell of the hoses drying in the tower, the oversized rubber boots, jackets and helmets. These smells, mixed in with the freshly washed floors and polished trucks, created that mysterious scent associated with all fire stations. Slowing down, I took a deep breath, closed my eyes and was transported back to my youth, to the fire station where my father worked for 35 years as head of fire maintenance.

I looked down to the end of the fire station and there it stood, sparkling gold to the sky, the fire pole. One day my dad let me and my older brother Jay slide down the pole, twice. In the corner of the station was the "creeper" used to slide under trucks when repairing them. Dad would say "Hold on" and he would spin me around until I was dizzy as a drunken sailor. It was better than any Tilt-A-Whirl ride I have ever been on.

Next to the creeper was an old soda machine that had the classic Coca-Cola logo on it. It still dispensed the original green 10-ounce bottles, but they were now 35 cents compared with the 10 cents they were back then. A trip to the soda machine was always the highlight of the visit with Dad to the station, my very own bottle of soda.

When I was 10 years old, I took two of my friends by the station to show off my dad and see if we could weasel some sodas out of him. After showing them around the station, I asked Dad if we could each have a soda before we went home for lunch.

I detected just the slightest hesitation in my father's voice that day, but he said "Sure" and gave us each a dime. We raced to the soda machine to see if our bottle had a cap with the illustrious star on the inside.

What a lucky day! My cap had a star. I was only two caps away from sending for my very own Davy Crockett hat.

We all thanked my father and headed home for lunch and a summer afternoon of swimming.

I came home early that day from the lake, and as I walked down the hall I heard my parents talking. Mom seemed upset with Dad, and then I heard my name mentioned: "You should have just said you didn't have money for sodas. Brian would have understood. That money was for your lunch. The kids have to understand that we don't have any extra money and you need to have your lunch."

My dad, in his usual way, just shrugged it off.

Before my mother knew I had overheard the conversation, I hurried up the stairs to the room I shared with my four brothers.

As I emptied my pockets, the bottle cap that had caused so many problems fell to the floor. I picked it up and was ready to put it with the other seven when I realized how great a sacrifice my father had made for that bottle cap.

That night I made a promise of repayment. Someday I would be able to tell my father that I knew of the sacrifice he made that afternoon and so many other days, and I would never forget him for it.

My father had his first heart attack at the young age of 47. I guess his lifestyle of working three jobs to support the nine of us finally caught up to him. On the evening of my parents' 25th anniversary, surrounded by all his family, the biggest, loudest, strongest of us all showed the first crack in the armor we as children thought would always be impenetrable.

Over the next eight years, my father battled back and forth, suffering another three heart attacks until he ended up with a pacemaker.

One afternoon my dad's old blue Plymouth wagon broke down, and he called me for a ride to take him to the doctor for his annual checkup. As I pulled into the station, I saw my dad outside with all the other firemen crowded around a brand-new pickup truck. It was a deep blue Ford pickup, and it was a beauty. I mentioned to my dad how nice it was, and he commented that someday he would own a truck like that.

We both laughed. This was always his dream—and it always seemed so unattainable.

At this point in my personal life, I was doing quite well in business, as were all my brothers. We offered to buy him a truck, but as he so aptly put it, "If I don't buy it, I won't feel like it's mine."

As my dad stepped out of the doctor's office I figured the gray pasty look on his face was from being poked, prodded and pricked with needles.

"Let's go," was all he said.

As we got into the car, I knew something was wrong. We drove off in silence and I knew Dad would tell me what was wrong in his own way.

I took the long way back to the station. As we drove by our old house, the ball field, lake and corner store, my dad started talking about the past and the memories each place held.

That's when I knew he was dying.

He looked at me and nodded.

I understood.

We stopped at Cabot's Ice Cream and had an ice cream together for the first time alone in 15 years. We talked, really talked that day. He told me how proud he was of all of us and that he wasn't afraid of dying. His fear was that he was going to be away from my mother.

I chuckled at him; never had a man been more in love with a woman than my dad.

He made me promise that day that I would never tell anyone of his impending death. As I agreed to his wishes, I knew that it was one of the toughest secrets I would ever have to keep.

At the time, my wife and I were looking for a new car or truck. My father knew the salesman at Cochituate Motors in Wayland, so I asked him if he would go with me to see what I could get for a trade-in toward a new car or truck.

As we entered the showroom, and I started talking with the salesman, I spotted Dad looking at the most beautiful, fully loaded chocolate-brown metal-flake pickup truck he or I had ever seen. I saw my dad run his hand over the truck like a sculptor checking his work.

"Dad, I think I should buy a truck. I want to look at

something small that is good on gas mileage."

As the salesman left the showroom to get the dealer plate, I suggested that we take the brown truck out for a ride.

"You can't afford this," he said.

"I know that, and you know that, but the salesman doesn't," I said.

As we pulled out onto Route 27, with my father behind the wheel, we both laughed like a couple of kids at the fast one we had pulled off. He drove for 10 minutes, commenting about how beautifully it rode while I played with all the bells and whistles.

When we returned to the showroom, we took out a small blue Sundowner truck. My dad commented that this was a better truck for commuting because of gas and all the miles I would be driving. I agreed with him and we returned and finalized the deal with the salesman.

I called my dad a few nights later and asked him if he would come with me to pick up the truck. I think he agreed so quickly just to get one final look at "his brown truck," as he called it.

When we pulled into the dealer's yard, there was my little blue Sundowner with a sold sticker on it. Next to it was the brown pickup, all washed and shiny, with a big SOLD sign on the window.

I glanced over at my father and saw the disappointment register on his face as he said, "Someone bought himself a beautiful truck."

I just nodded and said, "Dad, would you go inside and tell the salesman I'll be right in as soon as I park the car?" As my father walked past the brown truck, he ran his hand along it and I could see the look of disappointment pass over him again.

I pulled my car around to the far side of the building and looked out the window at the man who had given up everything for his family. I watched as the salesman sat him down, handed him a set of keys to his truck—the brown one—and explained that it was for him from me and this was our secret.

My dad looked out the window, our eyes met, and we both nodded and laughed at each other.

I was waiting outside my house when my dad pulled up that night. As he stepped out of his truck, I gave him a big hug and a kiss and told him how much I loved him, and reminded him this was our secret.

We went for a drive that evening. Dad said he understood the truck, but what was the significance of the Coca-Cola bottle cap with the star in the center taped to the steering wheel?

Brian Keefe

A Sandpiper to Bring You Joy

Several years ago, a neighbor related to me an experience that happened to her one winter on a beach in Washington State. The incident stuck in my mind and I took note of what she said. Later, at a writers' conference, the conversation came back to me and I felt I had to set it down. Here is her story, as haunting to me now as when I first heard it:

She was six years old when I first met her on the beach near where I live. I drive to this beach, a distance of three or four miles, whenever the world begins to close in on me.

She was building a sand castle or something and looked up, her eyes as blue as the sea.

"Hello," she said. I answered with a nod, not really in the mood to bother with a small child.

"I'm building," she said.

"I see that. What is it?" I asked, not caring.

"Oh, I don't know. I just like the feel of the sand."

That sounds good, I thought, and slipped off my shoes. A sandpiper glided by.

"That's a joy," the child said.

"It's what?"

"It's a joy. My mama says sandpipers come to bring us joy."

The bird went glissading down the beach. "Good-bye, joy," I muttered to myself, "hello, pain," and turned to walk on. I was depressed; my life seemed completely out of balance.

"What's your name?" She wouldn't give up.

"Ruth," I answered. "I'm Ruth Peterson."

"Mine's Windy." It sounded like Windy. "And I'm six."

"Hi, Windy."

She giggled. "You're funny," she said. In spite of my gloom I laughed too and walked on.

Her musical giggle followed me. "Come again, Mrs. P.," she called. "We'll have another happy day."

The days and weeks that followed belonged to others: a group of unruly Boy Scouts, PTA meetings, an ailing mother.

The sun was shining one morning as I took my hands out of the dishwater. "I need a sandpiper," I said to myself, gathering up my coat.

The never-changing balm of the seashore awaited me. The breeze was chilly, but I strode along, trying to recapture the serenity I needed. I had forgotten the child and was startled when she appeared.

"Hello, Mrs. P.," she said. "Do you want to play?"

"What did you have in mind?" I asked, with a twinge of annoyance.

"I don't know. You say."

"How about charades?" I asked sarcastically.

The tinkling laughter burst forth again. "I don't know what that is."

"Then let's just walk." Looking at her, I noticed the delicate fairness of her face.

"Where do you live?" I asked.

"Over there." She pointed toward a row of summer cottages. Strange, I thought, in winter.

"Where do you go to school?"

"I don't go to school. Mommy says we're on vacation."

She chattered little-girl talk as we strolled up the beach, but my mind was on other things. When I left for home, Windy said it had been a happy day. Feeling surprisingly better, I smiled at her and agreed.

Three weeks later, I rushed to my beach in a state of near panic. I was in no mood even to greet Windy. I thought I saw her mother on the porch and felt like demanding she keep her child at home.

"Look, if you don't mind," I said crossly when Windy caught up with me, "I'd rather be alone today." She seemed unusually pale and out of breath.

"Why?" she asked.

I turned on her and shouted, "Because my mother died!"—and thought, my God, why was I saying this to a little child?

"Oh," she said quietly, "then this is a bad day."

"Yes, and yesterday and the day before that and—oh, go away!"

"Did it hurt?"

"Did what hurt?" I was exasperated with her, with myself.

"When she died?"

"Of course it hurt!" I snapped, misunderstanding, wrapped up in myself. I strode off.

A month or so after that, when I next went to the beach, she wasn't there. Feeling guilty, ashamed and admitting to myself I missed her, I went up to the cottage after my walk and knocked at the door. A drawn-looking young woman with honey-colored hair opened the door.

"Hello," I said. "I'm Ruth Peterson. I missed your little girl today and wondered where she was."

"Oh yes, Mrs. Peterson, please come in."

"Wendy talked of you so much. I'm afraid I allowed her to bother you. If she was a nuisance, please accept my apologies."

"Not at all—she's a delightful child," I said, suddenly realizing that I meant it. "Where is she?"

"Wendy died last week, Mrs. Peterson. She had leukemia. Maybe she didn't tell you."

Struck dumb, I groped for a chair. My breath caught.

"She loved this beach; so when she asked to come, we couldn't say no. She seemed so much better here and had a lot of what she called happy days. But the last few weeks she declined rapidly. . . ." Her voice faltered. "She left something for you . . . if only I can find it. Could you wait a moment while I look?"

I nodded stupidly, my mind racing for something, anything, to say to this lovely young woman.

She handed me a smeared envelope, with MRS. P printed in bold, childish letters.

Inside was a drawing in bright crayon hues—a yellow beach, a blue sea, a brown bird. Underneath was carefully printed:

A SANDPIPER TO BRING YOU JOY

Tears welled up in my eyes, and a heart that had almost forgotten how to love opened wide. I took Wendy's mother in my arms. "I'm sorry, I'm sorry, I'm so sorry," I muttered over and over, and we wept together.

The precious little picture is framed now and hangs in my study. Six words—one for each year of her life—that speak to me of inner harmony, courage, undemanding love. A gift from a child with sea-blue eyes and hair the color of sand—who taught me the gift of love.

Mary Sherman Hilbert

The Most Caring Child

Author and lecturer Leo Buscaglia once talked about a contest he was asked to judge. The purpose of the contest was to find the most caring child. The winner was a four-year-old child whose next-door neighbor was an elderly gentleman who had recently lost his wife. Upon seeing the man cry, the little boy went into the old gentleman's yard, climbed onto his lap and just sat there. When his mother asked him what he had said to the neighbor, the little boy said, "Nothing, I just helped him cry."

Ellen Kreidman
Submitted by Donna Bernard

ZIGGY© ZIGGY AND FRIENDS, INC. Reprinted with permission of Universal Press Syndicate. All rights reserved.

Information Please

When I was quite young, my family had one of the first telephones in our neighborhood. I remember well the polished oak case fastened to the wall on the lower stair landing. The shiny receiver hung on the side of the box. I even remember the number—105. I was too little to reach the telephone, but used to listen with fascination when my mother talked to it. Once she lifted me up to speak to my father, who was away on business. Magic!

Then I discovered that somewhere inside that wonderful device lived an amazing person—her name was "Information Please" and there was nothing she did not know. My mother could ask her for anybody's number; when our clock ran down, Information Please immediately supplied the correct time.

My first personal experience with this genie-in-the-receiver came one day while my mother was visiting a neighbor. Amusing myself at the toolbench in the basement, I whacked my finger with a hammer. The pain was terrible, but there didn't seem to be much use crying because there was no one home to offer sympathy. I walked around the house sucking my throbbing finger, finally arriving at the stairway. The telephone! Quickly I ran for the footstool in the parlor and dragged it to the landing. Climbing up, I unhooked the receiver and held it to my ear. "Information Please," I said into the mouthpiece just above my head.

A click or two, and a small, clear voice spoke into my ear. "Information."

"I hurt my fingerrr—" I wailed into the phone. The tears came readily enough, now that I had an audience.

"Isn't your mother home?" came the question.

"Nobody's home but me," I blubbered.

"Are you bleeding?"

"No," I replied. "I hit it with the hammer and it hurts."

"Can you open your icebox?" she asked. I said I could.

"Then chip off a little piece of ice and hold it on your finger. That will stop the hurt. Be careful when you use the ice pick," she admonished. "And don't cry. You'll be all right."

After that, I called Information Please for everything. I asked for help with my geography and she told me where Philadelphia was, and the Orinoco—the romantic river I was going to explore when I grew up. She helped me with my arithmetic, and she told me that a pet chipmunk—I had caught him in the park just the day before—would eat fruit and nuts.

And there was the time that Petey, our pet canary, died. I called Information Please and told her the sad story. She listened, then said the usual things grown-ups say to soothe a child. But I was unconsoled: Why was it that birds should sing so beautifully and bring joy to whole families, only to end as a heap of feathers feet up, on the bottom of a cage?

She must have sensed my deep concern, for she said quietly, "Paul, always remember that there are other worlds to sing in."

Somehow I felt better.

Another day I was at the telephone. "Information," said the now familiar voice.

"How do you spell fix?" I asked.

"Fix something? F-I-X."

At that instant my sister, who took unholy joy in scaring me, jumped off the stairs at me with a banshee shriek—"Yaaaaaaaaaa!" I fell off the stool, pulling the receiver out of the box by its roots. We were both terrified—Information Please was no longer there, and I was not at all sure that I hadn't hurt her when I pulled the receiver out.

Minutes later there was a man on the porch. "I'm a telephone repairman. I was working down the street and the operator said there might be some trouble at this number." He reached for the receiver in my hand. "What happened?"

I told him.

"Well, we can fix that in a minute or two." He opened the telephone box, exposing a maze of wires and coils, and fiddled for a while with the end of the receiver cord, tightening things with a small screwdriver. He jiggled the hook up and down a few times, then spoke into the phone. "Hi, this is Pete. Everything's under control at 105. The kid's sister scared him and he pulled the cord out of the box."

He hung up, smiled, gave me a pat on the head and walked out the door.

All this took place in a small town in the Pacific Northwest. Then, when I was nine years old, we moved across the country to Boston—and I missed my mentor acutely. Information Please belonged in that old wooden box back home, and I somehow never thought of trying the tall, skinny new phone that sat on a small table in the hall.

Yet, as I grew into my teens, the memories of those childhood conversations never really left me; often in moments of doubt and perplexity I would recall the serene sense of security I had when I knew that I could call Information Please and get the right answer. I appreciated now how very patient, understanding and kind she was to have wasted her time on a little boy.

A few years later, on my way west to college, my plane put down in Seattle. I had about half an hour between plane connections, and I spent 15 minutes or so on the phone with my sister who lived there now, happily mellowed by marriage and motherhood. Then, really without thinking what I was doing, I dialed my hometown operator and said, "Information Please."

Miraculously, I heard again the small, clear voice I knew so well: "Information."

I hadn't planned this, but I heard myself saying, "Could you tell me, please, how to spell the word 'fix'?"

There was a long pause. Then came the softly spoken answer. "I guess," said Information Please, "that your finger must have healed by now."

I laughed. "So it's really still you. I wonder if you have any idea how much you meant to me during all that time. . . ."

"I wonder," she replied, "if you know how much you meant to me? I never had any children, and I used to look forward to your calls. Silly, wasn't it?"

It didn't seem silly, but I didn't say so. Instead I told her how often I had thought of her over the years, and I asked if I could call her again when I came back to visit my sister after the first semester was over.

"Please do. Just ask for Sally."

"Good-bye, Sally." It sounded strange for Information Please to have a name. "If I run into any chipmunks, I'll tell them to eat fruit and nuts."

"Do that," she said. "And I expect one of these days you'll be off for the Orinoco. Well, good-bye."

Just three months later I was back again at the Seattle airport. A different voice answered, "Information," and I asked for Sally.

"Are you a friend?"

"Yes," I said. "An old friend."

"Then I'm sorry to have to tell you. Sally had only been working part-time in the last few years because she was ill. She died five weeks ago." But before I could hang up, she said, "Wait a minute. Did you say your name was Villiard?"

"Yes."

"Well, Sally left a message for you. She wrote it down."

"What was it?" I asked, almost knowing in advance what it would be.

"Here it is, I'll read it—'Tell him I still say there are other worlds to sing in. He'll know what I mean.'"

I thanked her and hung up. I did know what Sally meant.

Paul Villiard

Two Nickels and Five Pennies

In the days when an ice cream sundae cost much less, a 10-year-old boy entered a hotel coffee shop and sat at a table. A waitress put a glass of water in front of him. "How much is an ice cream sundae?"

"Fifty cents," replied the waitress.

The little boy pulled his hand out of his pocket and studied a number of coins in it. "How much is a dish of plain ice cream?" he inquired.

Some people were now waiting for a table and the waitress was a bit impatient. "Thirty-five cents," she said brusquely.

The little boy again counted the coins. "I'll have the plain ice cream," he said.

The waitress brought the ice cream, put the bill on the table, and walked away. The boy finished the ice cream, paid the cashier and departed. When the waitress came back, she began wiping down the table and then swallowed hard at what she saw. There, placed neatly beside the empty dish, were two nickels and five pennies—her tip.

The Best of Bits & Pieces

The Ice Cream Girl

Eleanor didn't know what was wrong with Grandma. She was always forgetting things, like where she put the sugar, when to pay her bills, and what time to be ready to be picked up for grocery shopping.

"What's wrong with Grandma?" Eleanor asked. "She used to be such a neat lady. Now she looks sad and lost and doesn't remember things."

"Grandma's just getting old," Mother said. "She needs a lot of love right now, dear."

"What's it like to get old?" Eleanor asked. "Does every-body forget things? Will I?"

"Not everyone forgets things when they get old, Eleanor. We think Grandma may have Alzheimer's dis-ease, and that makes her forget more. We may have to put her in a nursing home to get the proper care she needs."

"Oh, Mother! That's terrible! She'll miss her own little house so much, won't she?"

"Maybe, but there isn't much else we can do. She'll get good care there and make some new friends."

Eleanor looked sorrowful. She didn't like the idea at all.

"Can we go and see her often?" she asked. "I'll miss

talking to Grandma, even if she does forget things."

"We can go on weekends," Mother answered. "We can take her a present."

"Like ice cream? Grandma loves strawberry ice cream!" Eleanor smiled.

"Strawberry ice cream it is!" Mother said.

The first time they visited Grandma in the nursing home, Eleanor wanted to cry.

"Mother, almost all of the people are in wheelchairs," she said.

"They have to be. Otherwise they'd fall," Mother explained. "Now when you see Grandma, smile and tell her how nice she looks."

Grandma sat all by herself in a corner of the room they called the sun parlor. She sat looking out at the trees.

Eleanor hugged Grandma. "Look," she said, "we brought you a present—your favorite, strawberry ice cream!"

Grandma took the Dixie cup and the spoon and began eating without saying a word.

"I'm sure she's enjoying it, dear," Eleanor's mother assured her.

"But she doesn't seem to know us." Eleanor was disappointed.

"You have to give her time," Mother said. "She's in new surroundings, and she has to make an adjustment."

But the next time they visited Grandma it was the same. She ate the ice cream and smiled at them, but she didn't say anything.

"Grandma, do you know who I am?" Eleanor asked.

"You're the girl who brings me the ice cream," Grandma said.

"Yes, but I'm Eleanor, too, your granddaughter. Don't you remember me?" she asked, throwing her arms around the old lady.

Grandma smiled faintly.

"Remember? Sure I remember. You're the girl who brings me ice cream."

Suddenly Eleanor realized that Grandma would never remember her. Grandma was living in a world all her own, in a world of shadowy memories and loneliness.

"Oh, how I love you, Grandma!" she said. Just then she saw a tear roll down Grandma's cheek.

"Love," she said. "I remember love."

"You see, dear, that's all she wants," Mother said. "Love."

"I'll bring her ice cream every weekend then, and hug her even if she doesn't remember me," Eleanor said.

After all, that was more important—to remember love rather than someone's name.

Marion Schoeberlein

How Magic Helped a Blind Girl See

My friend Whit is a professional magician, and he was hired by a restaurant in Los Angeles to perform walk-around, close-up magic each evening for the patrons as they ate their dinners. One evening he walked up to a family and, after introducing himself, pulled out a deck of cards and began performing. Turning to a young girl sitting at the table, he asked her to select a card. The girl's father informed him that Wendy, his daughter, was blind.

Whit replied, "That's okay. If it's all right with her, I'd like to try a trick anyway." Turning to the girl, Whit said, "Wendy, would you like to help me with a trick?"

Being a little shy, she shrugged her shoulders and said, "Okay."

Whit took a seat across from her at the table and said, "I'm going to hold up a playing card, Wendy, and it's going to be one of two colors, either red or black. What I want you to do is use your psychic powers and tell me what color the card is, red or black. You got it?" Wendy nodded.

Whit held up the king of clubs and said, "Wendy, is this a red card or a black card?"

After a moment, the blind girl replied, "Black." Her family smiled.

Whit held up the seven of hearts and said, "Is this a red card or a black card?"

Wendy said, "Red."

Then Whit held up a third card, the three of diamonds and said, "Red or black?"

Without hesitating, Wendy said, "Red!" Her family members giggled nervously. He went through three more cards, and she got all three right. Incredibly, she was six for six! Her family couldn't believe how lucky she was.

On the seventh card, Whit held up the five of hearts and said, "Wendy, I want you to tell me the *value* and *suit* of this card . . . whether it's a heart, diamond, club or spade."

After a moment, Wendy replied confidently, "It's the five of hearts." Her family let out a gasp; they were stunned!

Her father asked Whit whether he was doing some kind of trick or real magic. Whit replied, "You'll have to ask Wendy."

The father said, "Wendy, how did you do it?" Wendy smiled and said, "It's magic!" Whit shook hands with the family, gave Wendy a hug, left his business card, and said good-bye. Clearly, he had created a magical moment that this family would never forget.

The question, of course, is how did Wendy know the color of the cards? Since Whit had never met her before that moment in the restaurant, he could not have told her ahead of time which cards were red and which were black. And since Wendy was blind, it was impossible for her to see the color or value of the cards when he held them up. How then?

Whit was able to create this once-in-a-lifetime miracle by using a secret code and some quick thinking. Earlier in his career, Whit had worked out a foot code for communicating information from one person to another without words. He had never had a chance to use the code until that moment in the restaurant. When Whit sat down across from Wendy and said, "I'm going to hold up a playing card, Wendy, and it's going to be one of two colors, either red or black," he tapped her foot (underneath the table) once when he said the word "red" and twice when he said "black."

Just to make sure she understood him, he repeated the secret signals by saying, "What I want you to do is use your psychic powers and tell me what color the card is, red (tap) or black (tap-tap), you got it?" When she nodded yes, he knew that she understood the code and was willing to play along. Her family assumed that when he asked her whether she "got it," he was referring to his verbal instructions.

How did he communicate the five of hearts to her? Simple. He tapped her foot five times to let her know it was a five. When he asked her whether the card was a heart, spade, club or diamond, he let her know the suit by tapping her foot as he said the word "heart."

The real magic of this story is the effect it had on Wendy. Not only did it give her a chance to shine for a few moments and feel special in front of her family, but it made her a star at home, as her family told all their friends about the amazing "psychic" experience.

A few months after this event took place, Whit received a package from Wendy. It contained a deck of Braille playing cards, along with a letter. In the letter, she thanked him for making her feel so special, and for helping her "see" for just a few moments. She said that she still hadn't told her family how she did the trick, even though they kept asking her. She concluded by saying that she wanted him to have the deck of Braille cards so he could come up with more tricks for blind people.

Michael Jeffreys

The Horai Box

I am only one, but still I am one; I cannot do everything, but still I can do something; and because I cannot do everything I will not refuse to do the something that I can do.

Edward E. Hale

"What part of 'no' don't you understand?" I asked Larry, my physician husband, when he insisted that I accompany him to a mid-December medical seminar at Lake Tahoe, located in Northern California.

"I'd rather not drive alone," Larry pleaded. "Tell you what. We'll drive up in *Zeus* (our motor home). You'll be warm and cozy, and can sew teddy bears while I'm at the meetings. We'll eat out; no cooking and no dishes." The prospect of replacing holiday turmoil with alpine serenity appealed to me, so the next morning I found myself seated alongside Larry in *Zeus* as we headed for Tahoe. The warm sunshine that had driven off the frost in the Sacramento Valley also dissipated any misgivings I may have secretly harbored.

But later, as the road climbed above the Sierra foothills,

threatening low-slung gray clouds billowed across the sun, transforming a bright sunny morning into a bleak, chilly afternoon. Larry turned on the radio. Instead of music, we were greeted by: "This is a weather advisory. A major storm is heading for the Sierra Nevadas. Motorists should carry chains and be prepared for snow—very heavy at times."

By the time we hit Donner Summit, snow had blanketed the road; headlights could barely pierce the white maelstrom. "I should have stayed home," I complained.

Larry reassured me, "Don't worry. Instead of Tahoe, we'll go to Reno. I know a small RV park where we can hole up, near casinos and restaurants, too. We can take in some shows and live high on the hog. We should be there in less than an hour."

And so we stayed—safe and sound in an RV park—with a blizzard and a mountain between us and home. It snowed the next day, and the next, and the next. We read everything we had and time was beginning to weigh heavily on our hands when Larry sprang his idea. "Let's throw a Christmas party. Right here! We'll invite everyone in the park. They must also be going bonkers by now."

"Great!" I agreed. "Where's my writing box? I'll make the invitations." My writing box is no ordinary box. Actually it looks like a miniature Japanese *tonsu*, a chest of drawers, but it measures only 20 inches long, 12 inches high, and 8 inches deep. All the corners are covered with thin right-angled black iron, the top compartment has a hinged cover and is only deep enough for a thin charcoal ink block and brushes, and the front is inset with seven drawers of different sizes.

Each drawer has its own tiny lock and was painstakingly cut, mitered and assembled with bamboo pegs in place of nails. The wood has acquired a patina of antique umber that could only come from beeswax rubbings and doting care throughout its 200 years of existence. Larry gave it to me shortly after we were married.

I opened the drawer that contained my inks and broad-nibbed pens. In bold calligraphy strokes, I created a half-dozen invitations: POTLUCK PARTY TONIGHT, 8 PM, MOTOR HOME ZEUS, SPACE 23, BRING A DISH FOR YOU AND YOUR NEIGHBOR. We signed our names, plowed through knee-deep snow and discreetly attached the invitations to door handles of vehicles that, by now, looked like poppy seeds scattered on a white rug.

At the appointed time, jovial strangers with mouth-watering foods, drinks and treats presented themselves at the door. We gossiped, exchanged adventure stories, told jokes and sang old songs. Two hours later, the company departed as spontaneously as they had appeared.

Just as I slipped off my shoes, a knock summoned me to the door.

"Excuse us for being so late," a voice in the darkness said. "We're the Millers, in the trailer next to you."

"Come in! Come in! Never too late for a bit of cheer," I said.

"I'm Albert Miller," said the young man with the frost-reddened nose, ears and cheeks, "and this is my wife, Sally." Sally timidly extended her hand, which we shook. Then she silently and languidly sank into an overstuffed reading chair.

Al, as our guest preferred to be called, told us about his job as a computer programmer, about his home near San Francisco and about his travels through the Western states over the past two months. Sally never spoke. It was hard to tell whether she was ill, tired or bored. When the spiced tea was served, she hesitantly took a sip, then tried to put the cup and saucer aside.

But to do so she had to move the writing box, which I had inadvertently left on the coffee table. I noticed as she pushed back her chestnut hair and focused her blue-green eyes on the intriguing box, her dour mask had dropped. She was much younger than I had originally surmised— perhaps not yet 30. But before I could determine whether this transformation was real or illusory, the sullen, apathetic facade recaptured her features and she retreated once more into her private world.

Both Larry and I caught ourselves staring at Sally, so I tried to relieve the tension by expounding about the box. "Most Japanese were illiterate in the early 1800s. These boxes were used by itinerant scribes who carried their writing equipment in them as they went from village to village."

The attempt to start an exchange of words and thoughts proved useless; Sally's mind was elsewhere. Al stood up and reached for his muffler, suggesting it was time to leave. After we exchanged good nights, Al haltingly added, "Your invitation said 'bring a dish.' Sally doesn't cook. But here's a copy of her book of verse. Sally used to write—quite well."

Moments later the pair exited into the night. "I've seen that face before," Larry said as soon as our visitors departed. "No, not the Sally Miller face—but that one she was wearing. Wish I could remember where."

The next morning's brilliance and warmth more than offset the previous days' dullness and cold, as if nature was trying to compensate for her capriciousness. While Larry and I were sweeping snow off the motor home roof, Al Miller came over and inquired, "Getting ready to leave?"

"Yup. Must get back to the daily grind," Larry said.

Al stomped the snow with his boots. Was he cold? No. I couldn't help but feel that he was summoning up enough courage to say something . . . waiting for an opportune moment to speak. "Before you leave, I want to apologize for last night," he said. "Sally suffers from depression. When we received the invitation, I coaxed

Sally out of the trailer, hoping that new people or the party might cheer her up. I was wrong. I'm sorry."

Al paused, fidgeting with his long muffler, then continued, "We—that is Sally—had a baby three months ago. All of those new-parent fears and worries proved needless because the little boy was strong and healthy when he was born. After being home four days we found him dead in his crib. Doctors called it SIDS. Ever hear of it? It means Sudden Infant Death Syndrome. No warning. No cause. No cure.

"That's when Sally went into a depression. Sure, doctors gave her tranquilizers and mood elevators, but they only mask the symptoms; they really don't help. When friends suggested that we get away from home, away from those haunting memories, I bought this trailer. We've been on the road ever since. Can't say it's helping much, either."

We tried to say something comforting, but nothing seemed appropriate. We just wished each other bon voyage and went to our separate vehicles.

"Now I know where I saw Sally Miller before," Larry exclaimed. "No, not the Sally Miller next door, but her zombie-like prototype. It was during my internship in a women's psychiatric hospital, where I saw depressed, melancholy, withdrawn women—just like Sally—hopelessly imprisoned within their vacant minds and spiritless bodies.

"Poor Sally. The outlook for recovery is as dismal today as it was in the 18th century, when victims were lowered into snake pits because people believed that a shock caused the malady and therefore another shock, even more horrible, would reverse it."

Larry kicked the tires, checked the oil and prepared for the trip home. But when he came into the motor home to wash up, he caught me emptying all the drawers and cubicles in my Japanese writing box.

"What are you doing?" he asked.

"I'm giving Sally the box," I replied. "I'm going to wrap it, put a ribbon on it and give it to Sally."

"Are you out of your gourd? Have you forgotten how much it has meant to both of us? How much it cost? Why? Why? And to a perfect stranger to boot!"

If there were any compelling reasons behind my erratic behavior, I was either not aware of them or saw no need to explain them. "It's mine and I can do what I want with it," I retorted testily. Without another word, I wrapped the box, enclosed a card, bolted over to the Millers and quickly shoved it through the door.

We barely talked most of the way home, afraid that words would deepen our rift. At day's end, when cold and darkness intensified the strain between us, I broke the silence. "Remember when Sally first saw and touched the writing box? Remember how her face lit up? I figured that if she owned the box it might trigger such escapes from her depression over and over again until she was better. You know, like sometimes a single puff will make a dying ember glow but several puffs will rekindle a fire."

"Still believe in fairies," Larry shot back. "You could just as well have given her one of your teddy bears for all the good it's going to do. Sally believes that Providence is using a stacked deck in the game of life. Depression is her sanctuary. Sooner or later, she'll end up on the funny farm."

Larry's assessment kept gnawing at my conscience because I subsequently received no thank-you or other acknowledgment from the Millers. Almost a year later, however, I came home and found our precious little box sitting on a table in the entry hall, deliberately placed there so it would be the first thing seen by anyone coming through the door.

"It was delivered this afternoon," Larry said. "It was addressed to both of us, so I unwrapped it. There's a letter too, but I thought you ought to open that." I tore open the envelope and read:

Dear Kathleen and Doc:

I know I've been remiss in not writing sooner, but perhaps after reading this letter, you will understand my reasons for not doing so—and hopefully forgive me.

I vaguely remember Al handing me your gift, unwrapping it, then ignoring it as I retreated into my solitude. The next morning, the first thing I saw after waking was the box. An errant beam of sunlight highlighted it, like a spotlight on a single performer in a darkened theater. Its simple lines and exquisite craftsmanship penetrated my muddled mind. I began to perceive elegance and beauty. I played with the drawer, the locks, hinges and drawer pulls, captivated by its detail and precision.

I quickly dressed and for the first time since I became ill—yes, let's call it depression because I can face that now—I went shopping. I bought wax and buffing cloths for my new box. The next day and daily thereafter, I went out looking for pens and inks and papers, exploring new places, meeting new people and thinking of poetry again.

When we returned home several weeks later, I started going to the library to read up on Japanese arts and crafts. I learned a lot about the box and the special techniques of Japanese wood crafting. I also became entranced with the works of Lafcadio Hearn, the English literary scholar who immigrated to Japan at the turn of the century, married there and spent the rest of his life translating Japanese folk-tales, legends and classics. In one of his stories he tells about Horai, a place where there is no winter and flowers never fade—and by reason of being young at heart, the people always smile. I named my box Horai.

I also went to the museum in San Francisco, where I could learn even more about the arts and culture of Japan. I am now a docent there. Al, of course, returned to work, and I, between my new avocation, museum work and household chores, was too busy and too excited to be depressed.

At this point, when I was so happy, I suppose I should have written to you, but then I found out I was pregnant. Old fears and doubts resurfaced, and I again put off writing. In any event, we had a lovely little girl in November—now two months old—at last I find myself free of the past. I can write to you honestly, appreciatively and candidly.

I've often wondered why you gave me the box. Was it pity? Was it a thoughtless impulse? No, these didn't fit. Then, one day I learned that Horai is also called Shinkoro, which means mirage—the vision of the intangible. Now I understood that through intuition you perceived the intangible. You sensed what the gift would do.

I am returning the Horai box, not that I love it less, but so that you may have it in your hand if you ever need it to sustain another hapless soul. Should this never be the case, then I hope it will forever serve as a happy reminder of our meeting.

Sincerely and gratefully,
Sally

P.S. Our little girl is named Kathleen.

Of course I had tears running down both cheeks as I finished the letter. Larry turned away, ostensibly to clean his glasses, but in spite of his stolid medical mien and earlier prognostication, I think I detected him blotting his eyes.

Now, whenever we take *Zeus* on the road, especially around Christmas, Larry admonishes me to take the Horai box. "It's a great symbol of good will to all men," he says. "Besides, it takes up less room than a Christmas tree."

Kathleen Podolsky

This is a true story. Names and identifying characteristics of individuals involved have been changed to protect their identity.

Manuel Garcia

Manuel Garcia, a proud youthful father
Was known on his block as a hard-working man.
With a wife and a family, a job and a future
He had everything going according to plan.

One day Manuel Garcia, complaining of stomach pains
Went to the clinic to find the cause.
His body was found to have cancerous tissue
Ignoring the order of natural laws.

So Manuel Garcia of Milwaukee County
Checked into the medical complex in town.
Suddenly seeing his thirty-nine years
Like the sand in an hourglass plummeting down.

"What are my choices?" cried Manuel Garcia.
"You've basically two," was the doctor's decree.
"Your cancer untreated will quickly be fatal,
But treatment is painful with no guarantees . . . "

And so it began, Manuel's personal odyssey—
Long sleepless nights in a chemical daze
With echoes of footsteps down long lonely corridors
Tolling his minutes and hours away.

With the knowledge that something inside was
　　consuming him
Manuel Garcia was filled with despair.
He'd already lost forty pounds to the cancer,
And now to the drugs he was losing his hair.

After nine weeks in treatment the doctor came calling.
Said "Manuel, we've done about all we can do.
Your cancer could go either way at this juncture;
It's out of our hands and it's now up to you."

Manuel looked in the mirror, a sad frightened stranger
So pale, so wrinkled, so lonely, so scared.
Diseased, isolated, and feeling unlovable—
One-hundred-twenty-six pounds and no hair.

He dreamed of his Carmen at sixty without him,
His four little children not having their dad,
Of Thursday night card games at Julio's,
And everything else he'd not done that he wished that
　　he had.

Awakened from sleep on the day of his discharge
By shuffling feet going all around his bed,
Manuel opened his eyes and thought he was still
　　dreaming—
His wife, and four friends with no hair on their heads.

He blinked and he looked again, not quite believing
The five shiny heads all lined up side by side.
And still to that point not a word had been spoken,
But soon they were laughing so hard that they cried.

And the hospital hallways were ringing with voices.
"Patron, we did this for you," said his friends.
And they wheeled him out to the car they had borrowed.
"Amigo, estamos contigo ves. . . ."

So Manuel Garcia returned to his neighborhood
Dropped off in front of his two-bedroom flat.
And the block seemed unusually deserted for Sunday;
He drew a deep breath and adjusted his hat.

But before he could enter, the front door flew open.
Manuel was surrounded with faces he knew—
Fifty-odd loved ones and friends of the family
With clean-shaven heads and the words "We love you!"

And so Manuel Garcia, a person with cancer,
A father, a husband, a neighbor, a friend,
With a lump in his throat said "I'm not one for speeches,
But here I have something that needs to be said.

"I felt so alone with my baldness and cancer.
Now you stand beside me, thank Heaven above.
For giving me strength that I need may God Bless you,
And long may we live with the meaning of love.

"For giving me strength that I need may God Bless you,
And long may we live with the meaning of love."

David Roth

A Taste of Freedom

*If you find it in your heart to care for somebody
else, you will have succeeded.*

Maya Angelou

I was terrified. I was being transferred from the Federal
Correctional Institute in Pleasanton, California, to the
Women's Federal Correctional Institute in Lexington,
Kentucky, which was notorious for its overcrowding and
violence.

Eight months earlier I had been convicted of fraud for
my participation in my father's business. Since I was a
child my father had abused me physically, mentally and
sexually, so when he came to me and asked me to take my
mother's place in the family business, I still saw him
through the eyes of that five-year-old girl who knew that
no one would help and nothing ever worked. It never
occurred to me to say "No." When the FBI showed up
months later and asked if those were my signatures on
the documents, I did what I had done since the time I was
a child. I said, "Yes, it was me, not my father." I took
responsibility for the crime and was sentenced to serve

my time in a maximum-security prison.

Before I went to prison, I entered an adult survivor program and began healing my childhood wounds. I learned about the effects of long-term abuse, and also that some of the memories and traumas could be healed. Because of my experience in the program I knew the violence, the chaos and the hyper-vigilance all around me were only outward manifestations of the chaos in my own mind, so I chose to change. I began to read books of truth and wisdom and began to write affirmations to remind myself who I truly was. When I heard the voice of my father in my mind saying "You are a nothing," I replaced it with the voice of God saying "You are my beloved child." Over and over, day after day I began changing my life thought by thought.

When I received word to "pack out," I thought I was being transferred to a minimum-security camp. In order to prevent escape plans, the guards do not tell you where you are going or when you are leaving. But I was sure I had completed my journey in maximum-security prison and surely deserved to be in a minimum-security camp.

Arriving at FCI Lexington was indeed a shock. I was terrified, but I immediately had one of those serendipitous moments in which I realized I was still in the palm of God's hand. When I was taken to my housing unit, instead of having a Kentucky-sounding name like Bluegrass, like most of the other units, the name of my unit was "Renaissance." The name of my housing unit meant "rebirth." Trusting God, I knew I would be safe. I simply had more to learn to be truly reborn.

The next day I was assigned to a work detail in building maintenance. It was our job to buff floors, put up sheet rock and learn similar skills we could carry with us back into society after our stay in prison. Our guard, Mr. Lear (not his real name), was also our teacher. Mr. Lear was extraordinary in that he was funny and kind.

Normally, there are only two rules between an inmate and a guard—the inmate does not trust the guard, and the guard does not believe anything an inmate has to say. But Mr. Lear was different. He tried to make our time with him not only informative, but fun. He never bent the rules, but he did not go out of his way to make our detail miserable by being sarcastic or demeaning.

I watched Mr. Lear for many days and saw him look at me with a funny expression on his face. I got that quite often since I looked like who I was—a suburban house-wife from Kansas. I did not look like I belonged in prison.

One day, Mr. Lear and I were alone on a detail, and he finally asked me, "What in the world are you doing in prison?" I told him the truth. He listened and asked if my father was in prison too. I told him no. There had been no physical criminal evidence pointing to him and, in fact, my sister and brothers had backed him in his story that I was lying about his involvement at all.

Mr. Lear appeared angry at this and asked me, "Then why are you so happy?" I began sharing with him the simple truths that I was learning, such as happiness and peace are found within. I spoke to him about the real meaning of freedom and about how you had to first believe before you could eventually see the results of your belief.

I then asked Mr. Lear some questions. I asked how he could come to work day after day teaching inmates who did not want to listen and ask them to be enthused about a job they had no desire to do. How did he continue to stay happy and kind when he was working with people who didn't want to be there in a system that was fraught with bitterness and anger?

Mr. Lear admitted it was hard and was, in fact, not his first job choice. He told me his dream was to be a full-time military person. But he was scared to act on this dream since he had the security of the prison job and had a wife and children to support.

I told him the desire in his heart was not placed there if there was no chance of fulfillment. I told him he could do anything he wanted, and I commented on the different degrees of prison we all experience.

These conversations continued to take place over several weeks, and my feeling of safety with Mr. Lear grew. I thought he was one guard I did not have to be afraid would suddenly take out his personal frustration or anger on me by accusing me of insubordination or outright disobedience, giving me extra detail or throwing me in segregation, as quite often happens in prison—especially to women inmates.

So you can imagine how shocked and saddened I felt when, for no reason that I could think of, Mr. Lear came to me and angrily said, "Mrs. Rogoff, I want you to go into my office, clean everything you see off of every shelf in there, and don't come out until there is not one item left!"

I had no idea what I had done to upset Mr. Lear, but of course I had no choice but to obey. I said "Yes, sir," and went into his office, my face burning with humiliation. My feelings were truly hurt. I thought he was different—I thought we had spoken person to person, but in reality, I was just another inmate to him.

Mr. Lear shut the door behind me and stood with his back to the door, looking up and down the hallway. I wiped the tears from my eyes and looked at all the shelves. Slowly, a huge smile came over my face. The shelves were completely empty, except for one juicy, red-ripe tomato and a shaker of salt. Mr. Lear knew I had been in prison for almost a year and had not eaten a fresh tomato in all that time. Mr. Lear not only snuck the tomato in from his own garden, he "pinned" for me, which meant he looked out to ensure no other guard would catch me. I proceeded to eat the most delicious piece of fruit in my life.

That simple act of kindness—treating me like a human being and not a number—helped me continue my journey of healing. I knew for sure that my stay in prison was not an accident, but an opportunity to heal my abuse issues at depth so that I could later heal others.

Mr. Lear was my guard, but he was also a friend. I have not seen him nor heard about him since my release from prison, but I cannot help but think of him every time I pull a tomato from my own garden. It is my hope that Mr. Lear is as free today as I am.

Barbara Rogoff

Compassion Is in the Eyes

It was a bitter cold evening in northern Virginia many years ago. The old man's beard was glazed by winter's frost while he waited for a ride across the river. The wait seemed endless. His body became numb and stiff from the frigid north wind.

He heard the faint, steady rhythm of approaching hooves galloping along the frozen path. Anxiously, he watched as several horsemen rounded the bend. He let the first one pass by without an effort to get his attention. Then another passed by, and another. Finally, the last rider neared the spot where the old man sat like a snow statue. As this one drew near, the old man caught the rider's eye and said, "Sir, would you mind giving an old man a ride to the other side? There doesn't appear to be a passageway by foot."

Reining his horse, the rider replied, "Sure thing. Hop aboard." Seeing the old man was unable to lift his half-frozen body from the ground, the horseman dismounted and helped the old man onto the horse. The horseman took the old man not just across the river, but to his destination, which was just a few miles away.

As they neared the tiny but cozy cottage, the horse-man's curiosity caused him to inquire, "Sir, I notice that you let several other riders pass by without making an effort to secure a ride. Then I came up and you immediately asked me for a ride. I'm curious why, on such a bitter winter night, you would wait and ask the last rider. What if I had refused and left you there?"

The old man lowered himself slowly down from the horse, looked the rider straight in the eyes, and replied, "I've been around these here parts for some time. I reckon I know people pretty good." The old-timer continued, "I looked into the eyes of the other riders and immediately saw there was no concern for my situation. It would have been useless even to ask them for a ride. But when I looked into your eyes, kindness and compassion were evident. I knew, then and there, that your gentle spirit would welcome the opportunity to give me assistance in my time of need."

Those heartwarming comments touched the horseman deeply. "I'm most grateful for what you have said," he told the old man. "May I never get too busy in my own affairs that I fail to respond to the needs of others with kindness and compassion."

With that, Thomas Jefferson turned his horse around and made his way back to the White House.

Anonymous
From Brian Cavanaugh's The Sower's Seeds

Warm in Your Heart

It was a bitterly cold Denver morning. The weather was unpredictable. First, a warming trend gave the snow a chance to melt and run away, slipping from sight into the storm drains or running silently along the curbs, across side yards and under fences to the low-lying areas where it completed its vanishing act. Then the cold returned with a vengeance, bringing yet another coat of the white powdered precipitation, freezing what little remained from winter's previous blast and hiding it, an icy trap for street people.

This was a day for staying home, for having a cold and waiting for Mom to bring a cup of soup. It was a day for listening to the all-news radio and imagining the possibility of being snowbound without being too inconvenienced. That was the way the day was supposed to be.

I had a job speaking at the Denver Convention Center to a couple hundred other people who, like me, were unable to have the sniffles and stay home for Mom to bring us soup. Instead, we gathered at the convention center, unable to do more about the weather than to talk about it.

I needed a battery for my wireless microphone. What a lousy time to have gotten lazy. . . . I had failed to pack a spare. There was no choice, really. I needed a battery. So I headed into the wind, head bowed, collar up, shuffling in too-thin dress shoes.

Each step brought my thin suit pants close to my backside. The material was cold and reminded me that my mother would have never let me out of the house had she known I had dressed so foolishly.

Around the corner, I spotted a small sign announcing that a 7-Eleven convenience store was within sight. If I walked quickly and lengthened my stride, I could reach the front door and shelter from the brisk wind without drawing a breath of lung-burning air. People who live in Denver like to play with outsiders by telling them that winter in Denver means enduring a pleasant kind of cold. "It's a much drier kind of cold," report the Denver folks, when their relatives ask how they like life in the Mile-High city. Drier, my foot! It's cold enough to give the famous brass monkey reason to move. And humidity, or the lack of it, doesn't seem all that important when gusts of 40-mile-an-hour Arctic reminders are blowing against your backside.

Inside the 7-Eleven were two souls. The one behind the counter wore a name badge saying she was Roberta. Judging by her appearance, Roberta probably wished that she were home bringing hot soup and soothing words to her own little one. Instead, she was spending her day manning an outpost for commerce in a nearly abandoned, downtown Denver. She would be a beacon, a refuge for the few who were foolish enough to be out and about on a day so cold.

The other refugee from the cold was a tall, elderly gentleman who seemed comfortable with his surroundings. He was in absolutely no hurry to step back through the front door and risk sailing through town at the mercy of the wind and ice-covered sidewalks. I couldn't help but think that the gentleman had lost his mind or his way. To be out on such a day, shuffling through the merchandise of a 7-Eleven, the man must be completely daft.

I didn't have time to be concerned with an old man who had taken leave of his senses. I needed a battery, and there were a couple hundred important people who had things left to do with their lives waiting for me back at the convention center. We had a purpose.

The old man somehow found his way to the counter ahead of me. Roberta smiled. He said not a single word. Roberta picked up each of his meager purchases and entered each amount into the cash register. The old man had dragged himself into the Denver morning for a lousy muffin and a banana. What a sorry mistake that was!

For a muffin and a banana, a sane man could wait until spring and then perhaps enjoy the opportunity to saunter the streets when they had returned to reasonableness. Not this guy. He had sailed his old carcass into the morning as if there were no tomorrow.

Perhaps there would be no tomorrow. After all, he was pretty old.

When Roberta had figured the total, a tired, old hand fished deep into the trench coat pocket. "Come on," I thought, "You may have all day, but I have things to do!"

The fishing hand caught a change purse as old as the man himself. A few coins and a wrinkled dollar bill fell onto the counter. Roberta treated them as though she were about to receive a treasure.

When the meager purchases had been placed into a plastic bag, something remarkable happened. Although not a word had been spoken by her elderly friend, an old, tired hand slowly extended over the counter. The hand trembled, then steadied.

Roberta spread the plastic handles on the bag and gently slipped them over his wrist. The fingers that dangled into space were gnarled and spotted with the marks of age.

Roberta smiled larger.

She scooped up the other tired, old hand and in an instant, she was holding them both, gathered in front of her brown face.

She warmed them. Top and bottom. Then sides.

She reached and pulled the scarf that had flown nearly off his broad but stooped shoulders. She pulled it close around his neck. Still he said not a single word. He stood as if to cement the moment in his memory. It would have to last at least until the morrow, when he would once again shuffle through the cold.

Roberta buttoned a button that had eluded the manipulation of the old hands.

She looked him in the eye and, with a slender finger, mockingly scolded him.

"Now, Mr. Johnson. I want you to be very careful." She then paused ever so slightly for emphasis and added sincerely, "I need to see you in here tomorrow."

With those last words ringing in his ears, the old man had his orders. He hesitated, then turned, and one tired foot shuffling barely in front of the other, he moved slowly into the bitter Denver morning.

I realized then that he had not come in search of a banana and a muffin. He came in to get warm. In his heart.

I said, "Wow, Roberta! That was really some customer service. Was that your uncle or a neighbor or someone special?"

She was almost offended that I thought that she only gave such wonderful service to special people. To Roberta, apparently, everyone is special.

Scott Gross

An Act of Kindness

You must give time to your fellow men—even if it's a little thing, do something for others—something for which you get no pay but the privilege of doing it.

Albert Schweitzer

President Abraham Lincoln often visited hospitals to talk with wounded soldiers during the Civil War. Once, doctors pointed out a young soldier who was near death and Lincoln went over to his bedside.

"Is there anything I can do for you?" asked the President.

The soldier obviously didn't recognize Lincoln, and with some effort he was able to whisper, "Would you please write a letter to my mother?"

A pen and paper were provided and the President carefully began writing down what the young man was able to say:

"My dearest mother, I was badly hurt while doing my duty. I'm afraid I'm not going to recover. Don't grieve too much for me, please. Kiss Mary and John for me. May God bless you and father."

The soldier was too weak to continue, so Lincoln signed the letter for him and added, "Written for your son by Abraham Lincoln."

The young man asked to see the note and was astonished when he discovered who had written it. "Are you really the President?" he asked.

"Yes, I am," Lincoln replied quietly. Then he asked if there was anything else he could do.

"Would you please hold my hand?" the soldier asked. "It will help to see me through to the end."

In the hushed room, the tall gaunt President took the boy's hand in his and spoke warm words of encouragement until death came.

The Best of Bits & Pieces

Two Families

One family, which had emigrated from Japan and settled at the turn of the century near San Francisco, had
established a business in which they grew roses and
trucked them into San Francisco three mornings a week.

The other family was a naturalized family from
Switzerland who also marketed roses, and both families
became modestly successful, as their roses were known in
the markets of San Francisco for their long vase-life.

For almost four decades the two families were neighbors, and the sons took over the farms, but then on
December 7, 1941, Japan attacked Pearl Harbor. Although
the rest of the family members were Americans, the father
of the Japanese family had never been naturalized. In the
turmoil and the questions about internment camps, his
neighbor made it clear that, if necessary, he would look
after his friend's nursery. It was something each family
had learned in church: Love thy neighbor as thyself. "You
would do the same for us," he told his Japanese friend.

It was not long before the Japanese family was transported to a barren landscape in Granada, Colorado. The
relocation center consisted of tar-paper-roofed barracks

surrounded by barbed wire and armed guards.

A full year went by. Then two. Then three. While the Japanese neighbors were in internment, their friends worked in the greenhouses, the children before school and on Saturdays; and the father's work often stretched to 16 and 17 hours a day. And then one day, when the war in Europe had ended, the Japanese family packed up and boarded a train. They were going home.

What would they find? The family was met at the train depot by their neighbors, and when they got to their home, the whole Japanese family stared. There was the nursery, intact, scrubbed and shining in the sunlight— neat, prosperous and healthy.

So was the balance in the bank passbook handed to the Japanese father. And the house was just as clean and welcoming as the nursery.

And there on the dining room table was one perfect red rosebud, just waiting to unfold—the gift of one neighbor to another.

Diane Rayner
Submitted by Carol Broadbent

Guests in the Night

Love cures people—both the ones who give it and the ones who receive it.

Dr. Karl Menninger

It was a family adventure trip. My wife, Judith, our two-year-old daughter, Leila, and I had rented a small camper and were traveling through Baja California. The day before our return to San Diego, we parked the camper near a beach for one last night in nature.

In the middle of the night I was awakened by Judith poking me with her elbow and yelling at me to get up. My first impressions were of noise and banging. Fairly disoriented, I jumped down out of our little loft-bed, and standing stark naked, faced the windshield.

What I saw woke me quickly out of my half-dazed state. The van was surrounded by masked men banging on the windows.

Having watched a lot of adventure movies, I always wondered what I would feel and do when confronted with danger. Well, I leapt right into the hero's role. I felt no fear—time to "save the family."

I dove for the driver's seat and turned the ignition. The camper had started perfectly at least 50 times that trip. Now it tried to turn over, sputtered a few times, and died. There was the sound of breaking glass, and a hand reached in through the driver's side window. I smashed the hand. (Non-violently of course! Actually, my lifelong inquiries about pacifism didn't stand a chance in the energy of the moment. I've often thought that I'm glad I didn't have a gun because I probably would have used it.)

My hand was bleeding from the broken glass. I figured I had one more chance to start the car. Having played hero successfully a thousand times in fantasy, I never doubted I would do it. I turned the key. The engine sputtered to life . . . and died. Then someone jammed a rifle into my throat. I remember this thought: "You mean I don't save the family?" I was really quite surprised.

One of the bandits, who spoke a little English, was yelling, "Money! Money!" The rifle still at my throat, I reached under the driver's seat and handed one of them my wallet through the broken window. I was hoping this was the end of it.

It wasn't.

Releasing the latch through the broken window, they opened the door. The man with the rifle pushed me hard and sent me sprawling onto the floor. They entered the camper.

They looked remarkably like Mexican bandits from a grade-B movie. They had standard-issue bandannas over their faces. There were four: the one with the rifle, one with a rusty carving knife, one with a huge machete and one unarmed. I was half surprised they weren't wearing bullet-filled bandoleers slung over the shoulders. Maybe their weapons were really props from Central Casting.

While one man held me to the floor with the rifle against my neck, the bandits started tearing the camper apart, yelling in Spanish.

It's interesting. While I could do something (or at least had the illusion of being able to do something) like start the car or save the family, I felt no fear, although there was adrenaline to spare. But as I lay naked on the floor, cold steel against my neck, I started feeling quite helpless. Then I felt afraid. I began to shake.

Now this was an interesting situation. I was just about to get pretty in tune with my fear; in fact, I was only a moment or two from losing it. In a fleeting shred of self-consciousness, I reminded myself that this might be an excellent time to meditate and seek guidance. I remember breathing into my heart and asking God for help.

I heard quite clearly this passage from the 23rd Psalm: "Thou shalt preparest a table before me in the presence of mine enemies."

These words were met inside with a resounding, "Huh? . . . I don't get it!"

Then I saw an image of myself, serving the bandits a feast. I thought to myself, "I'm living in a reality where bandits have attacked me, I'm resisting, and it's a generally bad scene.

"Well, what if this wasn't so? What if they weren't bandits? What if they were old friends of ours, come to visit us out of the cold desert night? What if I were glad to see them, and welcomed them as I would honored guests? What if I prepared a table for them?"

While one aspect of me was busy fantasizing horrendous scenes of rape and murder, a clear, quiet space opened inside that was intrigued by this new possibility. These too are children of God. How many times have I declared that my purpose is to serve others? Well, here they are!

I looked at the bandits from this more heartfelt awareness. "Wait a minute! These aren't bandits! They're kids!"

It was suddenly apparent that these "bandits" were

quite young, obviously inexperienced and rather inept. They also seemed nervous. Their violence and yelling seemed more a product of their fear than their power. Also, in their thrashing about, they were making a terrific mess of things and losing a lot of the good loot. In a rather bizarre flash of insight, I saw that "serving a table" in this moment meant to help them do a better job of robbing us.

I turned to the young man who spoke English and said, "Hey, you're missing some of the best stuff! Under that pile over there is a very nice camera."

He gave me a peculiar look.

He yelled something in Spanish to one of the other young men, who found the camera buried where I had pointed. "Thirty-five millimeter . . . takes great pictures!" I offered helpfully.

I spoke to the English-speaking man again. "Your friends are making such a mess, you're going to miss things. I'd be happy to show you where all the good stuff is."

He looked at me strangely again. My responses were clearly not matching his script for bandits and victims. As I pointed out other items and their hiding places, his suspicion gave way. I offered to get things for him and his friends.

The next thing we knew, it was *show and tell.* "Nice guitar!" I demonstrated a few chords. "Who plays? Here, do you want it? . . . Sony Walkman, headsets, batteries, some tapes! Who wants it?" I thought about the Native American giveaway of the giveaway. I realized that given our respective access to money, it seemed right somehow that they should receive our goods, a kind of balancing of wealth. I began to enjoy the feeling of gifting them. I tried to think which of our possessions they would most enjoy.

Although my out-of-role behavior was clearly having some impact on the scene, it was not yet a total transformation. The young man with the carving knife seemed particularly erratic, perhaps drug-intoxicated. Every few minutes he pushed me or yelled at me. His English vocabulary seemed to consist of: "Drugs! Booze! More money!" He found a bottle of Lomotil (for diarrhea) in a kitchen drawer. I tried to convince him that he didn't want the pills, though when he became violent about it, I must confess the thought, "It serves you right" crossed my mind.

My English-speaking "friend" increasingly began to play a calming role with the others.

Well, I'd given away everything I could think of. I looked toward the back of the van where Judith and Leila were huddled, wrapped in a blanket. Judith, of course, was having her own inner adventure, managing her fears of rape for herself and kidnapping of our child. Leila, who in her whole two years of life had never encountered someone who wasn't "good," kept interjecting things like, "Daddy, who dese nice men?"

I thought to myself, "What's next?" Then I found myself spontaneously asking, "Would you like something to eat?" The English-speaking young man translated. Four pairs of incredulous eyes looked at me as I proceeded to open the refrigerator. Now we had a cultural problem. As I surveyed the shelves of tofu, sprouts, yogurt and nut butters, I had that sinking feeling like when you're hosting a dinner party and someone shows up on a special diet. It was obvious that we had nothing recognizable as food. Then I saw a nice red Delicious apple. "Okay, that's normal food." I took out the apple and held it out toward the man with the machete. This felt like an important moment. In most cultures, the sharing of food is a kind of communion, an acknowledgment of friendship, or declaration of peace. As I continued to hold out the apple toward him, I sensed him struggling for a moment, in his own way letting go of the roles in which we had met. For an instant he smiled, then took hold of the apple. I flashed on the image of E.T. extending his light-tipped finger. As our hands met on the apple, I felt a subtle exchange of energy.

Well, we had given presents and shared food. Now the English-speaking man said we were going for a ride. Fear came back. I didn't know where they were taking us. If they were going to kill us, this was as good a place as any. They didn't seem competent enough to pull off a kidnapping and ransom. I suggested that they take the car and leave us here. We were in the middle of nowhere, but anything seemed better than going driving with them. We exchanged views on this several times, then all of a sudden they were back to threatening me with weapons. I got it. As soon as I switched back into fear mode, they became bandits again. "Okay Let's go!"

I climbed in the back next to Judith and Leila, and away we went. I had my pants on now, which further improved my state of mind. I flipped in and out of realities, at some moments, just driving through the desert. Then, seeing lights, I planned how I might open the door and push Judith and Leila out if we slowed down near people.

As we drove along, I asked myself, "What would I do if I were driving along with my honored guests?" Sing, of course!

Judith, Leila and I started singing:

> *Listen, listen, listen to my heart's song.*
> *Listen, listen, listen to my heart's song.*
> *I will never forget you, I will never forsake you.*
> *I will never forget you, I will never forsake you.*

Leila kept smiling her outrageously cute smile. She'd catch the eye of one or another of the young men. Several times I saw them trying to keep it straight. ("Come on kid, cut it out. I'm trying to be a bandit.") Then they'd smile despite themselves.

They seemed to like the singing. We did. Then I realized I was failing to be a good host. They didn't know any of the songs. I thought for a moment. Inspiration!

Guantanamera, guajira, guantanamera.
Guantanamera. . . .

That did it. They began singing along. The energy came together. No more bandits and victims. Feet were tapping and spirits lifted as we sailed through the desert night.

We passed through a village without a chance for my great rescue attempt. Then the lights faded away as we entered some remote, hilly country. We pulled down a dark, dirt road, and the RV came to a halt. Judith and I looked at each other as we both had the thought that they were going to kill us. We rested deeply in each others' eyes.

Then they opened the door and began to get out. Evidently, they lived far from the scene of the robbery. They had driven themselves home!

Several of them said "Adios" as they exited. Finally, there was just my English-speaking friend. In halting English he struggled to communicate. "Please forgive us. My *hombres* and me, we are poor people. Our fathers are poor. This is what we do for making the money. I'm sorry. We didn't know it was you. You are such a good man. And your wife and child, so nice."

He apologized again and again. "You are good people. Please do not think bad of us. I hope this won't ruin your vacation."

Then he reached into his pocket and took out my wallet. "Here." He handed me back my MasterCard. "We can't really use this. Better you take it." He also gave me my driver's license. As one of his hombres stared in amazement, he peeled off a few Mexican bills. "Here, for the gasoline."

I was at least as amazed as his fellow bandits. He's giving my money back to me! He wants to make things right between us.

Then he took my hand. He looked into my eyes, and the veils were gone between us. Just for a moment, we rested in that place. Then he said, "Adios": "with God."

Our bandit guests disappeared into the night. Then my family held each other and cried.

Robert Gass

Appointment with Love

Six minutes to six, said the great round clock over the information booth in Grand Central Station. The tall young Army lieutenant who had just come from the direction of the tracks lifted his sunburned face, and his eyes narrowed to note the exact time. His heart was pounding with a beat that shocked him because he could not control it. In six minutes, he would see the woman who had filled such a special place in his life for the past 13 months, the woman he had never seen, yet whose written words had been with him and sustained him unfailingly.

He placed himself as close as he could to the information booth, just beyond the ring of people besieging the clerks. . . .

Lieutenant Blandford remembered one night in particular, the worst of the fighting, when his plane had been caught in the midst of a pack of Zeros. He had seen the grinning face of one of the enemy pilots.

In one of his letters, he had confessed to her that he often felt fear, and only a few days before this battle, he had received her answer: "Of course you fear . . . all brave men do. Didn't King David know fear? That's why he wrote the 23rd Psalm. Next time you doubt yourself, I want you to hear my voice reciting to you: 'Yea, though I walk through the valley of the shadow of death, I shall fear no evil, for Thou art with me'." And he had remembered; he had heard her imagined voice, and it had renewed his strength and skill.

Now he was going to hear her real voice. Four minutes to six. His face grew sharp.

Under the immense, starred roof, people were walking fast, like threads of color being woven into a gray web. A girl passed close to him, and Lieutenant Blandford started. She was wearing a red flower in her suit lapel, but it was a crimson sweet pea, not the little red rose they had agreed upon. Besides, this girl was too young, about 18, whereas Hollis Meynell had frankly told him she was 30. "Well, what of it?" he had answered. "I'm 32." He was 29.

His mind went back to that book—the book the Lord Himself must have put into his hands out of the hundreds of Army library books sent to the Florida training camp. *Of Human Bondage*, it was; and throughout the book were notes in a woman's writing. He had always hated that writing-in habit, but these remarks were different. He had never believed that a woman could see into a man's heart so tenderly, so understandingly. Her name was on the bookplate: Hollis Meynell. He had got hold of a New York City telephone book and found her address. He had written, she had answered. Next day he had been shipped out, but they had gone on writing.

For 13 months, she had faithfully replied, and more than replied. When his letters did not arrive, she wrote anyway, and now he believed he loved her, and she loved him.

But she had refused all his pleas to send him her photograph. That seemed rather bad, of course. But she had explained: "If your feeling for me has any reality, any honest basis, what I look like won't matter. Suppose I'm beautiful. I'd always be haunted by the feeling that you had been taking a chance on just that, and that kind of love would disgust me. Suppose I'm plain (and you must admit that this is more likely). Then I'd always fear that you were going on writing to me only because you were lonely and had no one else. No, don't ask for my picture. When you come to New York, you shall see me and then you shall make your decision. Remember, both of us are free to stop or to go on after that—whichever we choose . . ."

One minute to six—he pulled hard on a cigarette.

Then Lieutenant Blandford's heart leaped higher than his plane had ever done.

A young woman was coming toward him. Her figure was long and slim; her blond hair lay back in curls from her delicate ears. Her eyes were blue as flowers, her lips and chin had a gentle firmness. In her pale green suit, she was like springtime come alive.

He started toward her, entirely forgetting to notice that she was wearing no rose, and as he moved, a small, provocative smile curved her lips.

"Going my way, soldier?" she murmured.

Uncontrollably, he made one step closer to her. Then he saw Hollis Meynell.

She was standing almost directly behind the girl, a woman well past 40, her graying hair tucked under a worn hat. She was more than plump; her thick-ankled feet were thrust into low-heeled shoes. But she wore a red rose in the rumpled lapel of her brown coat.

The girl in the green suit was walking quickly away.

Blandford felt as though he were being split in two, so keen was his desire to follow the girl, yet so deep was his longing for the woman whose spirit had truly companioned and upheld his own; and there she stood. Her pale, plump face was gentle and sensible; he could see that now. Her gray eyes had a warm, kindly twinkle.

Lieutenant Blandford did not hesitate. His fingers gripped the small, worn, blue leather copy of *Of Human Bondage*, which was to identify him to her. This would not be love, but it would be something precious, something perhaps even rarer than love—a friendship for which he had been and must ever be grateful.

He squared his broad shoulders, saluted and held the book out toward the woman, although even while he spoke he felt shocked by the bitterness of his disappointment.

"I'm Lieutenant John Blandford, and you—you are Miss Meynell. I'm so glad you could meet me. May . . . may I take you to dinner?"

The woman's face broadened in a tolerant smile. "I don't know what this is all about, son," she answered. "That young lady in the green suit—the one who just went by—begged me to wear this rose on my coat. And she said that if you asked me to go out with you, I should tell you that she's waiting for you in that big restaurant across the street. She said it was some kind of a test. I've got two boys with Uncle Sam myself, so I didn't mind to oblige you."

Sulamith Ish-Kishor

Whoever Finds This, I Love You!

On a quiet street in the city a little old man walked along
Shuffling through the autumn afternoon,
And the autumn leaves reminded him of other summers
    come and gone.
He had a long lonely night ahead, waiting for June.

Then among the leaves near an orphan's home a piece of
    paper caught his eye,
And he stooped to pick it up with trembling hands.
As he read the childish writing the old man began to cry
'Cause the words burned inside him like a brand.

"Whoever finds this, I love you, whoever finds this, I
    need you
I ain't even got no one to talk to
So whoever finds this, I love you!"

The old man's eyes searched the orphan's home and
    came to rest upon a child
With her nose pressed up against the window pane.
And the old man knew he found a friend at last, so he
    waved to her and smiled

And they both knew they'd spend the winter laughing
    at the rain.

And they did spend the winter laughing at the rain
Talking through the fence and exchanging little gifts
    they had made for each other.
The old man would carve toys for the little girl.
She would draw pictures for him of beautiful ladies
Surrounded by green trees and sunshine, and they
    laughed a lot.

But then on the first day of June the little girl ran to the
    fence
To show the old man a picture she drew, but he wasn't
    there.
And somehow the little girl knew he wasn't coming back
So she went to her room, took a crayon and paper and
    wrote . . .

"Whoever finds this, I love you, whoever finds this, I
    need you
I ain't even got no one to talk to
So whoever finds this, I love you!"

Author Unknown

An Afternoon in the Park

There once was a little boy who wanted to meet God. He knew it was a long trip to where God lived, so he packed his suitcase with Twinkies and a six-pack of root beer and he started his journey.

When he had gone about three blocks, he met an old woman. She was sitting in the park just staring at some pigeons. The boy sat down next to her and opened his suitcase. He was about to take a drink from his root beer when he noticed that the old lady looked hungry, so he offered her a Twinkie. She gratefully accepted it and smiled at him. Her smile was so pretty that the boy wanted to see it again, so he offered her a root beer. Once again she smiled at him. The boy was delighted!

They sat there all afternoon eating and smiling, but they never said a word.

As it grew dark, the boy realized how tired he was and he got up to leave, but before he had gone more than a few steps, he turned around, ran back to the old woman and gave her a hug. She gave him her biggest smile ever.

When the boy opened the door to his own house a

short time later, his mother was surprised by the look of joy on his face.

She asked him, "What did you do today that made you so happy?"

He replied, "I had lunch with God." But before his mother could respond, he added, "You know what? She's got the most beautiful smile I've ever seen!"

Meanwhile, the old woman, also radiant with joy, returned to her home.

Her son was stunned by the look of peace on her face and he asked, "Mother, what did you do today that made you so happy?"

She replied, "I ate Twinkies in the park with God." But before her son responded, she added, "You know, he's much younger than I expected."

Julie A. Manhan

The Little Boy and the Old Man

Said the little boy, "Sometimes I drop my spoon."
Said the little old man, "I do that too."
The little boy whispered, "I wet my pants."
"I do that too," laughed the old man.
Said the little boy, "I often cry."
The old man nodded. "So do I."
"But worst of all," said the boy, "it seems
Grown-ups don't pay attention to me."
And he felt the warmth of a wrinkled old hand.
"I know what you mean," said the little old man.

Shel Silverstein
Submitted by Ruth Wiele

What's Really Important

A few years ago at the Seattle Special Olympics, nine contestants, all physically or mentally disabled, assembled at the starting line for the 100-yard dash. At the gun they all started out, not exactly in a dash, but with the relish to run the race to the finish and win.

All, that is, except one boy who stumbled on the asphalt, tumbled over a couple of times, and began to cry. The other eight heard the boy cry. They slowed down and paused. Then they all turned around and went back. Every one of them. One girl with Down's syndrome bent down and kissed him and said, "This will make it better." Then all nine linked arms and walked together to the finish line.

Everyone in the stadium stood, and the cheering went on for 10 minutes.

Author Unknown
Submitted by Bob French

Not a One!

Little Chad was a shy, quiet young man. One day he came home and told his mother that he'd like to make a valentine for everyone in his class. Her heart sank. She thought, "I wish he wouldn't do that!" because she had watched the children when they walked home from school. Her Chad was always behind them. They laughed and hung on to each other and talked to each other. But Chad was never included. Nevertheless, she decided she would go along with her son. So she purchased the paper and glue and crayons. For three weeks, night after night, Chad painstakingly made 35 valentines.

Valentine's Day dawned, and Chad was beside himself with excitement. He carefully stacked them up, put them in a bag, and bolted out the door. His mother decided to bake him his favorite cookies and serve them nice and warm with a cool glass of milk when he came home from school. She just knew he would be disappointed and maybe that would ease the pain a little. It hurt her to think that he wouldn't get many valentines—maybe none at all.

That afternoon she had the cookies and milk on the table. When she heard the children outside, she looked out the window. Sure enough, there they came, laughing and having the best time. And, as always, there was Chad in the rear. He walked a little faster than usual. She fully expected him to burst into tears as soon as he got inside. His arms were empty, she noticed, and when the door opened she choked back the tears.

"Mommy has some cookies and milk for you," she said.

But he hardly heard her words. He just marched right on by, his face aglow, and all he could say was: "Not a one. Not a one."

Her heart sank.

And then he added, "I didn't forget a one, not a single one!"

Dale Galloway

Teddy Bear

I was on the outskirts of a little Southern town, trying to reach my destination before the sun went down. The old CB was blaring away on channel 1-9 when there came a little boy's voice on the radio line. And he said, "Breaker 1-9, is anyone there? Come on back, truckers, and talk to Teddy Bear."

I keyed the mike and said, "You got it, Teddy Bear."

The little boy's voice came back on the air, "'Preciate the break. Who we got on the other end?" I told him my handle and then he began. "Now I'm not supposed to bother you fellas out there. Mom says you're busy and for me to stay off the air. But you see, I get lonely and it helps to talk 'cause that's about all I can do. I'm crippled and cannot walk."

I came back and told him to fire up that mike and I'd talk to him as long as he'd like.

"This was my dad's radio," the little boy said. "But I guess its mine and mom's now 'cause my daddy's dead. Dad had a wreck about a month ago. He was trying to get home in a blinding snow. Mom has to work now to make ends meet. I'm not much help with my crippled feet. She says not to worry, that we'll make it all right. But I hear her crying sometimes late at night. Ya know, there's one thing I want more than anything else to see. Ah, I know you guys are too busy to bother with me. But, ya see, my dad used to take me for rides when he was home. But I guess that's all over now since my daddy's gone."

Not one breaker came in on the CB as that little crippled boy talked to me. I tried hard to swallow the lump; it just would not stay down as I thought about my boy in Greenville Town.

"Dad was going to take Mom and me with him later on this year. Why, I remember him saying, 'Someday this ol' truck will be yours, Teddy Bear.' But I know I will never get to ride in an 18-wheeler again. But this old base will keep me in touch with all my trucker friends. Teddy Bear's going to back out now and leave you alone 'cause it's almost time for Mom to come home. But you give me a shout when you're passing through and I'll be happy to come back to you."

Well, I came back and said, "Before you go 10-10, what's your home 20, little CB friend?" Well, he gave me his address and I didn't hesitate one second 'cause this hot load of freight was just gonna have to wait. I turned that truck around on a dime and headed for Jackson Street 229. As I rounded the corner, I got one heck of a shock: 18-wheelers lined up for three city blocks. Why, I guess every trucker from miles around had caught Teddy Bear's call, and that little boy was having a ball. For as fast as one driver could carry him in, another would carry him to his truck and take off again. Well, you better believe I took my turn at riding Teddy Bear. And then I carried him back in and put him down in his chair. Buddy, if I never live to see happiness again, I want you to know I saw it that day in the face of that little man. We took up a collection before his momma came home. Each driver said good-bye and then they were all gone. He shook my hand with a mile-long grin and he said, "So long, trucker; I'll catch ya again."

I hit that interstate with tears in my eyes. I turned on the radio and got another surprise. "Breaker 1-9," came a voice on the air, "just one word of thanks from Momma Teddy Bear. We wish each and every one a special prayer for you, 'cause you just made my little boy's dream come true. I'll sign off now before I start to cry. May God ride with you; 10-4 and good-bye."

Dale Royal, Tommy Hill, Red Sovine and
J. William Denny

2

ON
PARENTING

Teach only love, for that is what you are!

A Course in Miracles

Paco, Come Home

In a small town in Spain, a man named Jorge had a bitter argument with his young son Paco. The next day Jorge discovered that Paco's bed was empty—he had run away from home.

Overcome with remorse, Jorge searched his soul and realized that his son was more important to him than anything else. He wanted to start over. Jorge went to a well-known store in the center of town and posted a large sign that read, "Paco, come home. I love you. Meet me here tomorrow morning."

The next morning Jorge went to the store, where he found no less than seven young boys named Paco who had also run away from home. They were all answering the call for love, each hoping it was his dad inviting him home with open arms.

Alan Cohen

Tommy's Essay

A gray sweater hung limply on Tommy's empty desk, a reminder of the dejected boy who had just followed his classmates from our third-grade room. Soon Tommy's parents, who had recently separated, would arrive for a conference on his failing schoolwork and disruptive behavior. Neither parent knew that I had summoned the other.

Tommy, an only child, had always been happy, cooperative and an excellent student. How could I convince his father and mother that his recent failing grades represented a broken-hearted child's reaction to his adored parents' separation and pending divorce?

Tommy's mother entered and took one of the chairs I had placed near my desk. Soon the father arrived. Good! At least they were concerned enough to be prompt. A look of surprise and irritation passed between them, and then they pointedly ignored each other.

As I gave a detailed account of Tommy's behavior and schoolwork, I prayed for the right words to bring these two together, to help them see what they were doing to their son. But somehow the words wouldn't come. Perhaps if they saw one of his smudged, carelessly done papers.

I found a crumpled tear-stained sheet stuffed in the back of his desk, an English paper. Writing covered both sides—not the assignment, but a single sentence scribbled over and over.

Silently I smoothed it out and gave it to Tommy's mother. She read it and then without a word handed it to her husband. He frowned. Then his face softened. He studied the scrawled words for what seemed an eternity.

At last he folded the paper carefully, placed it in his pocket, and reached for his wife's outstretched hand. She wiped the tears from her eyes and smiled up at him. My own eyes were brimming, but neither seemed to notice. He helped her with her coat and they left together.

In his own way God had given me the words to reunite that family. He had guided me to the sheet of yellow copy paper covered with the anguished outpouring of a small boy's troubled heart.

The words, "Dear Mother . . . Dear Daddy . . . I love you . . . I love you . . . I love you."

Jane Lindstrom

Barney

A four-year-old girl was at the pediatrician's office for a check-up. As the doctor looked into her ears with an otoscope, he asked, "Do you think I'll find Big Bird in here?" The little girl stayed silent.

Next, the doctor took a tongue depressor and looked down her throat. He asked, "Do you think I'll find the Cookie Monster down there?" Again, the little girl was silent.

Then the doctor put a stethoscope to her chest. As he listened to her heart beat, he asked, "Do you think I'll hear Barney in here?"

"Oh, no!" the little girl replied. "Jesus is in my heart. Barney's on my underpants."

Source Unknown
Submitted by Marilyn Thompsen

Almie Rose

It was at least two months before Christmas, when nine-year-old Almie Rose told her father and me that she wanted a new bicycle. Her old Barbie bicycle was just too babyish, and besides, it needed a new tire.

As Christmas drew nearer, her desire for a bicycle seemed to fade—or so we thought, as she didn't mention it again. Merrily, we started purchasing the latest rage—Baby-Sitter's Club dolls—and beautiful story books, a doll house, a holiday dress and toys. Then, much to our surprise, on December 23rd she proudly announced that she "really wanted a bike more than anything else."

Now we didn't know what to do. It was just too late, what with all the details of preparing Christmas dinner and buying last-minute gifts, to take the time to select the "right bike" for our little girl. So here we were—Christmas Eve around 9:00 P.M., having just returned from a wonderful party, contemplating our evening ahead—hours of wrapping children's presents, parents' presents, a brother's presents and friends' presents. With Almie Rose and her six-year-old brother, Dylan, nestled snug in their beds, we could now think only of the bicycle, the guilt and the idea that we were parents who would disappoint their child.

That's when my husband, Ron, was inspired. "What if I make a little bicycle out of clay and write a note that she could trade the clay model in for a real bike?" The theory, of course, being that since this is a high-ticket item and she is "such a big girl," it would be much better for her to pick it out. So he spent the next five hours painstakingly working with clay to create a miniature bike.

Three hours later, on Christmas morning, we were so excited for Almie Rose to open the little heart-shaped package with the beautiful red and white clay bike and the note. Finally, she opened and read the note aloud.

She looked at me and then at Ron and said, "So, does this mean that I trade in this bike that Daddy made me for a real one?"

Beaming, I said, "Yes."

Almie Rose had tears in her eyes when she replied, "I could never trade in this beautiful bicycle that Daddy made me. I'd rather keep this than get a real bike."

At that moment, we would have moved heaven and earth to buy her every bicycle on the planet!

Michelle Lawrence

Why I Wear a Plastic Dinosaur

The soul is healed by being with children.

Fyodor Dostoyevski

Why would a leader of the community, a respected family man, shamelessly walk around with a plastic dinosaur attached to his suit?

The set-up occurred one day as I was pulling out of my driveway, in a hurry to run an errand. I spied my son running toward me, his tiny hand outstretched.

He smiled, his tender eyes aglow with excitement. "I've got a present for you, Daddy."

"Really?" I said, feigning interest, frustrated at the delay and hoping he would hurry up.

Then he slowly opened his fingers to reveal a five-year-old's treasure. "I found them for you, Daddy." In those small hands were a white marble, an old and bent metal race car, a broken rubber band and several other items I can't recall. How I wish now that I could remember all the little-boy treasures. "Take them, Daddy—they're for you," he gushed with pride.

"I can't right now, Son. I've got to go somewhere. Why don't you go put them on top of the freezer in the garage for me?"

His smile fell, but he obediently started walking into the garage, and I drove off. From the moment I started down the street I felt remorse. I made a mental note that when I returned I would accept my gift with more graciousness and gratitude.

When I returned, I found him. "Hey, Son, where are those neat toys you had for me?"

His expression was blank. "Well, I didn't think you wanted them so I gave them to Adam." Adam is a little boy who lives down the street, and I pictured him accepting these treasures with a great deal more gratitude and excitement than I had.

His decision hurt, but I deserved it. Not simply because it highlighted my thoughtless reaction to his gesture, but because it triggered memories of another little boy I remembered.

Childhood Hurt

It was his older sister's birthday, and the boy had been given two dollars to buy something for her at the old five-and-dime. He toured the toy department repeatedly without success.

It had to be very special. He finally spied it sitting on a shelf, fairly shouting for attention. A beautiful plastic bubble gum machine, filled with brightly colored, chewy treasures. He wanted to show it to her almost as soon as he brought it home, but valiantly resisted the urge.

Later, at the birthday party attended by her young friends, she began to open her new gifts. With every present opened she squealed with delight.

And with each squeal, the little boy felt more apprehensive. These girls were from wealthier families that could afford to spend far more than two dollars. Their gifts were expensive and shiny and talked and went potty. His little package grew increasingly smaller and more insignificant.

Yet he managed to remain eager to see her eyes sparkle as she opened his gift. After all, she hadn't received anything she could eat or collect pennies with.

She finally opened his gift and he immediately saw her momentary disappointment.

She was slightly embarrassed at it. Suddenly the beautiful bubble gum machine looked like the plastic, cheap toy it was. To maintain her standing among her peers, she couldn't acknowledge the gift with too much enthusiasm. There was momentary silence as she deliberated her response.

Then she smiled knowingly at her friends, and turned to her brother with a safely patronizing tone and said, "Thank you, it's just what I wanted." Several girls tried unsuccessfully to contain their giggles.

She quickly returned to her next birthday game, and the little boy looked away, hurt and confused. The toy that had seemed so wondrous in the five-and-dime now seemed small and cheap.

He slowly picked it up, walked outside to the back porch, and began to cry. His cheap little gift didn't belong with the other ones; it was merely an embarrassment.

The laughing and celebrating continued inside, which only increased his pain. Soon his mother appeared and asked why he was crying. He explained as best he could between muffled sobs.

She listened silently, then returned inside. In a few moments, his sister appeared alone. He could tell by her expression that she had been sent, but her genuine remorse reminded him that she hadn't intended to be mean or hurtful. She was only eight years old, and unaccustomed to the task of balancing the difficult demands of people's feelings and queen-for-a-day euphoria.

She explained kindly in her grown-up eight-year-old way that she really did like his bubble-gum toy very much. He said he understood, and he did. She was just being nice.

Now it had come full circle. A new generation was faced with the same choice, except this new generation was mine. This little fellow would decide for himself whether it really is the thought that counts, and my response would play a large part in his decision.

The Ultimate Gift

We are repeatedly told growing up that the price of a gift isn't important, it's the thought that counts. But that can be hard to believe when Daddy gushes over an expensive new toy, but ignores a primitive token of love painstakingly created with tiny hands and huge hearts that care far more deeply about him than the hands that assembled that expensive new bike or CD player.

Which leads me to the daunting question I had to face that Christmas, the Christmas that my children were given money to buy presents at a school "Mistletoe Mall."

Mistletoe Mall is a kindergarten through sixth grade holiday emporium of "unique" items (what retail stores wouldn't carry if you paid them). However, all the gifts are designed for a child's budget, and they love it.

They had bought me presents and were trying very hard to keep from telling me what I was to receive—especially my son. He would tease me with my gift, which lay "creatively" wrapped under the tree. But not a day went by that he didn't make me guess what it might be.

On Christmas morning, very early, it was thrust at me first thing by my excited and impatient son, who insisted I open his first. He was giddy with excitement and sure I would never receive a gift of this caliber again. I excitedly opened the package and looked inside. There it was, truly the most beautiful present I had ever received. But I was no longer looking at it through 35-year-old eyes, jaded by promises of "newest technology" and "faster, easier and more economical." Instead, I once again looked at it through excited five-year-old eyes.

It was a several-inch long, green plastic dinosaur of the *Tyrannosaurus Rex* variety. But my son quickly pointed out its best feature. Its front claws were also clips so you could—you guessed it—wear it all the time.

I will never forget his eyes as I looked at him that Christmas morning. They were filled with expectation, hopefulness and love—the kind found only in very young eyes.

History was repeating itself. That small, blond-haired blue-eyed face was asking me the same question I had asked years before. Is it really the thought that counts? I thought of how he must have agonized at the Mistletoe Mall to find a jewel among all the paraphernalia that would best communicate his feelings of love to his daddy.

I answered his question the only way a five-year-old would understand. I immediately put it on and raved how "cool" it was and confirmed that, yes, he was right. I did love it. For the next several weeks I went literally every-where with a plastic dinosaur clipped to my lapel. Strangely, no one seemed to notice, especially when I was in the presence of my son. No one, that is, except him.

It has occurred to me that the expression on the face of young children giving gifts of the heart, especially at Christmas, is dramatically different from that of adults trying to buy love with expensive CDs or jewelry.

Last Christmas, two children from our neighborhood presented our children with handmade paper Christmas stockings, weighted down with treasures and held together by thousands of staples.

Inside were odd pieces of Christmas candy, favorite toys of old and once-loved figurines. The children were from a broken home and didn't have much money, but you could tell from their beaming faces that extra helpings of love and thought had been stapled into those childlike versions of gold, frankincense and myrrh.

When does the thought stop counting? It is a question I have asked myself time and time again. I guess it stops counting the moment the rewards for the most precious acts we perform for each other are reduced to their strictly commercial value.

The dollar amount of my son's presents wouldn't amount to pennies, but they are worth their weight in gold to me.

So the next time you see someone wearing a crude paper tie or a "cool" five-cent (rub-on) caterpillar tattoo that doesn't quite fit the mold of respectable adult fashion, don't bother feeling sorry for him. If you tell him he looks stupid, he'll just smile and say, "Maybe, but I've got a five-year-old son who thinks I'm the best thing since peanut butter, and there isn't enough money in the U.S. Treasury to make me take it off."

That's why I wear a plastic dinosaur.

Dan Schaeffer

The Coolest Dad in the Universe

He was 50 years old when I was born, and a "Mr. Mom" long before anyone had a name for it. I didn't know why he was home instead of Mom, but I was young and the only one of my friends who had their dad around. I considered myself very lucky.

Dad did so many things for me during my grade school years. He convinced the school bus driver to pick me up at my house instead of the usual bus stop that was six blocks away. He always had my lunch ready for me when I came home—usually a peanut butter and jelly sandwich that was shaped for the season. My favorite was at Christmas. The sandwiches would be sprinkled with green sugar and cut in the shape of a tree.

As I got a little older and tried to gain my independence, I wanted to move away from those "childish" signs of his love. But he wasn't going to give up. In high school and no longer able to go home for lunch, I began taking my own. Dad would get up a little early and make it for me. I never knew what to expect. The outside of the sack might be covered with his rendering of a mountain scene (it became his trademark) or a heart inscribed with "Dad-n-Angie K.K." in its center. Inside there would be a napkin with that same heart or an "I love you." Many times he would write a joke or a riddle, such as "Why don't they ever call it a momsicle instead of a popsicle?" He always had some silly saying to make me smile and let me know that he loved me.

I used to hide my lunch so no one would see the bag or read the napkin, but that didn't last long. One of my friends saw the napkin one day, grabbed it, and passed it around the lunch room. My face burned with embarrassment. To my astonishment, the next day all my friends were waiting to see the napkin. From the way they acted, I think they all wished they had someone who showed them that kind of love. I was so proud to have him as my father. Throughout the rest of my high school years, I received those napkins, and still have a majority of them.

And still it didn't end. When I left home for college (the last one to leave), I thought the messages would stop. But my friends and I were glad that his gestures continued.

I missed seeing my dad every day after school and so I called him a lot. My phone bills got to be pretty high. It didn't matter what we said; I just wanted to hear his voice. We started a ritual during that first year that stayed with us. After I said good-bye he always said, "Angie?"

"Yes, Dad?" I'd reply.

"I love you."

"I love you, too, Dad."

I began getting letters almost every Friday. The front-desk staff always knew who the letters were from—the return address said "The Hunk." Many times the envelopes were addressed in crayon, and along with the enclosed letters were usually drawings of our cat and dog, stick figures of him and Mom, and if I had been home the weekend before, of me racing around town with friends and using the house as a pit stop. He also had his mountain scene and the heart-encased inscription, Dad-n-Angie K.K.

The mail was delivered every day right before lunch, so I'd have his letters with me when I went to the cafeteria. I realized it was useless to hide them because my roommate was a high school friend who knew about his napkins. Soon it became a Friday afternoon ritual. I would read the letters, and the drawing and envelope would be passed around.

It was during this time that Dad became stricken with cancer. When the letters didn't come on Friday, I knew that he had been sick and wasn't able to write. He used to get up at 4:00 A.M. so he could sit in the quiet house and do his letters. If he missed his Friday delivery, the letters would usually come a day or two later. But they always came. My friends used to call him "Coolest Dad in the Universe." And one day they sent him a card bestowing that title, signed by all of them. I believe he taught all of us about a father's love. I wouldn't be surprised if my friends started sending napkins to their children. He left an impression that would stay with them and inspire them to give their own children their expression of their love.

Throughout my four years of college, the letters and phone calls came at regular intervals. But then the time came when I decided to come home and be with him because he was growing sicker, and I knew that our time together was limited. Those were the hardest days to go through. To watch this man, who always acted so young, age past his years. In the end he didn't recognize who I was and would call me the name of a relative he hadn't seen in many years. Even though I knew it was due to his illness, it still hurt that he couldn't remember my name.

I was alone with him in his hospital room a couple of days before he died. We held hands and watched TV. As I was getting ready to leave, he said, "Angie?"

"Yes, Dad?"

"I love you."

"I love you, too, Dad."

Angie K. Ward-Kucer

Workin' Man

I was never one to eavesdrop when someone was having
a chat.
But late one night as I came through our yard, I found I
was doing just that.
My wife was talking to our youngest son as he sat on the
kitchen floor,
So I stopped quietly to listen just outside the back
screen door.

Seems she'd heard some kids all bragging about their
daddy's jobs.
How they all were big executives . . . and then they
asked our Bob,
"What fine career does your father have?" their queries
all began.
Bob mumbled low as he looked away, "He's just a
workin' man."

My good wife waited 'til they all had just left, then called
our young boy in.
She said, "I have something to tell you, Son," as she
kissed his dimpled chin.
"You said your dad's just a workin' man, and what you
said was true.
But I doubt if you know what that really means, so I'll
explain it to you."

"In all the sprawling industries that make our country
  great.
In all the shops and stores and trucks that daily haul our
  freight . . .
Whenever you see a new house built, remember this, my
  son.
It took the common workin' man to get that big job done!"

"It's true—executives have nice desks and stay real clean
  all day.
They plan big projects to achieve . . . send memos to relay.
But to turn their dreams into fact, remember this, my son.
It takes the common workin' man to get those big jobs
  done!"

"If all the bosses left their desks and knocked off for a year.
The wheels of industry still could turn—running in high
  gear.
If men like your dad aren't on the job, that industry can't
  run.
It takes the common workin' man to get the big jobs done!"

Well, I choked back a tear and cleared my throat as I
  entered through the door.
My young son's eyes lit up for joy as he jumped up off the
  floor.
He gave me a hug as he said, "Hey, Dad, I'm so proud to
  be your son . . .
'Cause you're one of the men—the special men—who get
  the big jobs done."

Ed Peterman

It's How You Play the Game That Counts

Donald Jenson was struck in the head by a thrown bat while umpiring a Little League game in Terre Haute, Indiana. He continued to work the game, but later that evening was placed in a hospital by a doctor. While being kept overnight for observation, Jenson wrote the following letter:

Dear Parent of a Little Leaguer:

I am an umpire. I don't do it for a living, but on Saturdays and Sundays for fun.

I've played the game, coached it and watched it. But somehow, nothing takes the place of umpiring. Maybe it's because I feel that deep down I'm providing a fair chance for all the kids to play the game without disagreements and arguments.

With all the fun I've had, there is still something that bothers me about my job. . . . Some of you folks don't understand why I'm there. Some of you think I'm there to exert authority over your son or daughter. For that reason, you often yell at me when I make a mistake, or encourage your son or daughter to say things that hurt my feelings.

How many of you really understand that I try to be perfect? I try not to make a mistake. I don't want your child to feel that he got a bad deal from an umpire.

Yet no matter how hard I try, I can't be perfect. I counted the number of calls I made in a six-inning game today. The total number of decisions, whether on balls and strikes or safes and outs, was 146.

I tried my best to get them all right, but I'm sure I missed some. When I figured out my percentage on paper, I could have missed eight calls today and still got about 95 percent of the calls right. . . . In most occupations that percentage would be considered excellent. If I were in school, that grade would receive an "A" for sure.

But your demands are higher than that. Let me tell you more about my game today.

There was one real close call that ended the game . . . a runner for the home team was trying to steal the plate on a passed ball. The catcher chased the ball down and threw to the pitcher covering the plate. The pitcher made the tag, and I called the runner out.

As I was getting my equipment to leave, I overheard one of the parents' comments: "It's too bad the kids have to lose because of rotten umpires. That was one of the lousiest calls I've ever seen."

Later at the concession stand, a couple of kids were telling their friends, "Boy, the umpires were lousy today. They lost the game for us."

The purpose of Little League is to teach baseball skills to young people. Obviously, a team that does not play well in a given game, yet is given the opportunity to blame that loss on an umpire for one call or two, is being given the chance to take all responsibility for the loss from its shoulders.

A parent or adult leader who permits the younger player to blame his or her failures on an umpire, regardless of the quality of that umpire, is doing the worst kind of injustice to that youngster. . . . Rather than learning responsibility, such an attitude is fostering an improper outlook toward the ideals of the game itself. The irresponsibility is bound to carry over to future years.

As I sit here writing this letter, I am no longer as upset as I was this afternoon. I wanted to quit umpiring. But fortunately, my wife reminded me of another situation that occurred last week.

I was behind the plate, umpiring for a pitcher who pantomimed his displeasure at any call on a borderline pitch that was not in his team's favor. One could sense that he wanted the crowd to realize that he was a fine, talented player who was doing his best to get along, and that I was a black-hearted villain who was working against him.

The kid continued in this vein for two innings . . . while at the same time yelling at his own players who dared to make a mistake. For two innings, the manager watched this. When the kid returned to the dugout to bat in the top of the third, the manager called him aside.

In a loud enough voice that I was able to overhear, the lecture went like this: "Listen, Son, it's time you made a decision. You can be an umpire, or an actor, or a pitcher. But you can only be one at a time when you're playing for me. Right now it is your job to pitch, and you are basically doing a lousy job. Leave the acting to the actors, the umpiring to the umpires, or you won't do any pitching here. Now what is it going to be?"

Needless to say, the kid chose the pitching route and went on to win the game. When the game was over the kid followed me to my car. Fighting his hardest to keep back the tears, he apologized for his actions and thanked me for umpiring his game. He said he had learned a *lesson that he would never forget.*

I can't help but wonder . . . how many fine young men are missing their chance to develop into outstanding ballplayers because their parents encourage them to spend time umpiring, rather than working harder to play the game as it should be played.

The following morning, Donald Jenson died of a brain concussion.

Danny Warrick
Submitted by Michael J. Bolander

Reprinted with special permission of King Features Syndicate.

No Charge

Our little boy came up to his mother in the kitchen one evening while she was fixing supper, and he handed her a piece of paper that he had been writing on. After his mom dried her hands on an apron, she read it, and this is what it said:

For cutting the grass	$5.00
For cleaning up my room this week	$1.00
For going to the store for you	.50
Baby-sitting my kid brother while you went shopping	.25
Taking out the garbage	$1.00
For getting a good report card	$5.00
For cleaning up and raking the yard	<u>$2.00</u>
Total owed:	$14.75

Well, I'll tell you, his mother looked at him standing there expectantly, and boy, could I see the memories flashing through her mind. So she picked up the pen, turned over the paper he'd written on, and this is what she wrote:

For the nine months I carried you while you were growing inside me, No Charge.

For all the nights that I've sat up with you, doctored and prayed for you, No Charge.

For all the trying times, and all the tears that you've caused through the years, there's No Charge.

When you add it all up, the cost of my love is No Charge.

For all the nights that were filled with dread, and for the worries I knew were ahead, No Charge.

For the toys, food, clothes, and even wiping your nose, there's No Charge, Son.

And when you add it all up, the full cost of real love is No Charge.

Well, friends, when our son finished reading what his mother had written, there were great big old tears in his eyes, and he looked straight up at his mother and said, "Mom, I sure do love you." And then he took the pen and in great big letters he wrote: "PAID IN FULL."

M. Adams

Recognize Your Winners

Everyone needs recognition for his accomplishments, but few people make the need known quite as clearly as the little boy who said to his father: "Let's play darts. I'll throw and you say 'Wonderful!'"

The Best of Bits & Pieces

Fran Tarkenton, former Minnesota Vikings quarterback, once called a play that required him to block onrushing tacklers.

NFL quarterbacks almost never block. They're usually vastly outweighed by defenders, so blocking exposes them to the risk of severe injury.

But the team was behind, and a surprise play was needed. Tarkenton went in to block, and the runner scored a touchdown. The Vikings won the game.

Watching the game films with the team the next day, Tarkenton expected a big pat on the back for what he'd done.

It never came.

After the meeting, Tarkenton approached coach Bud Grant and asked, "You saw my block, didn't you, Coach? How come you didn't say anything about it?"

Grant replied, "Sure, I saw the block. It was great. But you're always working hard out there, Fran. I figured I didn't have to tell you."

"Well," Tarkenton replied, "if you ever want me to block again, you do!"

Don Martin

Courage of the Heart

I sit on the rickety auditorium chair with the camcorder on my shoulder and I can feel the tears well up in my eyes. My six-year-old daughter is on stage, calm, self-possessed, centered and singing her heart out. I am nervous, jittery and emotional. I try not to cry.

"Listen, can you hear the sound, hearts beating all the world around?" she sings.

Her little round face turns up to the light, a little face so dear and familiar and yet so unlike my own thin features. Her eyes—eyes so different from mine—look out into the audience with total trust. She knows she is loved.

"Up in the valley, out on the plains, everywhere around the world, heartbeats sound the same."

The face of her birth mother looks out at me from the stage. The eyes of a young woman that once looked into mine with trust now gaze into the audience. These features my daughter inherited from her birth mother—eyes that tilt up at the corners, and rosy, plump little cheeks that I can't stop kissing.

"Black or white, red or tan, it's the heart of the family of man . . . oh, oh beating away, oh, oh beating away," she finishes.

The audience goes wild. I do, too. Thunderous applause fills the room. We rise as one to let Melanie know we loved it. She smiles; she already knew. Now I am crying. I feel so blessed to be her mom. She fills me with so much joy that my heart actually hurts.

The heart of the family of man . . . the heart of courage that shows us the path to take when we are lost . . . the heart that makes strangers one with each other for a common purpose: this is the heart Melanie's birth mother showed to me. From deep inside the safest part of herself, Melanie heard her birth mother. This heart of courage belonged to a 16-year-old girl, a girl who became a woman because of her commitment to unconditional love. She was a woman who embraced the concept that she could give her child something no one else ever could: a better life than she had.

Melanie's heart beats close to mine as I hold her and tell her how great she performed. She wiggles in my arms and looks up at me. "Why are you crying, Mommy?"

I answer her, "Because I am so happy for you and you did so well, all by yourself!" I can feel myself reach out and hold her with more than just my arms. I hold her with love for not only myself, but for the beautiful and courageous woman who chose to give birth to my daughter, and then chose again to give her to me. I carry the love from both of us . . . the birth mother with the courage to share, and the woman whose empty arms were filled with love . . . *for the heartbeat that we share is one.*

Patty Hansen

Legacy of an Adopted Child

Once there were two women who never knew each other.
One you do not remember, the other you call Mother.
Two different lives shaped to make you one.
One became your guiding star. The other became your
     sun.
The first one gave you life, and the second taught you to
     live it.
The first gave you a need for love, the second was there to
     give it.
One gave you a nationality, the other gave you a name.
One gave you a talent, the other gave you aim.
One gave you emotions, the other calmed your fears.
One saw your first sweet smile, the other dried your tears.
One sought for you a home that she could not provide,
The other prayed for a child and her hope was not denied.
And now you ask me through your tears
The age-old question, unanswered through the years.
Heredity or environment. Which are you a product of?
Neither, my darling. Neither. Just two different kinds of
     love.

Author Unknown

What It Means to Be Adopted

Teacher Debbie Moon's first-graders were discussing a picture of a family. One little boy in the picture had different color hair than the other family members.

One child suggested that he was adopted, and a little girl named Jocelynn Jay said, "I know all about adoptions because I'm adopted."

"What does it mean to be adopted?" asked another child.

"It means," said Jocelynn, "that you grew in your mother's heart instead of her tummy."

George Dolan

Class Reunion

I was minding my own business a few weeks ago when I got "the call"—that dreaded, shrill ringing of my telephone bearing news just short of a death in the family. It was a former high school classmate asking my assistance in our 20-year class reunion.

Could it be 20 years already? I shuddered. Cold chills went up and down my spine as tiny beads of sweat popped out on my forehead. What had I done with my life the past 20 years? My mother told me I'd have to deal with this some day, but I had laughed it off, just like I laughed off those embarrassing pink plastic curlers she used to wear in her hair. (I picked up a set at a garage sale just last week. Got a great deal on them, too!)

It's amazing how a brief phone call can totally turn one's life upside down. Suddenly, I began hearing those 1970s songs (now known as "oldies") in a different arrangement, realizing that Mick Jagger was over 50, "Smoke on the Water" never did make any sense at all, and my "Seasons in the Sun" had literally faded into oblivion. Had the sun set on me already?

I glanced in the mirror. (Okay, I stared in the damned mirror.) I examined every tiny little crevice and pore, starting with my hairline, down past those patronizing "smile lines" to the base of my neck. No double chin yet, I thought.

The next few weeks were pure hell. Each day began with a grueling training program—a 6:30 A.M. run in a futile attempt to bounce off that unsightly baggage that had somehow accumulated on my thighs overnight. I went shopping for the perfect dress—you know, the one that would make me look 20 years younger. I found out that they stopped selling them around 1975. Three dresses later, I came to my senses. There was only one logical explanation: I was having a mid-life crisis.

I realized that the funny, crunching noise I heard each night as I climbed the stairs was really my knees. I had seriously considered adding potty training to my résumé as one of my greatest accomplishments. Bran flakes had become a part of my daily routine—and not because they were my favorite cereal. I held Tupperware parties just so I could count how many friends I had.

Life just hadn't turned out the way I'd planned. Sure, I was happy. I had a wonderful husband and two great kids in the center of my life. But somehow, working part-time as a secretary and mom hardly fit my definition of someone my classmates had voted as "most likely to succeed." Had I really wasted 20 years?

Just about the time I was ready to throw in the towel and my invitation, my seven-year old tapped me on the shoulder. "I love you, Mom. Give me a kiss."

You know, I'm actually looking forward to the next 20 years.

Lynne C. Gaul

The Gift

It was a warm summer day when the gods placed it in her hands. She trembled with emotion as she saw how fragile it appeared. This was a very special gift the gods were entrusting to her. A gift that would one day belong to the world. Until then, they instructed her, she was to be its guardian and protector. The woman said she understood and reverently took it home, determined to live up to the faith the gods had placed in her.

At first she barely let it out of her sight, protecting it from anything she perceived to be harmful to its well-being; watching with fear in her heart when it was exposed to the environment outside of the sheltered cocoon she had formed around it. But the woman began to realize that she could not shelter it forever. It needed to learn to survive the harsh elements in order to grow strong. So with gentle care she gave it more space to grow, enough to allow it to grow wild and untamed.

Sometimes she would lie in bed at night, feelings of inadequacy overwhelming her. She wondered if she was capable of handling the awesome responsibility placed on her. Then she would hear the quiet whispers of the gods reassuring her that they knew she was doing her best. And she would fall asleep feeling comforted.

The woman grew more at ease with her responsibility as the years passed. The gift had enriched her life in so many ways by its very presence that she could no longer remember what her life had been like before receiving it, nor imagine what life would be like without it. She had all but forgotten her agreement with the gods.

One day she became aware of how much the gift had changed. It no longer had a look of vulnerability about it. Now it seemed to glow with strength and steadiness, almost as if it were developing a power within. Month after month she watched as it became stronger and more powerful, and the woman remembered her promise. She knew deep within her heart that her time with the gift was nearing an end.

The inevitable day arrived when the gods came to take the gift and present it to the world. The woman felt a deep sadness, for she would miss its constant presence in her life. With heartfelt gratitude, she thanked the gods for allowing her the privilege of watching over the precious gift for so many years. Straightening her shoulders, she stood proud, knowing that it was, indeed, a very special gift. One that would add to the beauty and essence of the world around it. And the mother let her child go.

Renee R. Vroman

3

ON
TEACHING
AND
LEARNING

Teachers are those who use themselves as bridges, over which they invite their students to cross; then having facilitated their crossing, joyfully collapse, encouraging them to create bridges of their own.

Nikos Kazantzakis

To Beth's First-Grade Teacher

I didn't know the man in front of me that morning. But I did notice that we both walked a little straighter, a little more proudly, as our daughters held our hands. We were proud but apprehensive on that important day. Our girls were beginning first grade. We were about to give them up, for a while at least, to the institution we call school. As we entered the building, he looked at me. Our eyes met just for a minute, but that was enough. Our love for our daughters, our hopes for their future, our concern for their well-being welled up in our eyes.

You, their teacher, met us at the door. You introduced yourself and showed the girls to their seats. We gave them each a good-bye kiss and then we walked out the door. We didn't talk to each other on the way back to the parking lot and on to our respective jobs. We were too involved thinking about you.

There were so many things we wanted to tell you, Teacher. Too many things were left unsaid. So I'm writing to you. I'd like to tell you the things we didn't have time for that first morning.

I hope you noticed Beth's dress. She looked beautiful in it. Now I know you might think that's a father's prejudice, but she thinks she looks beautiful in it, and that's what's really important. Did you know we spent a full week searching the shopping malls for just the right dress for that special occasion? She wouldn't show you, but I'm sure she'd like you to know that she picked that dress because of the way it unfurled as she danced in front of the mirrors in the clothing store. The minute she tried it on, she knew she'd found her special dress. I wonder if you noticed. Just a word from you would make that dress all the more wondrous.

Her shoes tell you a lot about Beth and a lot about her family. At least they're worth a minute of your time. Yes, they're blue shoes with one strap. Solid, well-made shoes, not too stylish, you know the kind. What you don't know is how we argued about getting the kind of shoes she said all the girls would be wearing. We said no to plastic shoes in purple or pink or orange.

Beth was worried that the other kids would laugh at her baby shoes. In the end she tried the solid blue ones on and, with a smile, told us she always did like strap shoes. That's the first-born, eager to please. She's like the shoes—solid and reliable. How she'd love it if you mentioned those straps.

I hope you quickly notice that Beth is shy. She'll talk her head off when she gets to know you, but you'll have to make the first move. Don't mistake her quietness for lack of intelligence. Beth can read any children's book you put in front of her. She learned reading the way it should be taught. She learned it naturally, snuggled up in her bed with her mother and me reading her stories at nap time, at bedtime, at cuddling times throughout the day. To Beth, books are synonymous with good times and loving family. Please don't change her love of reading by making the learning of it a burdensome chore. It has taken us all her life to instill in her the joy of books and learning.

Did you know that Beth and her friends played school all summer in preparation for their first day? I should tell you about her class. Everybody in her class wrote something every day. She encouraged the other kids who said they couldn't think of anything to write about. She helped them with their spelling. She came to me upset one day. She said you might be disappointed in her because she didn't know how to spell "subtraction." She can do that now. If you would only ask her. Her play school this summer was filled with positive reinforcement and the quiet voice of a reassuring teacher. I hope that her fantasy world will be translated into reality in your classroom.

I know you're busy with all the things that a teacher does at the beginning of the school year, so I'll make this letter short. But I did want you to know about the night before that first day. We got her lunch packed in the Care Bear lunch box. We got the backpack ready with the school supplies. We laid out her special dress and shoes, read a story, and then I shut off the lights. I gave her a kiss and started to walk out of the room. She called me back in and asked me if I knew that God wrote letters to people and put them in their minds.

I told her I never had heard that, but I asked if she had received a letter. She had. She said the letter told her that her first day of school was going to be one of the best days of her life. I wiped away a tear as I thought: *Please let it be so.*

Later that night I discovered a note Beth left me. It read, "I'm so lucky to have you for a dad."

Well, Beth's first-grade teacher, I think you're so lucky to have her as a student. We're all counting on you. Every one of us who left our children and our dreams with you that day. As you take our youngsters by the hand, stand a little taller and walk a little prouder. Being a teacher carries with it an awesome responsibility.

Dick Abrahamson

Mr. Washington

One day in 11th grade, I went into a classroom to wait for a friend of mine. When I went into the room, the teacher, Mr. Washington, suddenly appeared and asked me to go to the board to write something, to work something out. I told him that I couldn't do it. And he said, "Why not?"

I said, "Because I'm not one of your students."

He said, "It doesn't matter. Go to the board anyhow."

I said, "I can't do that."

He said, "Why not?"

And I paused because I was somewhat embarrassed. I said, "Because I'm Educable Mentally Retarded."

He came from behind his desk and he looked at me and he said, "Don't ever say that again. Someone's opinion of you does not have to become your reality."

It was a very liberating moment for me. On one hand, I was humiliated because the other students laughed at me. They knew that I was in Special Education. But on the other hand, I was liberated because he began to bring to my attention that I did not have to live within the context of what another person's view of me was.

And so Mr. Washington became my mentor. Prior to this experience, I had failed twice in school. I was identified as Educable Mentally Retarded in the fifth grade, was put back from the fifth grade into the fourth grade, and failed again when I was in the eighth grade. So this person made a dramatic difference in my life.

I always say that he operates in the consciousness of Goethe, who said, "Look at a man the way that he is, he only becomes worse. But look at him as if he were what he could be, and then he becomes what he should be." Like Calvin Lloyd, Mr. Washington believed that "Nobody rises to low expectations." This man always gave students the feeling that he had high expectations for them and we strove, all of the students strove, to live up to what those expectations were.

One day, when I was still a junior, I heard him giving a speech to some graduating seniors. He said to them, "You have greatness within you. You have something special. If just one of you can get a glimpse of a larger vision of your-self, of who you really are, of what it is you bring to the planet, of your specialness, then in a historical context, the world will never be the same again. You can make your parents proud. You can make your school proud. You can make your community proud. You can touch mil-lions of people's lives." He was talking to the seniors, but it seemed like that speech was for me.

I remember when they gave him a standing ovation. Afterwards, I caught up to him in the parking lot and I said, "Mr. Washington, do you remember me? I was in the auditorium when you were talking to the seniors."

He said, "What were you doing there? You are a junior."

I said, "I know. But that speech you were giving, I heard your voice coming through the auditorium doors. That speech was for me, Sir. You said they had greatness within them. I was in that auditorium. Is there greatness within me, Sir?"

He said, "Yes, Mr. Brown."

"But what about the fact that I failed English and math and history, and I'm going to have to go to summer school. What about that, Sir? I'm slower than most kids. I'm not as smart as my brother or my sister who's going to the University of Miami."

"It doesn't matter. It just means that you have to work harder. Your grades don't determine who you are or what you can produce in your life."

"I want to buy my mother a home."

"It's possible, Mr. Brown. You can do that." And he turned to walk away again.

"Mr. Washington?"

"What do you want now?"

"Uh, I'm the one, Sir. You remember me, remember my name. One day you're gonna hear it. I'm gonna make you proud. I'm the one, Sir."

School was a real struggle for me. I was passed from one grade to another because I was not a bad kid. I was a nice kid; I was a fun kid. I made people laugh. I was polite. I was respectful. So teachers would pass me on, which was not helpful to me. But Mr. Washington made demands on me. He made me accountable. But he enabled me to believe that I could handle it, that I could do it.

He became my instructor my senior year, even though I was Special Education. Normally, Special Ed students don't take Speech and Drama, but they made special provisions for me to be with him. The principal realized the kind of bonding that had taken place and the impact that he'd made on me because I had begun to do well academically. For the first time in my life I made the honor roll. I wanted to travel on a trip with the drama department and you had to be on the honor roll in order to make the trip out of town. That was a miracle for me!

Mr. Washington restructured my own picture of who I am. He gave me a larger vision of myself, beyond my mental conditioning and my circumstances.

Years later, I produced five specials that appeared on public television. I had some friends call him when my program, "You Deserve," was on the educational television channel in Miami. I was sitting by the phone waiting when he called me in Detroit. He said, "May I speak to Mr. Brown, please?"

"Who's calling?"

"You know who's calling."

"Oh, Mr. Washington, it's you."

"You were the one, weren't you?"

"Yes, Sir, I was."

Les Brown

Faith, Hope and Love

At the age of 14 I was sent away to Cheshire Academy, a boarding school in Connecticut for boys who had problems at home. My problem was my alcoholic mother, who had torn apart our family with her dysfunctional behavior. After my parents divorced, I baby-sat my mother until I failed every course in eighth grade. My father and a school headmaster decided that a disciplinary boarding school that excelled in sports (and was a good distance from my alcoholic mother) might give me a chance to graduate from high school.

At orientation my freshman year at Cheshire, the last man to speak was the head disciplinarian—Fred O'Leary. He was a former All-American football player at Yale, a very large man. He had jowls and a huge neck; he looked like the Yale mascot "The Bulldog." As he moved his large frame forward toward the microphone to speak, everyone got real quiet. An upper-classman next to me said, "Kid, don't ever let this man see you. Cross the street or whatever. Just don't let this man know that you exist!"

Mr. O'Leary's speech to the school assembly that night was short and to the point: "Don't, I repeat, don't go off campus, don't smoke, don't drink. No contact with town girls. If you break these rules, there will be hell to pay, plus I will personally kick your ass!" Just when I thought he was finished, in a much lower tone, he said, "If you ever have any problems, the door to my office is open to you." How that stuck in my mind!

As the school year wore on, my mother's drinking got worse. She called me in my dorm at all hours of the day and night. With her slurred words, she'd beg me to drop out and move back home with her. She promised she would quit drinking and we could go to Florida on vacation, and on and on. I loved her. It was hard to say no to her and my insides turned upside-down with every call. I felt guilt. I felt shame. I was very, very confused.

One afternoon while in freshman English, I was thinking about the call from my mother the night before and my emotions got the better of me. I could feel the tears coming fast, so I asked my professor if I could be excused.

"Excused for what?" asked my professor.

"To see Mr. O'Leary," I answered. My classmates froze and stared at me.

"What have you done, Peter? Maybe I can help," my professor suggested.

"No! I want to go to Mr. O'Leary's office now," I said. As I left class, all I could think of were those words, "My door is open."

Mr. O'Leary's office was off a large lobby in the main hall. The door to his office had a big glass pane so you could see inside. Whenever someone was in serious trouble, he would pull them inside his office, slam the door and lower the window shade. Often you could hear him yelling, "You were seen smoking behind the town fire station last night with another guy and that town girl from the coffee shop!" There would be hell to pay for that unfortunate soul.

There was a line outside his office at all times: academy boys with all kinds of problems, sitting there with their tails between their legs. As I took my place in line, the other boys asked me what I had done wrong.

"Nothing," I said.

"Are you crazy? Get out of here, now!" they cried, but I could think of nowhere else to go.

Finally, it was my turn. Mr. O'Leary's office door opened and I was staring straight into the jowls of discipline. I was shaking and feeling foolish, but I had this crazy hunch that something or someone had put me in front of this man—the most feared man on campus. I looked up; our eyes met.

"What are you here for?" he barked.

"At orientation you said your door was open if anyone had a problem," I stammered.

"Come in," he said as he pointed to a big green arm chair and pulled the shade down over the door. Then he walked behind his desk and sat down and looked at me.

I looked up, opened my mouth and the tears ran down my face. "My mother is an alcoholic. She gets drunk and calls me on the phone. She wants me to quit school and move home. I don't know what to do. I'm scared, afraid. Please don't think I'm crazy or a fool."

I buried my head in my knees and began to cry uncontrollably. Oblivious to my surroundings, I didn't hear this large, ex-athlete move quietly from behind his desk, come around and stand beside the little adolescent boy sobbing in the big green chair. One of God's lost children in a dark, cold place.

Then it happened—one of those miracles that God makes happen through people. Mr. O'Leary's large hand gently touched my shoulder; his thumb rested on my neck.

Softly, I heard this dreaded giant of discipline say, "Son, I know how you feel. You see, I'm an alcoholic, too. I will do everything I can to help you and your mother. I will have my friends in Alcoholics Anonymous make contact with her today."

In that instant, I had a moment of clarity. I knew things were going to get better, and I wasn't scared anymore. With his hand resting on my shoulder, I felt I had been touched by God, by Christ, by Moses. Faith, Hope and Love became real to me for the first time. I could see them, taste them, and I was filled with faith, hope and love for everyone around me. The most feared man on campus became my secret friend, and I checked in with him religiously, once a week. Whenever I passed his table at lunch time, I got a quick glance and friendly wink. My heart soared with pride that this feared man of discipline took such a gentle, loving interest in me.

I reached out and, in my moment of need . . . He was there.

Peter Spelke
with a little help from Dawn Spelke
and Sam Dawson

The name Fred O'Leary is a pseudonym. The name has been changed to protect the privacy of the actual individual.

The Shoes

What do we live for if not to make life less difficult for each other?

George Eliot

During the 1930s, things were really rough in all the mining and manufacturing places everywhere. In my old hometown in western Pennsylvania, men by the thousands walked the streets looking for work. My older brothers were among these. Not that the family went hungry, mind you, but we didn't eat much.

Since I was one of the younger boys in a large family, all my clothes were hand-me-downs. Long pants would be bobbed knee length, and the cut-off legs used to patch or reinforce the cut-down trousers. Shirts would be made over. But shoes—shoes were a different story. Shoes would be worn right down to the ground. They would be literally worn out, being cast aside only when the bare feet came through the leather.

I can remember that before getting the oxfords, I wore a pair of shoes with split sides and loose soles completely free at the front that made slapping sounds as I walked. I cut two bands off an old inner tube and slipped them over my toes to hold those shoe soles down.

I had a sister then. She and her husband had moved west and settled down in Colorado. When she could, she helped out by sending us their old clothes.

One day before Thanksgiving we received a box of such things from her. All of us gathered round it. Nestled in the corner were the shoes. I didn't know what kind they were at the time. My mother didn't either, come to think of it, nor did my dad, nor any of the boys. They all thought like I did, that those shoes were some my sister had grown tired of.

My mother looked down at my feet coming out through my old shoes, and then leaned over the box and brought out those gift shoes and held them out to me. I put my hands behind me, looked around the family circle, and began to cry softly to myself. It's a wonder none of my brothers laughed at me or called me cry baby.

It's still painful after 30 years to think about it. My mother took me aside and told me she was sorry, but there were no other shoes for me to wear and with winter coming on, I'd simply have to make use of them. My dad patted me but didn't say anything. My favorite brother, Mike, roughed up my hair and told me everything would be all right.

Finally, when I was all alone, I put on my sister's shoes. They were tan colored and had pointy toes and kind of high heels but they felt pretty good. I sat there staring through my tears at them, sobbing softly to myself.

Next day I got up and dressed for school, taking as much time as I could, and leaving to the very last those shoes. I felt my eyes filling up again but fought the tears back. I finally had to get to school, so I took the back way and didn't run into anybody till I was in the school yard. There stood Timmy O'Toole, my only enemy, older and taller than me, and, like me, in Miss Miller's class.

He took one look at my sister's shoes, grabbed my arm, and began to yell, "Evan's wearing girls' shoes! Evan's wearing girls' shoes!" Oh, I could have pounded him soft but he was so much bigger and tougher than me! He wouldn't let me go at first. He kept it up till he had a big ring of kids around us. I don't know what I'd have done, but suddenly there was Ol' Man Weber, the principal.

"Come in," he said, "it's time for the tardy bell." I made a dash for the door and got into our room before Timmy could torment me any more.

I sat quietly with my eyes down and my feet pulled up under me, but even this didn't stop him. He kept it up and kept it up. Every time he'd come by my desk, he'd do a little dance and call me Edna and make some silly crack about my sister's shoes.

By midmorning we were talking about the winning of the West, and Miss Miller told us a lot about the pioneers out in Kansas and Colorado and Texas and other places. About this time Ol' Man Weber came into our room and stood just inside the door, listening quietly.

I was like all the other boys before that morning. That is, I didn't like Ol' Man Weber much. He was supposed to be real mean. He had a bad temper. He favored girls.

He stood inside the door of our room. Now none of us knew, excepting maybe Miss Miller, that Ol' Man Weber had once lived on an Oklahoma ranch. Miss Miller turned to him and asked if he would care to join the discussion, and much to our surprise he did. Only instead of telling the usual kind of thing, Ol' Man Weber began talking about a cowboy's life and about Indians, things like that. He even sang a couple of cowboy songs! He went on like that for 40 minutes.

It was nearing noon and about time for us to go home for lunch, when Ol' Man Weber started up my aisle, still speaking. Suddenly he paused near my desk and went silent. I looked up into his face and realized that he was staring down under my desk, gazing at my sister's shoes.

I could feel my face getting red as I began to move my feet up under me. But before I could ease them up he whispered, "Cowboy oxfords!"

I said, "Sir?"

And again he said, "Cowboy oxfords!" And then in a pleased voice, as the other children strained to see what he was staring at and hear what he was saying, he exclaimed, "Why, Evan, where on earth did you get those cowboy oxfords?"

Well, soon everybody in the room was gathered as near to him and me as they could get, even Miss Miller. And everybody was saying, "Evan's got a genuine pair of cowboy oxfords!" It was easily the happiest day of my life.

Since there wasn't much time left anyway, Mr. Weber told Miss Miller it would be all right, provided Evan was agreeable, to let the boys and girls get a real good look at those cowboy oxfords. Well, everybody including Timmy O'Toole filed past my desk and peered at my beautiful shoes. I felt like a giant but knew from my mother that I should avoid pride, so I sat there trying not to be too big-headed. Finally, it was lunch time.

I could hardly get outside, for everybody wanted to walk next to me. Then everybody wanted to try 'em on, my cowboy oxfords, I mean. I said I'd have to think it over. After all!

That afternoon I asked Mr. Weber what he thought about letting everybody try on my cowboy oxfords, and he thought and thought about it. Finally he said it would be all right to let the boys try them on but certainly not the girls. After all, girls aren't ever to wear cowboy oxfords. It was funny that Mr. Weber thought about it the same way I did.

So I let all the boys in my room try them on, even Timmy O'Toole, though I made him go last. And he was the only one besides me that they fit. He wanted me to write my sister and see if she could find a pair for him. I didn't ask her, though. I had the only pair of cowboy oxfords in town, and I really liked it that way.

Paul E. Mawhinney

Bonehead

As long as I live, I won't forget when I met Alvin C. Hass for the first time in 1991. The other inmate in the prison class didn't use the name "Alvin Hass" when he introduced us—not even close! He introduced Alvin as "Bonehead." Immediately, I felt uncomfortable with Alvin's nickname. The tall, soft-spoken inmate wouldn't look at me as he shook my hand. Needless to say, "Bonehead" was bald-headed. The hair that he had on the sides went way down past his shoulders. I felt as though I were staring at him and tried not to look. But there was a large (and very intimidating) tattoo on top of his bald head. (Yes! A tattoo on his head!) The tattoo was of Harley-Davidson wings and covered the entire top of his head.

As a teacher, I try to maintain excellent composure during stressful times, and I made it through that first day of class. At the end of the period, "Bonehead" slipped me a note while he was filing out of the classroom. I thought, "Oh no! He's telling me that I'm going to be 'taken out' by his other 'Harley' buddies if I don't give him a good grade or something like that." A little later, I had a chance to read the note. It said, "Teach [he always called me "Teach"], breakfast is an important meal and if you're not in by then you're in big trouble!—Bonehead, the Mountain Hippie."

Bonehead completed a series of six classes with me over many months. He was an excellent student who seldom spoke. However, he handed me a note nearly every day with some type of saying, tidbit, anecdote or other wise advice for life. I looked forward to receiving them and became a little disappointed if by chance he didn't give me one. I still have them all today.

Bonehead and I clicked. Somehow, I knew that each time I opened my mouth to teach, he understood me. He silently soaked up everything I said. We were connected.

At the conclusion of the course, each student received a certificate. Bonehead had completed the course doing excellent work the entire way through and I was excited to give him his certificate.

We were alone when I presented his certificate of completion. I shook his hand and briefly told him what a pleasure it was to have had him in my classes and that I appreciated his hard work, excellent attendance and superior attitude. His response stayed with me and continues to make a deep impression on my life. In that soft voice of his, Bonehead said, "Thank you, Larry. You're the first teacher in my life that ever told me I did anything right."

As I walked away, I was awash with emotion. I could hardly hold back the tears thinking that in all of Bonehead's growing-up years, no one ever told him he had done anything right.

Now, I'm from the "old school." I was raised in a conservative setting and I believe criminals must pay for their wrongdoings and be held accountable. Yet I've asked myself several times, "Could it be, by chance, just by chance, that Bonehead's never hearing 'you did that right' or 'Good job' might have had anything at all to do with why he ended up in prison?"

That moment's experience implanted into my heart

the desire to make sure I acknowledge, in a positive way, every student that does something "right."

Thanks, Bonehead, for telling me that I, too, did something right.

Larry Terherst

"Maybe you didn't notice, kid, but we have a dress code here."

FARCUS ©1994 FARCUS CARTOONS. Distributed by Universal Press Syndicate. Reprinted with permission. All rights reserved.

Footprints on My Heart

Some people come into our lives and quickly go. Some stay for a while and leave footprints on our heart and we are never, ever the same.

Source Unknown

On a bitterly cold January day a new student walked into my fifth-grade class for students with learning disabilities, leaving his footprints on my heart. The first time I saw Bobby, he was wearing a tank top and a pair of threadbare jeans, obviously too small, despite the cold weather. One of his shoes was missing a lace, and it flopped up and down when he walked. Even if he had been wearing a decent set of clothes, Bobby wouldn't have looked like a normal child. He had a haunted, neglected, lost look about him that I had never seen before and hope that I never see again.

Not only did Bobby look strange, but his behavior was so bizarre that I was convinced he belonged in a classroom that taught social skills. Bobby thought that a rounded sink in the hallway was a urinal, his normal tone of voice was a yell, he was obsessed with Donald Duck and he never made eye contact with anyone. He blurted out comments continuously during class. Once he proudly announced to everyone that the P.E. teacher told him that he smelled bad and had made him put on deodorant.

Not only were his social skills atrocious, but his academic skills were nonexistent. Bobby was 11 years old and he couldn't read or write. He couldn't even write the letters of the alphabet. To say that he didn't fit in among my classroom students was an understatement.

I was sure that Bobby was misplaced in my room. I checked his records and was shocked to learn that his I.Q. was normal. What could account for his bizarre behavior? I talked with the school counselor, who told me that he had met Bobby's mother. He said, "Bobby is a lot closer to normal than she is." I searched the records further and found that Bobby had been placed in foster care for the first three years of his life. After that he was returned to his mother and they had moved to a different town at least once a year. So that was it. Bobby's intelligence was normal, and despite his odd behavior, he would remain in my room.

I hate to admit it, but I resented him being in my class. My room was crowded enough and I already had several demanding students. I had never tried to teach someone whose abilities were at such a low level It was a struggle to even plan lessons for him. The first few weeks he was at school I would wake up to find my stomach in knots, dreading to go to work. There were days when I would drive to school and hope that he wouldn't be there. I took pride in being a good teacher, and I was disgusted with myself for not liking him and not wanting him in my class.

Despite the fact that he drove me crazy, I tried valiantly to treat him like all of the other students. I never allowed anyone to pick on him in my classroom. However, outside of the room, the students made a game out of being mean to him. They were like a pack of wild animals attacking one of their own for being sick or hurt.

About a month after he started at the school, Bobby came into my room with his shirt torn and his nose bloodied. He had been jumped on by a group of my students. Bobby sat down at his desk and pretended that nothing was wrong. He opened his book and tried to read it as blood and tears mingled and dripped onto the pages. Outraged, I sent Bobby to the nurse and unleashed a verbal fury on the students who had hurt him. I told them that they ought to be ashamed of themselves for not liking him because he was different. I yelled that just because he acted strangely, this was even more reason to treat him kindly. At some point during my verbal assault, I started to listen to my own words and I resolved that I would have to change *my* thoughts toward him as well.

That incident changed how I felt about Bobby. I finally saw past his bizarre behavior and saw a little boy in desperate need of someone to care about him. I realized that the true test of a teacher was not just teaching academics but meeting the needs of the students. Bobby had extraordinary needs that I had to fill.

I started buying Bobby clothes from the Salvation Army. I knew that the students made fun of him because he only had three shirts. I carefully chose clothing that was in good condition and in style. He was thrilled with the clothes and it improved his self-esteem tremendously. I escorted Bobby to classes whenever he was worried about being beaten up. I spent extra time with him before school working on homework.

It was amazing to see the change in Bobby that resulted from the new clothes and extra attention. He came out of his shell and I found that he really was a likeable child. His behavior improved and he even started making brief eye contact with me. I no longer dreaded going to work. I actually looked forward to seeing him coming down the hallway in the morning. I worried about him when he was absent. I noticed that as my attitude toward him changed, so did the behavior of the other students. They stopped picking on him and included him as a part of the group.

One day Bobby brought a note to school that said he would be moving in two days. I was heartbroken. I hadn't managed to get him all of the clothes I wanted to. I went to a store on my break and bought him an outfit. I gave it to him and told him that it was his good-bye present. When he saw the tags on the clothes he said, "I can't ever remember wearing brand-new clothes before."

Some of my students found out that Bobby was moving, and after class several of them asked if they could give him a good-bye party the next day. I said, "Sure," but I thought to myself, "They can't remember to do their homework. There's no way they can organize a party by tomorrow morning." To my surprise they did. The next morning they brought in a cake, streamers, balloons and presents for Bobby. His tormentors had become his friends.

On Bobby's last day of school, he walked into my classroom carrying a huge backpack filled with children's books. He enjoyed the party, and, after things had settled down, I asked him what he was doing with all of the books. He said, "The books are for you. I have lots of books so I thought maybe you should have some." I was sure that Bobby didn't have anything of his own at home, certainly not books. How could a child who at one time only had three shirts have lots of books?

As I looked through the books, I found that most of them were library books from various places where he had lived. Some of the books had written in them, "Teacher's personal copy." I knew that the books didn't really belong to Bobby and that he had acquired them through questionable means. But he was giving me all that he had to give. Never before had anyone ever given me such a wonderful gift. Except for the clothes on his back, which I had given him, Bobby was giving me all that he owned.

As Bobby left that day he asked me if he could be my pen pal. He walked out of my room with my address, leaving me his books and his footprints forever on my heart.

Laura D. Norton

4

ON DEATH AND DYING

Do not stand at my grave and weep.
I am not there.
I do not sleep.
I am a thousand winds that blow.
I am the diamond glint on snow.
I am the sunlight on ripened grain.
I am the autumn rain.
When you awake in the morning hush,
I am the swift uplifting rush
Of birds circling in flight.
I am the stars that shine at night.
Do not stand at my grave and weep.
I am not there.
I do not sleep.

Author Unknown

The Golden Crane

As a teacher of origami (the ancient Japanese art of paper folding) at the LaFarge Lifelong Learning Institute in Milwaukee, Wisconsin, Art Beaudry was asked to represent the school at an exhibit at a large mall in Milwaukee.

He decided to take along a couple hundred folded paper cranes to pass out to people who stopped at his booth.

Before that day, however, something strange happened—a voice told him to find a piece of gold foil paper and make a gold origami crane. The strange voice was so insistent that Art actually found himself rummaging through his collection of origami papers at home until he found one flat, shiny piece of gold foil.

"Why am I doing this?" he asked himself. Art had never worked with the shiny gold paper; it didn't fold as easily or neatly as the crisp multicolored papers. But that little voice kept nudging. Art harrumphed and tried to ignore the voice. "Why gold foil anyway? Paper is much easier to work with," he grumbled.

The voice continued. "Do it! And you must give it away tomorrow to a special person."

By now Art was getting a little cranky. "What special person?" he asked the voice.

"You'll know which one," the voice said.

That evening Art very carefully folded and shaped the unforgiving gold foil until it became as graceful and delicate as a real crane about to take flight. He packed the exquisite bird in the box along with about 200 colorful paper cranes he'd made over the previous few weeks.

The next day at the mall, dozens upon dozens of people stopped by Art's booth to ask questions about origami. He demonstrated the art. He folded, unfolded and refolded. He explained the intricate details, the need for sharp creases.

Then there was a woman standing in front of Art. The special person. Art had never seen her before, and she hadn't said a word as she watched him carefully fold a bright pink piece of paper into a crane with pointed, graceful wings.

Art glanced up at her face, and before he knew what he was doing, his hands were down in the big box that contained the supply of paper cranes. There it was, the delicate gold-foil bird he'd labored over the night before. He retrieved it and carefully placed it in the woman's hand.

"I don't know why, but there's a very loud voice inside me telling me I'm supposed to give you this golden crane. The crane is the ancient symbol of peace," Art said simply.

The woman didn't say a word as she slowly cupped her small hand around the fragile bird as if it were alive. When Art looked up at her face, he saw tears filling her eyes, ready to spill out.

Finally, the woman took a deep breath and said, "My husband died three weeks ago. This is the first time I've been out. Today . . ." she wiped her eyes with her free hand, still gently cradling the golden crane with the other.

She spoke very quietly. "Today is our golden wedding anniversary."

Then this stranger said in a clear voice, "Thank you for this beautiful gift. Now I know that my husband is at peace. Don't you see? That voice you heard, it's the voice of God and this beautiful crane is a gift from Him. It's the most wonderful 50th wedding anniversary present I could have received. Thank you for listening to your heart."

And that's how Art learned to listen very carefully when a little voice within him tells him to do something he may not understand at the time.

Patricia Lorenz

If I Had Only Known

For everything you have missed, you have gained something else.

Ralph Waldo Emerson

When Reba McEntire recorded the song "If I Had Only Known," people wanted to know how the song came to be written. The song might never have been created if I could have received my driver's license the same day all my friends did.

In Clovis, New Mexico, where I was raised, you can get your driver's license at 15, but only if you've successfully completed Driver's Education. Nearly everybody in my class turned 15 during the ninth grade. On the last day of school when they passed their Driver's Ed test, they could get their licenses. The excitement and anticipation on that final day of junior high was almost unbearable to us. I'm sure it was completely unbearable to our teachers. Even though I wouldn't turn 15 until we started 10th grade, I was thrilled that my friends would be driving. Never again would we be hauled around like cattle by our mothers. At last we would be FREE.

My dad saw the situation differently, as dads so often do. He was a loving father, and very protective. When I got home from school that day, chattering away about the fun things Dena, Lori, Debi, Kristi, and Johnna and I were planning, my dad sat me down for one of those dreaded talks that begin with, "This is going to hurt me a lot worse than it's going to hurt you." He didn't think my friends would be safe drivers yet. He was afraid I would wind up in a car accident. He said he didn't want me to go places with them driving until we started school again in the fall.

My heart dropped as fast as that one big tear fell to my jawline. I could see what my dad could not. I saw myself spending the long, precious days of summer alone. Wrestling a lump in my throat the size of a basketball, I tried to reason, using the only thing teenagers can think of, like, "But Dad, it's not fair" and "But Dad, all the other kids get to." As always, it was no use. He had laid down the law. I could still go places with my friends, but only if their mothers drove us.

Remembering what it was like to be 15, take a wild guess at how many teenage girls with new driver's licenses would ask their mothers to drive them, just so the girl down the street could go. The answer is zero, *nada*, zip, none. My only hope for seeing my friends was to sit on the front lawn in the hot sun, pretending to read *Seventeen* magazine. I thought that if they noticed how lonely I was, they'd stop and talk before zipping out of the neighborhood in their moms' cars. Most days, they didn't.

I could've disobeyed my dad. I could've sneaked out of the house to meet the girls and go driving. I chose not to. I spent those summer days disappointed and disheartened, unnaturally separated from my friends at a time when friends mean everything. My experience that summer leads me to believe, though, that there is sometimes a reward for integrity in the face of hardship. Sometimes, an angel is moved by a brave, sad face. My angel was my great-aunt, my Aunt Dorothy. A phone call from her later that summer changed everything.

Dorothy was a bookkeeper out at Doc Stewart Chevrolet. Everybody said that she and her sister Katheryne were the most beautiful girls in eastern New Mexico when they were younger. As they grew older, it became clear that their beauty was not just on the surface, but from deep within. Aunt Dorothy always wore a big smile with her round brown glasses and wavy blonde hair. She loved people with such enthusiasm that you couldn't help feeling better about yourself around her. She had never called me before, but she called that day to ask if I'd like to help out at the dealership.

My mom, who was on summer break from teaching, drove me out there early every morning so I could work with Aunt Dorothy and the secretaries—Creola, Sonya and Lynn.

Those women treated me so big. Most mornings, they complimented me on my outfits, playfully saying they hated me because I could eat three chocolate donuts for breakfast and stay skinny. After a week or two, Creola mentioned that I was always singing. When she said that, I stopped, but they got me to start again because they said too many grown-ups are afraid to sing while they work. They wanted to know what I thought about deep stuff like destiny, religion and politics. What a hoot it would be now to hear what I said. I'm sure that when I went to get my morning Dr. Pepper, they shared the secret chuckles that all grown-ups have over the opinions of a teenager they love.

Creola, Sonya and Lynn didn't care whether I could drive. I earned their respect by my ability (or maybe it was just my eager willingness) to tackle any task. I carried heavy boxes of folders up the tiny stairway to the attic. I cleaned out dusty old cabinets, bulging with unorganized files. I learned all the important grown-up stuff, like how to curve your fingers when you reach down into a file, so you won't drive a staple under your fingernail. Like how to shoot purchase orders up the suction tube to the parts department, and how to tell if one of the salesmen was having an affair.

The best part of my job was that after I finished my work, I could play on the typewriter, teaching myself how to type. Since I wanted to be a writer someday, my dad said typing would be important. I'd take a nice, clean sheet of Doc Stewart Chevrolet stationery and type silly stuff as fast as I could think it. *My name is Jana Lee Stanfield. Stars shibing right abode me* [sic]. *Never will I have chicken feet for breakfast.*

Aunt Dorothy often took me with her to lunch. Our favorite spot was Twin Cronnie. Don't ask me what a cronnie is. All I can tell you is that the place was a drive-in with car-hops and it had a big sign with two hot dogs jitterbugging.

We'd order chicken-fried steak fingers in big boxes with gravy, french fries and Texas toast. Sitting in her car, we'd eat lunch and talk about important things, like what high school was like in 1943, and how Uncle Joe lost part of his lung in the war, and why my cousin Judy got married so young. Sometimes a carload of my friends would drive up. Even though I longed to be with them, I was proud that I had a job and I was proud that Aunt Dorothy was my friend.

By the end of that summer, I saved enough money to buy all my own clothes for school. I bought little flowered T-shirts and baggy, high-waisted pants in three colors with narrow belts. A few days before school started, I cut my hair off short like the girls in *Seventeen* magazine. All of us girls know that a drastic change in your hair is a symbol of a change in your life.

I started high school feeling different in a real good

way—older and stronger and more confident. The most amazing thing happened. For the first time in my life, I became popular at my school. I barely got my driver's license before I got Homecoming Court, Student Council, and then the honor that meant so much to me after those lonely days, Class Favorite.

You know how a teenager's life goes. After that summer I didn't have much time to see Aunt Dorothy. I'd stop by maybe once a year to take her out for steak fingers, and to give Creola, Sonya and Lynn the satisfaction of knowing that all those chocolate donuts caught up with me.

When I finally graduated from college, Aunt Dorothy and Uncle Joe were there cheering. Aunt Dorothy gave me a beautiful filigree bracelet she got on their vacation. Underneath the cotton was a gift even more precious to me. Folded up small was a dusty old sheet of Doc Stewart stationery. *My name is Jana Lee Stanfield. Stars shibing right abode me. Never will I have chicken feet for breakfast.*

I was living in Nashville six years later, trying without much success to be a songwriter when Aunt Dorothy was diagnosed with cancer. She fought it so bravely, hating to lose her pretty blonde hair, but never losing her warm smile, peeking out from that thick blonde wig. It was Christmas when I saw her last. Not long after that, I got a call from my cousin Judy. Aunt Dorothy was slipping away quickly, but was still well enough to talk a little on the phone if I wanted to say good-bye. Judy gave me Aunt Dorothy's number at the hospital in New Mexico.

Holding that small slip of paper with her number, I thought about how the smallest thing a person does with love can make the biggest difference in our lives. Calling Aunt Dorothy that day was one of the most painful things I have ever experienced. I told her how much I loved her. I thanked her for reaching out to me when I needed somebody I thanked her for always seeing the best in everyone she cared about. I didn't want to hang up. I wanted to hang on. I wanted that moment to last. I wanted to stop the clock and go back to spend more time with her.

After Aunt Dorothy and I said our last "I love you," I hung up the phone and sobbed into the silence of my empty apartment. I thought about all the people who touch our lives with their kindness and then disappear before we ever thank them or tell them how much they mean to us.

On a lonely Sunday a few weeks later, the words to "If I Had Only Known" came in a flood of tears. Since I didn't know much about writing melodies yet, I took the unfinished lyrics to the most talented songwriter I knew, Craig Morris, and asked if he could craft something beautiful from my simple words.

In the same way that Aunt Dorothy turned my life around when I was 14, she had turned it around again by inspiring "If I Had Only Known."

If I had only known it was our last walk in the rain
I'd keep you out for hours in the storm
I would hold your hand, like a lifeline to my heart
And underneath the thunder we'd be warm
If I had only known it was our last walk in the rain

If I had only known I'd never hear your voice again
I'd memorize each thing you ever said
And on these lonely nights, I could think of them once
  more
And keep your words alive inside my head
If I had only known I'd never hear your voice again

You were the treasure in my heart
You were the one who always stood beside me
So unaware, I foolishly believed that you would always
  be there

But then there came a day when I closed my eyes
And you slipped away

If I had only known it was my last night by your side
I'd pray a miracle would stop the dawn
And when you smiled at me, I would look into your eyes
And make sure you know my love for you goes on and on
If I had only known, If I had only known

The love I would've shown
If I had only known

Reba McEntire recorded the song in remembrance of her band members who were killed in a plane crash. It has since been used to raise money for St. Jude's Children's Hospital, to educate teenagers about the dangers of underage drinking, and to bring attention to the needs of AIDS patients. It has been sung and quoted at countless funerals and even a high school graduation. The song's popularity in the movie *8 Seconds* made it possible for me to start doing concerts with a positive message in elementary schools, middle schools and high schools all over the country. If I had only known.

Jana Stanfield

"If I Had Only Known" by Craig Morris/Jana Stanfield
©1991, Alabama Band Music (a division of Wildcountry, Inc.)/Jana Stantunes. Used by permission. All rights reserved.

A Trucker's Last Letter

Steamboat Mountain is a man-killer, and truckers who haul the Alaska Highway treat it with respect. Particularly in the winter, the road curves and twists over the mountain and sheer cliffs drop away sharply from the icy road. Countless trucks and truckers have been lost there and many more will follow their last tracks.

On one trip up the highway, I came upon the Royal Canadian Mounted Police and several wreckers winching the remains of a semi up the steep cliff. I parked my rig and went over to the quiet group of truckers who were watching the wreckage slowly come into sight.

One of the Mounties walked over to us and spoke quietly.

"I'm sorry," he said, "the driver was dead when we found him. He must have gone over the side two days ago when we had a bad snowstorm. There weren't many tracks. It was just a fluke that we noticed the sun shining off some chrome."

He shook his head slowly and reached into his parka pocket.

"Here, maybe you guys should read this. I guess he lived for a couple of hours until the cold got to him."

I'd never seen tears in a cop's eyes before—I always figured they'd seen so much death and despair they were immune to it, but he wiped tears away as he handed me the letter. As I read it, I began to weep. Each driver silently read the words, then quietly walked back to his rig. The words were burned into my memory and now, years later, that letter is still as vivid as if I were holding it before me. I want to share that letter with you and your families.

December, 1974

My Darling Wife,

This is a letter that no man ever wants to write, but I'm lucky enough to have some time to say what I've forgotten to say so many times. I love you, sweetheart.

You used to kid me that I loved the truck more than you because I spent more time with her. I do love this piece of iron—she's been good to me. She's seen me through tough times and tough places. I could always count on her in a long haul and she was speedy in the stretches. She never let me down.

But you want to know something? I love you for the same reasons. You've seen me through the tough times and places, too.

Remember the first truck? That run down 'ol' corn-binder' that kept us broke all the time but always made just enough money to keep us eating? You went out and got a job so that we could pay the rent and the bills. Every cent I made went into the truck while your money kept us in food with a roof over our heads.

I remember that I complained about the truck, but I don't remember you ever complaining when you came home tired from work and I asked you for money to go on the road again. If you did complain, I guess I didn't hear you. I was too wrapped up with my problems to think of yours.

I think now of all the things you gave up for me. The clothes, the holidays, the parties, the friends. You never complained and somehow I never remembered to thank you for being you.

When I sat having coffee with the boys, I always talked about my truck, my rig, my payments. I guess I forgot you were my partner even if you weren't in the cab with me. It was your sacrifices and determination as much as mine that finally got the new truck.

I was so proud of that truck I was bursting. I was proud of you too, but I never told you that. I took it for granted you knew, but if I had spent as much time talking with you as I did polishing chrome, perhaps I would have.

In all the years I've pounded the pavement, I always knew your prayers rode with me. But this time they weren't enough.

I'm hurt and it's bad. I've made my last mile and I want to say the things that should have been said so many times before. The things that were forgotten because I was too concerned about the truck and the job.

I'm thinking about the missed anniversaries and birthdays. The school plays and hockey games that you went to alone because I was on the road.

I'm thinking about the lonely nights you spent alone, wondering where I was and how things were going. I'm thinking of all the times I thought of calling you just to say hello and somehow didn't get around to. I'm thinking of the peace of mind I had knowing that you were at home with the kids, waiting for me.

The family dinners where you spent all your time telling your folks why I couldn't make it. I was busy changing oil; I was busy looking for parts; I was sleeping because I was leaving early the next morning. There was always a reason, but somehow they don't seem very important to me right now.

When we were married, you didn't know how to change a light bulb. Within a couple of years, you were fixing the furnace during a blizzard while I was waiting for a load in Florida. You became a pretty good mechanic, helping me with repairs, and I was mighty proud of you when you jumped into the cab and backed up over the rose bushes.

I was proud of you when I pulled into the yard and saw you sleeping in the car waiting for me. Whether it was two in the morning or two in the afternoon you always looked like a movie star to me. You're beautiful, you know. I guess I haven't told you that lately, but you are.

I made lots of mistakes in my life, but if I only ever made one good decision, it was when I asked you to marry me. You never could understand what it was that kept me trucking. I couldn't either, but it was my way of life and you stuck with me. Good times, bad times, you were always there. I love you, sweetheart, and I love the kids.

My body hurts but my heart hurts even more. You won't be there when I end this trip. For the first time since we've been together, I'm really alone and it scares me. I need you so badly, and I know it's too late.

It's funny I guess, but what I have now is the truck. This damned truck that ruled our lives for so long. This twisted hunk of steel that I lived in and with for so many years. But it can't return my love. Only you can do that.

You're a thousand miles away but I feel you here with me. I can see your face and feel your love and I'm scared to make the final run alone.

Tell the kids that I love them very much and don't let the boys drive any truck for a living.

I guess that's about it, honey. My God, but I love you very much. Take care of yourself and always remember that I loved you more than anything in life. I just for-got to tell you.

> *I love you,*
> *Bill*

Rud Kendall
Submitted by Valerie Teshima

For the Love of a Child

Seventeen-year-old Mike Emme drove a '67 Ford Mustang. It had sat neglected in a Colorado field undriven for over seven years before he bought it, rebuilt it and painted it bright yellow. A gifted student, Mike was a happy, helpful young man with a future as bright and cheerful as his car. Friends called him "Mustang Mike."

"I wish I could have learned how to hate," the note read. "Don't blame yourselves. Mom and Dad, I love you. Remember, I'll always be with you." It was signed, "Love, Mike 11:45."

Mike's summer love had been terminated abruptly by his girlfriend's engagement to someone else on August 23. On September 8, in a move that stunned all who knew him, Mike slipped into the front seat of his bright yellow Mustang, closed the door and shot himself.

At 11:52 his parents, Dar and Dale Emme, and his brother, Victor, pulled into their driveway behind Mike's bright yellow Mustang—seven minutes too late.

By noon the next day, teenagers started arriving at the Emme home wearing T-shirts bearing the words "IN MEMORY OF MIKE EMME" imprinted above a bright yellow Mustang. (They had been created by Mike's best friend, Jarrod, and Jarrod's mom.)

A stream of stories that went on for days began emerging. Most were news to Mike's family. Some went clear back to grade school times, when he had shared his lunch with a less fortunate child or contributed his lunch money to some fund drive.

A stranger phoned to share how her car had broken down late one night, leaving her and her two small children stranded on a dark road. Mike had stopped, shown her his driver's license to assure her he would not harm them, got her car started, and followed them home to be sure they arrived safely.

A classmate from a single-parent family revealed that Mike had canceled his order for a brand-new, completely built Mustang transmission, which he had saved up for to put in his own car, and bought two used ones from the salvage yard instead so that this classmate could get his car running too.

Next came a young girl who disclosed that had it not been for Mike, she would not have been able to go to the Homecoming dance. When Mike heard that she did not have the money to buy an evening dress, he paid for a very nice dress that she had found in a used-clothing store.

When Mike was 14, his niece was born severely handicapped. Mike learned how to remove the tracheotomy tube from her throat, should an emergency arise, and replace it with a new one; how to perform CPR on her; and how to use sign language to sign songs with her because the tracheotomy tube, without which she would die, prevented her from talking. Their favorite song to sign has a chorus that says, "God is watching us from a distance . . ." It seemed like Mike was always there to give happiness, a hand or a hug.

Teenagers gathered at the Emme home to comfort the family and each other. They discussed the tragedy of teen suicide and the fact that the highest number of teen suicides are gifted (high I.Q.) children. They learned that suicide is the sixth most common cause of death of children ages 5 to 14 and the third most common in those ages 15 to 24. They discovered that each year suicide takes the life of over 7,000 children between the ages of 10 and 19, and that it is now becoming epidemic even in our elementary schools. Someone mentioned a study that compared adolescents who committed suicide but who had no apparent mental disorders with kids of the same age who did not commit suicide. It found only one difference—a loaded gun in the house.

As they explored what they themselves might be able to do to prevent this type of tragedy, someone looked up, saw a bright yellow Mustang on one of the T-shirts, and the Yellow Ribbon Project was born. Linda Bowles, a family friend, brought over a large roll of yellow ribbon and printed up little business-card-size papers containing instructions on how to use the ribbons. They read:

> "YELLOW RIBBON PROJECT"
> In loving memory of Michael Emme
>
> THIS RIBBON IS A LIFELINE: It carries the message
> that there are those who care and will help. If you
> (or anyone else) are in need and don't know how to
> ask for help, take this, or any yellow ribbon or
> card, to a counselor, teacher, priest, rabbi, minister,
> parent, or friend and say:
> "I'D LIKE TO USE MY YELLOW RIBBON."

Sitting on the Emmes' living room floor, Mike's friends shared their stories, their grief and their tears as they mourned the loss of their friend by pinning a piece of yellow ribbon on each instruction card.

Five hundred of these yellow ribbons were placed in a basket set out at Mike's memorial service. By the end of the service, the basket was empty, and 500 little yellow ribbons, complete with instruction cards, had begun their mission of saving other children from suicide. In just its first few weeks, the Yellow Ribbon Project prevented three teen suicides that we know of, and was soon introduced in all of Colorado's high schools. It has been growing ever since.

Because of the internal nature of depression, loneliness and fear, thousands of our very fine children—who appear to be perfectly happy—are screaming silently in the deepest of emotional pain. What can we do?

Free ribbons and suggestions are available at The Yellow Ribbon Project, P.O. Box 644, Westminster, CO 80030, or call (303) 429-3530.

Thea Alexander

The Last Dance

One of my first tasks as a boy was to help gather firewood. I loved it. I went with my father out into the woods to cut and split the firewood. We were men working together as mighty lumberjacks, doing our share to keep our house and women warm. Yes, he taught me to be a provider. It was a wonderful feeling. Oftentimes he bet me that I could not split a big old knotty cut of wood, say, in 500 strokes. Oh, how I tried! Most of the time I won, but I think he always gave me plenty of strokes because he saw how proud and happy I was on that last powerful stroke (499th) when the piece of wood finally split. With runny noses from the cold, we then pulled the sled of wood home, heading in for some grub and a warm relaxing fire.

When I was in first grade, my father and I watched television together on Tuesday nights: *Wyatt Earp, Cheyenne, Maverick* and *Sugar Loaf.* He totally convinced me that he rode with them in his past. He was always able to tell me what was going to happen before it happened. That is why I believed him. He said he knew them so well he could predict their actions. Boy, was I proud; my father was a real cowboy who rode with the best. I went to school and told this to my friends. They laughed at me and told me my father was lying to me. To defend his honor, I constantly got into fights. One day I was beat up pretty badly. Seeing my torn pants and split lip, my teacher pulled me to the side to find out what had happened. One thing led to another, and my father had to tell me the truth. Needless to say, I was crushed, but I still loved him dearly.

My father started to play golf when I was about 13 years old. I was his caddie. He would let me hit a few shots when we got away from the clubhouse. I fell in love with the game and became good at it. Once in a while Dad brought two of his friends along. When Dad and I took them on in a skins game and won, I beamed with joy. We were a team.

Both my father and mother's second love (us kids being the first) was dancing. Together they were fabulous. The ballroom crowd nicknamed my parents, Marvin and Maxine, the great M & M's of the dance floor. It was their romantic fantasy come true. I never saw Mom and Dad with anything but smiles on their faces when they were dancing. My two sisters, Nancy and Julie, and I always went along to the wedding dances. What a blast!

After church on Sunday mornings, my Dad and I were in charge of preparing breakfast. While we waited for the oatmeal and raisins to cook, we practiced our tap-dance routine on Mom's clean, newly waxed floor. She never complained.

As I got older, our relationship seemed to grow apart. When I entered junior high school, extracurricular activities started to consume my time. My peer group were jocks and musicians—we played sports, played in a band and chased girls. I remember how hurt and lonely I was when Dad began working at night and no longer came to any of my activities. I submerged myself in hockey and golf. My angry attitude was, "I'll show you. I will be the best even without you there." I was captain of both the hockey and golf teams, but he did not come to *one* of my games. I felt as if his lack of attention was conditioning me to be a bitter survivor in life. I needed him. Didn't he know?

Drinking alcohol became a part of the social scene for me. Dad no longer seemed like a hero, but more like a person who did not understand my feelings or that I was going through a very difficult time. Once in a while when we were both drinking and getting high, things seemed to get closer between us, but the special feelings of the past were just not there. From the time I was 15 until I was 26, we never said we loved each other. Eleven years!

Then it happened. One morning Dad and I were getting ready for work. He was shaving and I noticed a lump on his throat. I asked, "Dad, what is that on your neck?"

"I don't know. I'm going to the doctor today to find out," he said.

That morning was the first time I saw Dad look so scared.

The doctor diagnosed the lump on Dad's throat as cancer, and for the next four months I saw my father die a little each day. He seemed so confused by what was happening. He was always so healthy; it was unbearable to see him go from 165 pounds of muscles and flesh to 115 pounds of skin and bones. I tried to get close to him, but I guess he had so much on his mind that he could not focus on me or our feelings toward each other.

This seemed to be the case until the night of Christmas Eve.

I arrived at the hospital that evening and discovered my mom and sister had both been there all day. I stood watch so they could go home and get some rest. Dad was asleep when I walked into his room. I sat in a chair beside his bed. From time to time he would wake up, but he was so weak that I could hardly hear what he had to say.

At about 11:30 P.M., I got sleepy, so I lay down and slept on a cot that an orderly had brought to the room. All of a sudden, my father awakened me. He was shouting out my name. "Rick! Rick!" As I sat up, I saw Dad sitting up in bed with a most determined look. "I want to dance. I want to dance, right now," he said.

At first I didn't know what to say or do, so I just sat there. Again he persisted. "I want to dance. Please, son, let's have this last dance." I went over to the bed, bowed slightly and asked, "Will you dance with me, Father?" It was amazing. I hardly had to help him up from the bed. His energy must have come from God's grace. Hand in hand, arms around each other, we danced around the room.

No writer has ever written words that could describe the energy and love that we shared that night. We became one, united in the true meaning of love, understanding and caring for each other. Our whole life together all seemed to be happening at that exact moment. The tap-dancing, hunting, fishing, golf—we experienced everything all at once. Time did not exist. We did not need a record player or radio, for every song that was ever written, or ever will be, was playing in the air. The small room was bigger than any ballroom in which I had ever danced. Dad's eyes lit up with a glitter and sorrowful joy I had never experienced before. Tears came to both of our eyes as we kept on dancing. We were saying good-bye, and with just a short time left we both realized once again how great it was to have this uncompromising love for each other.

When we stopped, I helped my father back into the bed, as he was now near exhaustion. With a firm grasp, he took my hand, looked straight into my eyes and said, "Thank you, my son. I am so glad that you are here with me tonight. It means so much to me." He died the following day on Christmas.

The last dance was God's gift to me on that Christmas Eve—a gift of happiness and wisdom as I found out just how strong and purposeful a love between a father and son can be.

Well, Pop, I do love you, and I look forward to our next dance in God's ballroom.

Rick Nelles

My Daddy

When I was three, my father passed away. But when I was seven, my mother remarried. And I became the luckiest little girl in the world. You see, I got to pick my daddy. After Mom and "Dad" had dated for a while, I said to my mother, "He's the one. We'll take him."

I got to be flower girl when Mommy and Daddy got married. That alone was wonderful. How many people can say they were in their parents' wedding (and actually walked down the aisle)?

My daddy had such pride in his family. (Two years later our family grew by one little sister.) People who barely knew us would say to my mother, "Charlie always looks so proud to be with you and the kids." It wasn't just materialistic. Daddy was proud of our intelligence, our beliefs, our common sense and our love of people (as well as my cute smile).

Right before I turned 17, something awful happened. My daddy got sick. After several days of tests, the doctors couldn't find anything wrong. "If we, *the omnipotent,* can't find anything—he must be well." They told Dad to return to work.

The next day he came home from work with tears streaming down his face. That's when we knew he was deathly ill. I had never seen my father cry before. Dad thought crying was a sign of weakness. (Which made for an interesting relationship, since—as a hormonal teenager—I cried at everything, including Hallmark commercials.)

Finally, we got Dad admitted into the hospital. He was diagnosed with pancreatic cancer. The doctors said that he could go at any time. But we knew better. We knew he had at least three more weeks. You see, my sister's birthday was the next week and mine was in three. My father would defy death—praying to God for strength—to hang on until after those events. He would not let us go through the rest of our lives with such a terrible memory on our birthdays.

The fact that life must go on is never more evident than when someone is dying. Dad wanted desperately for us to keep living our lives. We wanted desperately for him to remain a part of it. We compromised. We agreed to continue doing our "normal" activities, but Dad was going to be an active part of those—even from the hospital.

After one of our daily visits, the man sharing Dad's room followed Mom into the hallway. "Charlie is always so quiet and positive when you are here. I don't think you realize how much pain he is in. He uses all of his strength and endurance to hide it."

My mother replied, "I know he is hiding it, but that is his way. He would never want us to suffer, and he knows how much it pains us to see him hurting."

For Mother's Day, we took all our gifts to the hospital. Dad met us in the lobby (since my little sister was too young to be allowed in his room). I bought a gift for Dad to give to Mom. We had a wonderful little party in our corner of the lobby.

The next week was my sister's birthday. Dad wasn't well enough to come downstairs, so we celebrated with cake and presents in the waiting area on his floor.

My prom was the following weekend. After the customary pictures at my house and my date's, we went to the hospital. Yes, I walked through the hospital in a full-length gown with a hoop. (I barely fit in the elevator.) I was a little embarrassed. But not when I saw the look on my daddy's face. He had waited so many years to see his little girl go to her first prom.

My sister's annual dance recital always had a dress rehearsal the day before the event. That's when family members could take pictures. Naturally, after the rehearsal we went to the hospital. My sister paraded through the hallways in her dance costume. Then she did her dance for Dad. He smiled throughout—although all that tapping was excruciatingly painful to his head.

My birthday came. We sneaked my sister into Dad's room, since he couldn't leave. (The nurses kindly looked in the other direction.) And again, we celebrated. But Dad was not in good shape. It was time for him to go, but he was holding out.

That night, the hospital called. Dad had taken a serious turn for the worse. A few days later, my daddy died.

One of the hardest lessons to learn from death is that life must go on. Dad insisted that we never stop living our lives. To the end, he was concerned about us and proud of us. His last request? That he be buried with a picture of his family in his pocket.

Kelly J. Watkins

Where Do the Sparrows Go When They Die?

A question I often asked myself as a child was, "Where do the sparrows go when they die?" I didn't know the answer then and I still wonder about it. Now I see a dead bird silenced by some evil force, and I know he didn't die. Something killed him: the elements took him away, a lost soul in the night.

When I was six, my best friend was a boy on my street. We used to play in my sandbox, talking of things long forgotten by grownups like never growing up, or the monsters under our beds and in dark closets. His name was Tommy, but I called him Sparrow because he was small for his age. It's ironic to think of that name now because he died, too.

I remember the day I found out Tommy was dying. I waited in the sandbox for him, half-heartedly building the castle we began the day before. Without Tommy I was only half, so I waited for what seemed like forever, and it began to rain. Then I heard a distant ring from the house. About 10 minutes later my mother came out, sheltered by her umbrella but her face wet just the same. We walked to the house. Just before we entered, I turned around and watched the rain beat down the sand castle Tommy and I built.

Once I was inside and had a cup of hot chocolate in my belly, my mother called me to the table. She put her hands on mine. They were shaking. I immediately felt it: something had happened to Tommy. She said doctors had performed some blood tests awhile back. When they received the test results, something showed up wrong. That something was leukemia. I didn't know what it was and I looked at my mother with confused eyes, but with a knowing and heavy heart. She said that people who had what Tommy got—no: *what got Tommy*—had to go away. I didn't want him to go away. I wanted him to stay, with me.

The next day I had to see Tommy. I had to see if it was all true, so I had the bus driver drop me off at his house instead of mine. When I reached the door, Tommy's mom said that he didn't want to see me. She had no idea how easily she could hurt a little girl. She broke my heart like a piece of cheap glass. I ran home in tears. After I returned home, Tommy called. He said to meet him at the sandbox after our parents went to bed, so I did.

He didn't look different, maybe a little paler, but it was Tommy. He did want to see me. We talked of those subjects incomprehensible to adults, and all the while we rebuilt our sand castle. Tommy said we could live in one just like it and never grow up. I believed him wholeheartedly. There we fell asleep, engulfed in true friendship, surrounded by warm sand and watched by our sand castle.

I woke up just before dawn. Our sandbox was like a desolate island surrounded by a sea of grass, interrupted only by the back patio and the street. A child's imagination is never-ending. The dew gave the imaginary sea a reflective shimmer, and I remember reaching out to touch the dew to see if it would make the make-believe water ripple, but it did not. I turned around, and Tommy jolted me back to reality. He was already awake, staring at the castle. I joined him, and there we sat, locked in the awesome magic the sand castle held for two small children.

Tommy broke the silence and said, "I'm going to the castle now." We moved like robots, as if we knew what we were doing, and I guess in some small way we did. Tommy laid his head on my lap and said drowsily, "I'm going to the castle now. Come visit; I'll be lonely." I promised him with all my heart that I would. Then he closed his eyes, and my Sparrow flew away to where I knew at that moment all the other sparrows went when they died. And there he left me, holding a soulless, crippled little bird in my arms.

I went back to Tommy's grave 20 years later and placed a small toy castle on it. On the castle I had engraved, "To Tommy, my Sparrow. I'll come to our castle someday, forever."

When I am ready, I'll go back to the place where our sandbox was and imagine our sand castle. Then my soul, like Tommy's, will turn into a sparrow and will fly back to the castle, and to Tommy, and to all the other little lost sparrows. A six-year-old again, who will never grow up.

Casey Kokoska

The Courage Not to Fight

Twilight shadows stole softly across the floor of my new apartment as I nursed my infant son, absorbed in the fresh wonder of motherhood. Long after I finished nursing, I held him close, hearing his tiny breathing, smelling his baby smell. Our small living room turned from mellow to cool dusk. I snapped on the lamp, bathing the room and us in a glow of happiness.

"This is our home, Wilson, cozy and safe," I whispered, kissing his soft cheek. Recently I'd separated from my husband and moved from Philadelphia, Pennsylvania, to Mount Kisco, New York.

At last my life was getting settled. I'd found a job as a domestic where I could keep Wilson with me. Our apartment was in a large complex, convenient to shopping and with wonderful neighbors. There was a big grassy lot and a playground. Important things for Wilson and his older sister, Yolaine, as they grew.

I was still holding this sweet burden of mine when he fell asleep. As I leaned back to rest, suddenly I jumped. A voice, soft and gentle, said, *You will only have Wilson for a short time. Teach him about God.*

My heart was pounding. "Was that you, Lord?" I asked, knowing it was. Shifting a sleeping Wilson to one arm, I went to the window and pulled the cord on the drapes.

Would I see an angel? There was only the dark silhouette of the maple tree blowing in the October wind. I hurried to the phone and called my mother.

Her calm, familiar voice reassured me. "Don't worry," she said. "Short time could mean a normal life span because the Bible says, 'A day with the Lord is as a thousand years.' Perhaps God has a special purpose for Wilson and wants you to start teaching him right away."

Of course! I began singing to him and talking to him of Jesus' love.

When Wilson was two he was diagnosed as having hemophilia. It would be hard and often painful for my son, especially since he was so active. But we could live with it.

Then when Wilson was four I got shattering news. Through an infusion of blood protein, he contracted the virus that causes AIDS. The doctor had tears as he told me. I looked this caring man in the eye and said, "My son will be the one in a million to beat this." The doctor didn't answer, but neither would he dash my hope. We immediately began with the drug AZT, which has prolonged the lives of many AIDS patients.

For five years Wilson continued with his normal routine. Then the virus struck. Still I couldn't believe he would die. I prayed hard.

During the last few months of second grade, Wilson began to downslide. He loved school. His teachers were great and wanted him there, despite his physical problems. He was an outgoing child who was popular with all the kids as well.

One day the school nurse called me at my desk where I was a receptionist at Mount Kisco Medical Group. Wilson had a seizure. He was going down the steps at recess and hit the wall, breaking his glasses. Would I please come right away?

I found him lying on a cot in the nurse's office, his face swollen and bruised. He was dazed but managed a feeble smile and tried to sit up. He was a fighter. I slipped his broken glasses in my purse, knowing they could easily be fixed, and wishing all of life was that simple. "Come on, honey," I said, my arm supporting him, "the doctor will adjust your medicine and it will be all right."

And it was. For a little while Wilson was back to his old self—almost. I'd watch him through the bedroom window of our apartment, where kids, just home from school, were gathering. They were skateboarding and after that, chasing one another around the jungle gym. There was a catch in my throat as Wilson drifted to the sidelines and sat lethargically on the grass, while Yolaine followed and kept an eye on him. After a while I heard his footsteps, weak and shuffling, on the outside stairs. I opened the door. "Wilson . . ."

"I'm all right, just tired," he said in his little-boy voice that belied man-size courage. As he reached for a book and slumped on the couch, I wondered if there were any limits to his bravery. There were.

Mid-June came, the last two weeks of school, and Wilson had to drop out. A crushing blow. He was running a high fever that wouldn't break and the doctor had him hospitalized.

Einstein Hospital in New York City's Bronx is an old, plain building fighting its age and looks with fresh paint. Wilson was in the pediatric bed next to a deep-sill window overlooking the street. It had a chair that folded back for me to sleep in at night. I used my vacation and sick time from work to stay with Wilson.

The next day my son was lying weak in bed, having just returned from a bone marrow scan. The doctor still hadn't found the cause of his fever. Fluid from an IV unit was dripping into Wilson's arm. I reached for my worn

Bible and opened it to where Jesus gathered the children on his lap. I read to Wilson, picturing those little ones climbing all over Jesus, His strong carpenter's arms holding them protectively and His eyes burning with love. I thought of those hands that healed all who came to Him when He was on earth, and I sent up another prayer.

Then came an ice-cold shock. Wilson looked up at me and said, "I know I'm dying, but I don't want to leave you yet."

I went numb. With all his medical problems—hepatitis, blood transfusions three or four times a week, limbs locking painfully from internal bleeding, seizures—he had never ever mentioned dying or giving up. Until now. He was a fighter, and it was important that he keep on fighting if he was going to live.

"Honey, you're not dying," I said. "You're sick, but we're going to fight to make you better. You're going to keep on taking your medicine. You'll get out of the hospital and ..."

I stopped. His eyes, glued to mine, were pleading. Suddenly I saw the depth of his terror, the awful weight of dying. Of leaving me, his family, friends, his room that meant so much to him, going out of his body and moving to an alien place called heaven. Unlike the visits to his uncle in Philadelphia, there would be no phone calls home. Total separation. I laid the Bible aside and stroked his thin arm. "Jesus loves you, even more than I do," I said. He fell asleep. I sat still in my chair, looking out the window at a lazy summer day. "Jesus," I began, remembering how easily Wilson prayed, about everything small and great, "I can't believe that he's going to die. But if it comes to that, help my son to know that heaven is wonderful like Your Word says. Help him not to be afraid."

Summer passed in a blur of hospital trips, ups and downs, hope and despair. Before I knew it, the nip of fall had arrived and the leaves were flaming ... then withering brown, then gone, and it was winter. Wilson was now bedridden at home.

As the winter wind beat against our building, I tried to think of a way to make Christmas special for Wilson. My mother had moved in with us so I could still go to work. "How about his own tree in his room?" she suggested. We got a table-sized one because his room was tiny. The lights winked at him all through the long nights when he couldn't sleep.

Christmas Day came. Family arrived and we celebrated. Wilson was propped up on pillows on the pullout sofa, his hand resting on one of his presents. There was a faraway look in his eyes that couldn't be penetrated, not even by the train set we surprised him with, though he managed a smile and ran the train around the track twice. He fell asleep from the effort.

I sank into a chair next to him. From the kitchen came the clatter of pots and pans, and the smells of ham, fried chicken, mashed potatoes and gravy. Wilson opened his eyes and immediately his face searched for mine, as if to confirm that he hadn't left me yet. I finally admitted it. My son was dying.

On January 12, a gray wintry day, I carried Wilson from his bed to the living room sofa. There I bundled him up for his last trip to the hospital. He looked around at each piece of furniture, each picture on the wall, the doorway, the kitchen table and the dishes drying in the sink, soaking himself in memories. "Jesus loves you," I said, praying that Wilson would know it. *Really* know it.

At the hospital my own strength was about gone, and as day stretched into night I felt strangely numb and detached, almost in shock. Doctors, nurses, family drifted in and out, urging me to sleep, telling me they'd wake me if anything happened—"anything" being the moment of death. The next morning came. Wilson was thirsty, but he couldn't swallow. The soft drink dribbled out of his mouth. As the day progressed he couldn't talk. I remembered a line from his favorite song and could still hear him at church, handsome in his suit, singing for all he was worth: "When I'm sick and can't get well, Lord, remember me. . . . Do Lord, oh do, Lord, oh do remember me, way beyond the blue."

Please, Jesus . . . it was dark again at a quarter to five, and suddenly Wilson became alert, opening his eyes and looking right at me.

"I'm going home, Mom."

How could I explain to him that this was impossible? "Wilson, Mommy can get oxygen for you, but you can't go home with the IV."

"No, Mom. I mean I'm going home to be with Jesus."

Home. He was calling heaven *home.* Gone was his dread of leaving me and all else he knew and felt connected to. Wilson's eyes were now focused beyond me. "Jesus is coming to get me. Okay, Mom?"

Jesus Himself coming to take Wilson home. "Yes, Wilson," I said. Fifteen minutes ticked by. My son's eyes closed. His breathing grew more labored. Then stopped. The doctor came in, leaned over and checked his pulse.

"He's gone," the doctor said gently, touching me. Involuntarily I screamed and grabbed my son by the shoulders. Wilson opened his eyes and started breathing again, a pleading look on his face, as if to say, "Let me go . . . home."

In my mind I could see Jesus waiting. "It's okay, honey. You can go now. Mommy's all right."

He smiled, stopped breathing and walked home with Jesus.

Denise Wicks-Harris
Submitted by Jane Hanna

Please Dress Me in Red

In my dual profession as an educator and health care provider, I have worked with numerous children infected with the virus that causes AIDS. The relationships that I have had with these special kids have been gifts in my life. They have taught me so many things, but I have especially learned that great courage can be found in the smallest of packages. Let me tell you about Tyler.

Tyler was born infected with HIV; his mother was also infected. From the very beginning of his life, he was dependent on medications to enable him to survive. When he was five, he had a tube surgically inserted in a vein in his chest. This tube was connected to a pump, which he carried in a small backpack on his back. Medications were hooked up to this pump and were continuously supplied through this tube to his bloodstream. At times, he also needed supplemental oxygen to support his breathing.

Tyler wasn't willing to give up one single moment of his childhood to this deadly disease. It was not unusual to find him playing and racing around his backyard, wearing his medicine-laden backpack and dragging his tank of oxygen behind him in his little wagon. All of us who knew Tyler marveled at his pure joy in being alive and the energy it gave him. Tyler's mom often teased him by telling him that he moved so fast she needed to dress him in red. That way, when she peered out the window to check on him playing in the yard, she could quickly spot him.

This dreaded disease eventually wore down even the likes of a little dynamo like Tyler. He grew quite ill and, unfortunately, so did his HIV-infected mother. When it became apparent that he wasn't going to survive, Tyler's mom talked to him about death. She comforted him by telling Tyler that she was dying too, and that she would be with him soon in heaven.

A few days before his death, Tyler beckoned me over to his hospital bed and whispered, "I might die soon. I'm not scared. When I die, please dress me in red. Mom promised she's coming to heaven, too. I'll be playing when she gets there, and I want to make sure she can find me."

Cindy Dee Holms

Don't Worry, It'll Be Alright

As a mother and as a school psychologist, I see many extraordinary friendships between children. My son Court and his friend Wesley share the very closest of friendships. Their relationship is truly exceptional.

Court has not had an easy childhood. He has been challenged with a speech and language handicap and gross motor delays. At age four, Court met Wesley in a Special Education preschool class. Wesley was suffering from a brain tumor, causing him to have similar developmental delays as Court. An instant bond developed and they became best friends. No day was complete for either boy if either one missed a day of school.

At age two, Wesley was diagnosed as having an "inoperable" tumor on his brain stem. He endured several unsuccessful surgeries. While the boys played, Wesley began to noticeably drag his leg. An MRI showed significant tumor growth. Once again, it was time for Wesley to undergo another operation, only this time the surgery would be in Oklahoma City.

Court and Wesley were blessed throughout their preschool years with a wonderful teacher. The children affectionately called her "Bachmann." She was the finest teacher I have ever met in my career as a school psychologist. Bachmann tried to explain and to prepare her class of language-delayed preschoolers about Wesley's surgery and trip to Oklahoma City. Court became very emotional and cried. He did not want his best friend to go so far away on an airplane, and he certainly did not want a doctor to hurt Wesley.

On departure day, Wesley and the entire class said their farewells. Tears rolled down Court's cheeks. Bachmann then dismissed the class to allow Court and Wesley private time to say good-bye. Court was afraid that he would never see his best friend again. Wesley, frail and much shorter than Court, hugged Court at chest level, looked knowingly up into Court's eyes and soothingly replied, "Don't worry, it'll be alright."

The operation was extremely dangerous, but Wesley pulled through once again. After many weeks, he returned to school. Court and Wesley became closer than before.

As the years passed by, Wesley had to have several more critical operations and had to be subjected to many experimental drugs. Each time, he suffered crippling side effects. Wesley spent much of his time confined to a wheelchair or having his frail body carried from place to place.

Wesley loved the school's Jog a-thons. Wesley would physically participate in any way possible. Although his legs failed him, those close to him didn't. One year, Wesley's mother pushed him in his wheelchair, with cheers of "Faster, Mom!" Another year, Wesley participated by being carried on the shoulders of another child's father.

At age 11, every surgery and alternative medicine had been exhausted. The tumor had taken over his delicate body. On March 9th of that year, Bachmann notified Court that it was time to really say good-bye to Wesley, his dear friend, forever. Wesley was now at home and was not expected to live.

By Court's 11th birthday, he had made great progress in his development. Academic difficulties were still apparent and running the Jog-a-thon was not Court's best event. The day after the phone call from Bachmann, Court ran in the Jog-a-thon. Court was recovering from a cold and asthma but convinced me to let him go to school. When I picked him up from school that afternoon, he said that his lungs were burning. He was holding a certificate and a shiny first-place ribbon. The certificate read, "First Place for Fifth-Graders awarded to Court in dedication to his friend Wesley."

Court, who is usually not an assertive, "take charge" child, insisted that we go to see Wesley that night. Wesley's mother arranged for us to visit him between medication times. Wesley was in bed in their family room. A soft light was shining on his fragile, angelic body, while Christian music played in the background. Between the cancer and the pain medication, Wesley could do very little. Occasionally, he was able to squeeze someone's finger and open one eye.

Bachmann was able to arouse Wesley and help him understand that Court was with him. Court held Wesley's hand as he showed Wesley the First Place certificate. Court expressed his deep feelings of desperately wanting to win for Wesley since Wesley was unable to be there. Wesley squeezed Court's finger and gave Court a look that was to be understood only for them. As Court leaned over to give Wesley a kiss, he whispered, "Good-bye Wesley, my friend. Don't worry. It'll be alright."

Wesley did live to see his 11th birthday, and then died that June. Court went through the formal motions of the funeral that one does, but when he was asked about how he was feeling, he explained that he had already said good-bye to his best friend and knew Wesley would be "alright."

I thought the story of their friendship was over when Wesley died. I was wrong. Exactly a year after Wesley's death, Court became violently ill with meningitis. While we were in the emergency room, Court desperately clutched onto me. We were both afraid. Court had the chills and could not stop shivering. While the doctor was completing the spinal tap, Court and I experienced a warmth and an indescribable calmness come over us. Court instantly relaxed and stopped shaking. After the doctor and nurse left the room, Court and I stared at each other. Court, fully composed, turned to me and said, "Mom, Wesley was here in this room and he said, 'Don't worry, it'll be alright.'"

I believe with all my heart that some friendships never die.

Janice Hunt

The Eternal Optimist

We have been lucky to be blessed with three sons. They have each brought us special joy with their individual personalities, but our middle son, Billy, is fondly known as the "eternal optimist." I wish that we could take credit for this attitude, but it's something he was born with! For example, he had always been an early riser and liked to get in our bed at 5 A.M. As he would crawl into our bed, we would admonish him to be quiet and go back to sleep. He would lie on his back and say in a falsetto whisper, "It's going to be a beautiful morning. I hear the birds singing."

When we would ask him to stop talking to us, he would reply, "I not talking to you; I talking to me!"

In kindergarten, he was asked to draw a tiger. Now, while optimism is Billy's strong suit, art is not, and his tiger came out with a crooked head and one eye that appeared to be shut. When his teacher asked him about why the tiger had one eye closed, he replied, "Because he's saying, 'Here's looking at you, kid!'"

Also, when he was five, he got into an argument with his older brother about whether a man on TV was bald. Billy said, "He's not bald. He's like Papa. He's only bald when he looks at you. When he walks away, he has lots of hair!"

These memories and many, many more led up to the ultimate optimistic statement. Our third son, Tanner, was stricken with hemolytic uremic syndrome on a Tuesday and died the following Sunday. Billy was seven. The night after Tanner's funeral I was putting Billy to bed. I often used to lie down beside him to discuss the day. On this particular night, we lay quietly in the dark with not much to say. Suddenly, from the dark, Billy spoke.

He said, "I feel sorry for us, but I almost feel more sorry for all those other people." I questioned him about which people he was talking about. He explained, "The people who never knew Tanner. Weren't we lucky to have had Tanner with us for 20 months. Just think, there are lots of people who were never lucky enough to know him at all. We are really lucky people."

Beth Dalton

To Remember Me

The day will come when my body will lie upon a white sheet neatly tucked under four corners of a mattress located in a hospital busily occupied with the living and the dying. At a certain moment a doctor will determine that my brain has ceased to function and that, for all intents and purposes, my life has stopped.

When that happens, do not attempt to instill artificial life into my body by the use of a machine. And don't call this my deathbed. Let it be called the Bed of Life, and let my body be taken from it to help others lead fuller lives.

Give my sight to the man who has never seen a sunrise, a baby's face or love in the eyes of a woman. Give my heart to a person whose own heart has caused nothing but endless days of pain. Give my blood to the teenager who was pulled from the wreckage of his car, so that he might live to see his grandchildren play. Give my kidneys to one who depends on a machine to exist from week to week. Take my bones, every muscle, every fiber and nerve in my body and find a way to make a crippled child walk.

Explore every corner of my brain. Take my cells, if necessary, and let them grow so that someday, a speechless boy will shout at the crack of a bat and a deaf girl will hear the sound of rain against her window.

Burn what is left of me and scatter the ashes to the winds to help the flowers grow.

If you must bury something, let it be my faults, my weaknesses and all prejudice against my fellow man.

Give my sins to the devil. Give my soul to God.

If, by chance, you wish to remember me, do it with a kind deed or word to someone who needs you. If you do all I have asked, I will live forever.

Robert N. Test
Submitted by Ken Knowles

Keep Your Fork

The sound of Martha's voice on the other end of the telephone always brought a smile to Brother Jim's face. She was not only one of the oldest members of the congregation, but one of the most faithful. Aunt Martie, as all the children called her, just seemed to ooze faith, hope and love wherever she went.

This time, however, there seemed to be an unusual tone to her words.

"Preacher, could you stop by this afternoon? I need to talk with you."

"Of course. I'll be there around three. Is that okay?"

As they sat facing each other in the quiet of her small living room, Jim learned the reason for what he sensed in her voice. Martha shared the news that her doctor had just discovered a previously undetected tumor.

"He says I probably have six months to live." Martha's words were certainly serious, yet there was a definite calm about her.

"I'm so sorry to . . ." but before Jim could finish, Martha interrupted.

"Don't be. The Lord has been good. I have lived a long life. I'm ready to go. You know that."

"I know," Jim whispered with a reassuring nod.

"But I do want to talk with you about my funeral. I

have been thinking about it, and there are things that I know I want."

The two talked quietly for a long time. They talked about Martha's favorite hymns, the passages of Scripture that had meant so much to her through the years, and the many memories they shared from the five years Jim had been with Central Church.

When it seemed that they had covered just about everything, Aunt Martie paused, looked up at Jim with a twinkle in her eye, and then added, "One more thing, preacher. When they bury me, I want my old Bible in one hand and a fork in the other."

"A fork?" Jim was sure he had heard everything, but this caught him by surprise. "Why do you want to be buried with a fork?"

"I have been thinking about all of the church dinners and banquets that I attended through the years," she explained. "I couldn't begin to count them all. But one thing sticks in my mind.

"At those really nice get-togethers, when the meal was almost finished, a server or maybe the hostess would come by to collect the dirty dishes. I can hear the words now. Sometimes, at the best ones, somebody would lean over my shoulder and whisper, 'You can keep your fork.' And do you know what that meant? Dessert was coming!

"It didn't mean a cup of Jell-O or pudding or even a dish of ice cream. You don't need a fork for that. It meant the good stuff, like chocolate cake or cherry pie! When they told me I could keep my fork, I knew the best was yet to come!

"That's exactly what I want people to talk about at my funeral. Oh, they can talk about all the good times we had together. That would be nice.

"But when they walk by my casket and look at my pretty blue dress, I want them to turn to one another and say, 'Why the fork?'

"That's what I want you to say. I want you to tell them that I kept my fork because the best is yet to come."

Roger William Thomas

There Are No Wheelchairs in Heaven

My grandfather was a Buddhist priest. At the time of his death, he was the highest-ranking Caucasian priest in the world. But it was not the distinction of his accolades that one noticed in grandfather's presence; it was the energy that emanated from within. Grandpa's clear green eyes sparkled with a mysterious vitality. Although a quiet man, he always stood out in a crowd. Grandfather had a radiance that emanated from within. Silence seemed to speak profoundly around him.

His wife, my grandmother, was a High Roman Catholic. Brilliant and energetic, she was a woman ahead of her time. I called her "Gagi" because the first word that came out of my mouth as a baby was "gaga," and she was sure I was trying to say her name. So Gagi it was, and is to this day.

Gagi had wrapped her life around her husband, becoming the source for all the income for themselves and their five children during their 50 years of marriage. Grandfather was thus freed to fulfill his mission as a priest and minister to the needy, as well as a host to the visiting dignitaries that frequented his temple from around the world. When Grandpa died, the light went out in Gagi's life, and a deep depression set in. Having lost her central focus, she retreated from the world and entered the stages of mourning and grief.

During those days, I made a habit of visiting her once a week, just to let her know that I was there for her.

Time passed, as always, and the healing of the heart took its true and natural course.

One day, some years later, I went to pay my usual visit to Gagi. I walked in to find her sitting in her wheelchair, beaming—alive with fire in her eyes. When I didn't comment soon enough about the obvious change in her demeanor, she confronted me.

"Don't you want to know why I'm so happy? Aren't you even curious?"

"Of course, Gagi," I apologized. "Tell me, why are you so happy? What has given you this new disposition?"

"Last night I got an answer. I finally know why God took your grandfather and left me behind," she declared.

"Why, Gagi?" I asked.

Then, as if imparting the greatest secret in the world, she lowered her voice and leaned forward in her wheelchair and confided in me. "Your grandfather knew the secret of a good life and he lived it every day. Your grandfather had become unconditional love in action. That's why he got to go first, and I had to stay behind." She paused thoughtfully, and then continued.

"What I thought was a punishment was, in fact, a gift. God let me stay behind so that I could turn my life into love. You see," she continued, "last night I was shown that you can't learn the lesson of love out there." She pointed to the sky as she spoke. "Love has to be lived here on earth; once you leave it's too late. So I was given the gift of life so that I can learn to live love here and now."

From that day on, my visits with Gagi were filled with a unique combination of both sharing and constant surprises. Even though her health was failing, she was really happy. Indeed, she finally had a reason for her life and a goal worth living for again.

Once, when I went up to see her, she pounded the arm of her wheelchair in excitement and said, "You'll never guess what happened this morning."

I responded that I couldn't and she continued with growing enthusiasm, "Well, this morning your uncle was angry with me over something I had done. I didn't even flinch. I received his anger, wrapped it in love and returned it with joy!" Her eyes twinkled as she added, "It was even kind of fun, and naturally, his anger dissolved."

Day after day passed, and visit after visit added up, while Gagi practiced her lessons in love—and all the while age continued to run its relentless course. Every visit was a new adventure as she shared her stories. She conquered mountains of habits within her and made herself constantly new. She was honestly giving birth to a new and vital being.

Over the years, her health gradually worsened. She went in and out of the hospital a lot. Finally, when she was 97, she entered the hospital just after Thanksgiving. I rode the elevator to the fourth floor and went to the nurses' station. "Which room is Mrs. Hunt in?" I asked.

The nurse on duty looked up quickly from her work, pulled her glasses off and replied, "You must be her granddaughter! She's expecting you and she asked us to keep an eye out for your arrival." She came out from behind the nurses' station saying, "Let me take you to her." As we started down the hallway, the nurse suddenly stopped, and looking directly into my eyes she said quietly, "Your grandmother is a special lady, you know. She's a light. The nurses on the floor all ask for her room when they're on duty. They love to take her medication to her because they all say that there's something about her." She paused, almost embarrassed at the thought of having said too much. "But, of course, you know that."

"She's special, all right," I reflected, and a small voice

whispered within, "Gagi has accomplished her goal. Her time is nearly done."

It was two days after Christmas. Having spent a couple of hours visiting with Gagi earlier that day, I was home in the evening relaxing when a voice suddenly came to me, "Get up! Go to the hospital, now! Don't hesitate! Go to the hospital now!"

I threw on a pair of jeans and a T-shirt, jumped into the car and sped to the hospital. Parking the car quickly, I broke into a run, racing the rest of the way to the elevator and up to the fourth floor. As I hit the door of her room, I looked in to see my aunt holding Gagi's head in her hands. She looked up with tears in her eyes. "She's gone, Trin," she said. "She left five minutes ago. You're the first one here."

My mind reeled as I moved to Gagi's bedside. In prayerful denial, my hand went out to test her heart. It was silent; Gagi was gone. I stood holding her still warm arm, looking down at the beautiful old body that had housed the soul of the woman I had adored. Gagi had cared for me during my early years. She had clothed me and paid my way through school when my parents were young and struggling to make ends meet. I was at a loss, unable to believe that my beloved grandmother, my dearest Gagi, was gone.

I remember the aching emptiness as I walked the floor around her bed that night, touching every part of her precious body. I was overwhelmed, flooded with impressions I'd never experienced before. Here were the arms and legs I knew so well, but where was she? Her body was vacant; so where had she gone? Deep in inner thought, I begged for an answer. One moment the body is animated by the soul and in the next moment it is gone, and nothing on earth can cause it to move or have life again. Where was Gagi? Where had she gone?

Suddenly there was a flash of light and a burst of energy. My grandmother was hovering near the ceiling above her empty body. The wheelchair was gone and she was dancing in light.

"Trin, I'm not gone!" she exclaimed. "I left my body but I'm still here. Look, Trin, I've got the use of my legs back. There are no wheelchairs in heaven, you know. I'm with your grandfather now and my joy is boundless. As you look down at my vacant body, realize the secret of life. Always remember that you cannot take anything physical with you when you leave. I couldn't take my body with me, nor all the money I earned in life, nor any of the things that I amassed. Even my most prized possession, your grandfather's wedding ring, had to stay behind when I left."

Gagi's light was very bright as she continued, "You're going to meet a lot of people, Trin, and you must share this truth with all whom you meet. Tell people that the only thing that we take with us when we leave is a record of how much love we gave away. Our life, my child, is measured in giving, not in taking." And with that my grandmother's light dissolved and disappeared.

Many years have passed since that bedside moment, yet my grandmother's message remains. It is indelibly inscribed on my heart, and written in the little things I try to do to improve my character daily. Gagi loved me with all her heart. In the course of her lifetime she had showered me with gifts, but I knew that she had just given me her final and greatest gift. In her death she renewed my life.

D. Trinidad Hunt

5

A
MATTER
OF
PERSPECTIVE

Things don't change. You change your way of looking, that's all.

Carlos Castaneda

Christmas

He had been inspecting the church before the parish-
ioners arrived for the first mass and had noted with
approval that the aisles and pews had been swept and
dusted after the midnight mass, and that any lost purses,
prayer books and gloves had been collected and sent to
the parish rectory.

It was a little before five in the morning. Outside it was
dark, and in the church, where only the old priest moved
about, the yellow light from the candles flickered and
threw shifting shadows on the arches and the stone floor.
Occasionally, a transient beam of candlelight dimly picked
out the rich colors of the stained glass windows. It was
cold, and except for the priest's slow tread, it was silent.

On his way back to the sacristy, he paused beside the
crèche to say a Christmas prayer of greeting to the Christ
Child. On the little model stage, with admirable realism,
the sacred scene was shown. Through the open door you
could see the night sky and the star that had led the shepherds to the stable; the shepherds, in fact, were just entering, in attitudes of adoration; livestock were in the stalls;
and in the center was the Holy Family, looking down into
the manger.

The priest frowned and leaned closer. The whisper of
his exclamation rustled through the church. The manger

was empty. The Christ Child—the little plaster doll that represented the infant savior—was gone.

Hurriedly, and with growing agitation, the priest made a search that started in the vicinity of the manger and then took him, bent and peering, through the aisles again. He called the church sexton, then the assistant pastor and all the parish fathers. But none of them could offer any explanation. They discussed it long; and in the end, shaking their heads and surveying one another sorrowfully, they accepted the truth they had been trying to evade. The figure of the infant savior had not been mislaid, or lost; it had been stolen.

With a solemnity befitting the occasion, the pastor reported the theft to the congregation that assembled for the first mass. In a voice stern and yet trembling with outraged emotion, he spoke of the shocking nature of the deed, and of the dreadful sacrilege that had been committed. His gaze swept the congregation, as if searching the innermost thoughts of each man and woman. "The Christ Child," he said, "must be returned to the crèche before this Christmas Day is over." Then, in silence, he strode from the pulpit.

At each succeeding mass he repeated this adjuration, but to no avail. The manger remained empty. Toward the end of Christmas afternoon the pastor, gray-faced and heavy-hearted, set out on a meditative stroll through the wintry streets of his parish.

It was while he was on this walk that he saw ahead of him one of the smallest members of his flock, a little boy of five or six named Johnny Mullaney. Shabbily bundled against the cold, Johnny was trudging up the sidewalk, dragging proudly behind him a toy express wagon, bright red and obviously Christmas new.

The priest was touched by the realization of the sacrifices and the scrimpings that the purchase of a toy like this must have entailed; for the family was poor. Here was a needed glow to warm his heart and to renew his faith in human nature. He quickened his step and overtook the little boy, intending to wish him a merry Christmas and to exclaim admiringly over the beauty of the wagon. But as he drew nearer, this benevolent plan was suddenly put out of his mind by the discovery that the wagon was not empty—it contained, in fact, the figure of the Christ Child, now wrapped and blanketed, but not quite hidden.

Grimly the priest stopped Johnny. Severely he lectured him. The boy was only a little boy, and one must, of course, make allowances—but nevertheless he was old enough to understand that stealing was a sin, and that to rob the church of a sacred image was a very great sin indeed. Now, in ringing tones, the priest made this plain to Johnny, who stood looking up at him with clear eyes that seemed guiltless—filling now, however, with what must be penitent tears.

"But, Father," the small boy quavered, when at last the priest had finished his tirade, "I didn't *steal* the Christ Child. It wasn't like that at all." He gulped, and went on: "It was just that I've been praying to Him for a red wagon for a Christmas present—and I promised Him that if I got it, I'd take Him out for the first ride."

Author Unknown
Submitted by Carolyn Bower

The Cookie Thief

A woman was waiting at an airport one night,
With several long hours before her flight.
She hunted for a book in the airport shop,
Bought a bag of cookies and found a place to drop.

She was engrossed in her book, but happened to see,
That the man beside her, as bold as could be,
Grabbed a cookie or two from the bag between,
Which she tried to ignore, to avoid a scene.

She read, munched cookies, and watched the clock,
As the gutsy "cookie thief" diminished her stock.
She was getting more irritated as the minutes ticked by,
Thinking, "If I wasn't so nice, I'd blacken his eye!"

With each cookie she took, he took one too.
When only one was left, she wondered what he'd do.
With a smile on his face and a nervous laugh,
He took the last cookie and broke it in half.

He offered her half, as he ate the other.
She snatched it from him and thought, "Oh brother,
This guy has some nerve, and he's also *rude*,
Why, he didn't even show any gratitude!"

She had never known when she had been so galled,
And sighed with relief when her flight was called.
She gathered her belongings and headed for the gate,
Refusing to look back at the "thieving ingrate."

She boarded the plane and sank in her seat,
Then sought her book, which was almost complete.
As she reached in her baggage, she gasped with surprise.
There was her bag of cookies in front of her eyes!

"If mine are here," she moaned with despair,
"Then the others were *his* and he tried to share!"
Too late to apologize, she realized with grief,
That *she* was the rude one, the ingrate, the thief!

Valerie Cox

The True Story of Arbutus and Sea Gull

My grandmother had an enemy named Mrs. Wilcox. Grandma and Mrs. Wilcox moved as brides into next-door houses on the sleepy elm-roofed Main Street of the tiny town in which they were to live out their lives. I don't know what started the war—that was long before my day—and I don't think that by the time I came along, over 30 years later, they remembered themselves what started it. But it was still being waged bitterly.

Make no mistake. This was no polite sparring match. This was war between ladies, which is total war. Nothing in town escaped repercussion. The 300-year-old church, which had lived through the Revolution, the Civil War and the Spanish-American War, almost went down when Grandma and Mrs. Wilcox fought the Battle of the Ladies' Aid. Grandma won that engagement, but it was a hollow victory. Mrs. Wilcox, since she couldn't be president, resigned from the Aid in a huff, and what's the fun of running a thing if you can't force your mortal enemy to "eat crow"?

Mrs. Wilcox won the Battle of the Public Library, getting her niece Gertrude appointed librarian instead of my Aunt Phyllis. The day Gertrude took over was the day Grandma stopped reading library books— "filthy germ things" they'd become overnight—and started buying her own.

The Battle of the High School was a draw. The principal got a better job and left before Mrs. Wilcox succeeded in having him ousted, or Grandma in having him given life tenure in office.

In addition to these major engagements, there was constant sallying and sniping back of the main line of fire. When, as children, we visited my grandmother, part of the fun was making faces at Mrs. Wilcox's impossible grandchildren—nearly as impossible as we were, I now see—and stealing grapes off the Wilcox side of the fence between the gardens. We chased the Wilcox hens, too, and put percussion caps, saved from July 4th, on the rails of the trolley line right in front of the Wilcox house, in the pleasant hope that when the trolley went by, the explosion—actually a negligible affair—would scare Mrs. Wilcox into fits.

One banner day, we put a snake into the Wilcox rain barrel. My grandmother made token protests, but we sensed tacit sympathy, so different from what lay back of my mother's no's, and went merrily on with our career of brattishness. If any child of mine . . . but that's another story.

Don't think for a minute that this was a one-sided campaign. Mrs. Wilcox had grandchildren, too, remember, more and tougher and smarter grandchildren than my grandmother had. Grandma didn't get off scot free. She had skunks introduced into her cellar. On Halloween all loose forgotten objects, such as garden furniture, miraculously flew to the ridgepole of the barn, whence they had to be lowered by strong men, hired at exorbitant day rates.

Never a windy washday went by but what the clothesline mysteriously broke, so that the sheets walloped around in the dirt and had to be done over. Some of these occurrences may have been acts of God, but the Wilcox grandchildren always got the credit.

I don't know how Grandma could have borne her troubles if it hadn't been for the household page of her daily Boston newspaper.

This household page was a wonderful institution. Besides the usual cooking hints and cleaning advice, it had a department composed of letters from readers to each other. The idea was that if you had a problem—or even only some steam to blow off—you wrote a letter to the paper, signing some fancy name like Arbutus. That was Grandma's pen name. Then some of the other ladies who had the same problem wrote back and told you what they had done about it, signing themselves One Who Knows or Xanthipee, or whatever. Very often, the problem disposed of, you kept on for years writing to each other through the columns of the paper, telling each other about your children and your canning and your new dining room suite.

That's what happened to Grandma. She and a woman called Sea Gull corresponded for a quarter of a century, and Grandma told Sea Gull things that she never breathed to another soul—things like the time she hoped that she was going to have another baby but didn't, and the time my Uncle Steve got you-know-what in his hair in school and how humiliated she was, although she got rid of them before anyone in town guessed. Sea Gull was Grandma's true bosom friend.

When I was about 16, Mrs. Wilcox died. In a small town, no matter how much you have hated your next-door neighbor, it is only common decency to run over and see what practical service you can do the bereaved.

Grandma, neat in a percale apron to show that she meant what she said about being put to work, crossed the two lawns to the Wilcox house, where the Wilcox daughters set her to cleaning the already immaculate front parlor for the funeral. And there on the parlor table in the

place of honor was a huge scrapbook, and in the scrapbook, pasted neatly in parallel columns, were her letters
to Sea Gull over the years and Sea Gull's letters to her.
Grandma's worst enemy had been her best friend.

That was the only time I remembered seeing my grandmother cry. I didn't know then exactly what she was crying about, but I do now. She was crying for all the wasted
years that could never be salvaged. Then I was impressed
only by the tears, and they made me remember that day
worthier of remembrance than a woman's tears. That was
the day when I first began to suspect what I now believe
with all my heart, and if ever I have to stop believing it, I
want to stop living. It is this:

People may seem to be perfectly impossible. They may
seem to be mean and small and sly. But if you will take 10
paces to the left and look again with the light falling at a
different angle, very likely you will see that they are generous and warm and kind. It all depends. It all depends on
the point from which you're seeing them.

Louise Dickinson Rich

Lady, Are You Rich?

They huddled inside the storm door—two children in ragged outgrown coats.

"Any old papers, lady?"

I was busy. I wanted to say no—until I looked down at their feet. Thin little sandals, sopped with sleet. "Come in and I'll make you a cup of hot cocoa." There was no conversation. Their soggy sandals left marks upon the hearthstone.

I served them cocoa and toast with jam to fortify against the chill outside. Then I went back to the kitchen and started again on my household budget. . . .

The silence in the front room struck through to me. I looked in.

The girl held the empty cup in her hands, looking at it. The boy asked in a flat voice, "Lady . . . are you rich?"

"Am I rich? Mercy, no!" I looked at my shabby slip covers.

The girl put her cup back in its saucer—carefully. "Your cups match your saucers." Her voice was old, with a hunger that was not of the stomach.

They left then, holding their bundles of papers against the wind. They hadn't said thank you. They didn't need to. They had done more than that. Plain blue pottery cups and saucers. But they matched. I tested the potatoes and stirred the gravy. Potatoes and brown gravy, a roof over our heads, my man with a good steady job—these things matched, too.

I moved the chairs back from the fire and tidied the living room. The muddy prints of small sandals were still wet upon my hearth. I let them be. I want them there in case I ever forget again how very rich I am.

Marion Doolan

The Flower in Her Hair

She always wore a flower in her hair. Always. Mostly I thought it looked strange. A flower in midday? To work? To professional meetings? She was an aspiring graphic designer in the large, busy office where I worked. Every day she'd sail into the office with its ultra-modern crisp decor, wearing a flower in her shoulder-length hair. Usually color-coordinated with her otherwise suitable attire, it bloomed, a small parasol of vivid color, pinned to the large backdrop of dark brunette waves. There were times, like at the company Christmas party, where the flower added a touch of festivity and seemed appropriate. But to work, it just seemed out of place. Some of the more "professionally-minded" women in the office were practically indignant about it, and thought someone ought to take her aside and inform her of the "rules" in being "taken seriously" in the business world. Others among us, myself included, thought it just an odd quirk and privately referred to her as "flower power" or "girl flower."

"Has flower power completed the preliminary design on the Wal-Mart project?" one of us would ask the other, with a small lopsided smile.

"Of course. It turned out great—her work has really blossomed," might be the reply, housed in patronizing smiles of shared amusement. We thought our mockery innocent at the time. To my knowledge no one had questioned the young woman as to why a flower accompanied her to work each day. In fact, we probably would have been more inclined to question her had she shown up without it.

Which she did one day. When she delivered a project to my office, I queried. "I noticed there is no flower in your hair today," I said casually. "I'm so used to seeing you wear one that it almost seems as if something is missing."

"Oh, yes," she replied quietly, in a rather somber tone. This was a departure from her usual bright and perky personality. The pregnant pause that followed blared loudly, prompting me to ask, "Are you okay?" Though I was hoping for a "Yes, I'm fine" response, intuitively, I knew I had treaded onto something bigger than a missing flower.

"Oh," she said softly, with an expression encumbered with recollection and sorrow. "Today is the anniversary of my mother's death. I miss her so much. I guess I'm a bit blue."

"I understand," I said, feeling compassion for her but not wanting to wade into emotional waters. "I'm sure it's very difficult for you to talk about," I continued, the business part of me hoping she would agree, but my heart understanding that there was more.

"No. It's okay, really. I know that I'm extraordinarily sensitive today. This is a day of mourning, I suppose. You see . . ." and she began to tell me the story.

"My mother knew that she was losing her life to cancer. Eventually, she died. I was 15 at the time. We were very close. She was so loving, so giving. Because she knew she was dying, she prerecorded a birthday message I was to watch every year on my birthday, from age 16 until I reached 25. Today is my 25th birthday, and this morning I watched the video she prepared for this day. I guess I'm still digesting it. And wishing she were alive."

"Well, my heart goes out to you," I said, feeling a great deal of empathy for her.

"Thank you for your kindness," she said. "Oh, and about the missing flower you asked about. When I was a little girl, my mother would often put flowers in my hair. One day when she was in the hospital, I took her this beautiful large rose from her garden. As I held it up to her nose so she could smell it, she took it from me, and without saying a word, pulled me close to her, stroking my hair and brushing it from my face, placed it in my hair, just as she had done when I was little. She died later that day." Tears came to her eyes as she added, "I've just always worn a flower in my hair since—it made me feel as though she were with me, if only in spirit. But," she sighed, "today, as I watched the video designed for me on this birthday, in it she said she was sorry for not being able to be there for me as I grew up, that she hoped she had been a good parent, and that she would like a sign that I was becoming self-sufficient. That's the way my mother thought—the way she talked." She looked at me, smiling fondly at the memory. "She was so wise."

I nodded, agreeing. "Yes, she sounds very wise."

"So I thought, a sign, what could it be? And it seemed it was the flower that had to go. But I'll miss it, and what it represents."

Her hazel eyes gazed off in recollection as she continued. "I was so lucky to have had her." Her voice trailed off and she met my eyes again, then smiled sadly. "But I don't need to wear a flower to be reminded of these things. I really do know that. It was just an outward sign of my treasured memories—they're still there even with the flower gone . . . but still, I will miss it . . . Oh, here's the project. I hope it meets with your approval." She handed me the neatly prepared folder, signed, with a hand-drawn flower, her signature trademark, below her name.

When I was young, I remember hearing the phrase, "Never judge another person until you've walked a mile in his shoes." I thought about all the times I had been insensitive about this young woman with the flower in her hair, and how tragic it was that I had done this in the absence of information, not knowing the young woman's fate and the cross that was hers to bear. I prided myself on knowing intricately each facet of my company, and knew precisely how each role and function contributed to the next. How tragic for me that I had bought into the notion that a person's personal life was unrelated to her professional life, and was to be left at the door when entering corporate life. That day I knew that the flower this young woman wore in her hair was symbolic of her outpouring of love—a way for her to stay connected to the young mother she had lost when she herself was a young girl.

I looked over the project she had completed, and felt honored that it had been treated by one with such depth and capacity for *feeling* . . . of *being*. No wonder her work was consistently excellent. She lived in her heart daily. And caused me to re-visit mine.

Bettie B. Youngs

Avalanche

To every disadvantage there is a corresponding advantage.

W. Clement Stone

It was our dream cabin—10,000 square feet of luxurious space overlooking a majestic waterfall on the back side of Mount Timpanogos, near the slopes of Robert Redford's famous Sundance Ski Resort. It took my wife and me several years to design, plan, build and furnish it.

But it took only 10 seconds to completely destroy it.

I remember the afternoon of the disaster as if it were yesterday. Thursday, February 13th, 1986, the day before our ninth anniversary. It had snowed heavily that day. About 40 inches. Still, my wife braved the weather for the 30-minute ride up the canyon from our home in Provo, Utah, to visit our newly completed mountain home. Taking our six-year-old son, Aaron, she left early that afternoon, stopping on the way to buy some ingredients for a cake to celebrate our special day. I was to join her later and bring Aimee, our nine-year-old daughter, and Hunter, our youngest son.

My first hint of danger came at about 3:00 P.M. with a call from the Sundance ski patrol.

"There's a problem at your cabin. You'd better come immediately."

They gave no more details. Although I was behind deadline in finishing up a book project, I left my computer and anxiously dashed up the canyon on snow-clogged roads. When I arrived at the ski resort, the director of the resort and his staff greeted me with somber looks on their faces.

"There's been a catastrophe at the cabin. We think your wife and son were there. Jump in my four-wheel drive. Let's go."

The cabin was adjacent to the main Sundance ski slope and was accessible only by a narrow, winding mountain road. As we frantically raced up the road, the high snow banks on either side made it seem as if we were winding through a labyrinth. As we rounded a curve in the road we met another vehicle coming down the narrow roadway. Both of us slammed on our brakes as we skidded into each other, with minor damage to both vehicles. After a brief exchange of information we continued our race up the narrow road until the copper roof of the cabin came into sight in the distance.

As we pulled near I spotted my wife and son in the roadway surrounded by several members of the Sundance ski patrol. As I jumped out of the vehicle and ran toward her, she pointed to the trees above the cabin. I was shocked by what I saw.

The swath of a monster avalanche had blasted down the mountainside, leaving massive trees snapped and broken in its wake like match sticks. I glanced again at the cabin and could now see how the avalanche had ripped through our mountain home. In seconds it had blown out all of the windows and piled tons and tons of snow into our huge living room, collapsing all the floors and completely destroying our dreams. What remained was just a shell. Outside, our carefully selected furniture lay smashed to bits in the snow. It was a scene of such shocking devastation, I shall never forget it.

The ski patrol hustled us out of the avalanche zone quickly, as new avalanches threatened. We returned home dazed, stunned, in shock. I must admit, the loss of the cabin really shook us. For months after, I wondered why we had been so unlucky as to lose our beautiful mountain home. Why did God allow such things to happen?

The story could end here. But then you wouldn't know of the miracle that happened that day. As it was, I, myself, didn't discover the miracle until eight months later.

At a business meeting, a colleague of mine asked me a seemingly simple question:

"Did your wife ever tell you that my wife and your wife almost had an accident on the road to your cabin on the day of your avalanche?"

"No," I replied. "What happened?"

"Well, my wife and our boys were staying at our Sundance cabin. Because of the heavy snow, they decided to leave and come back home. Before leaving the cabin, one of the boys suggested that they offer a prayer for a safe trip home. They bowed their heads and offered a brief prayer and then started down the narrow road. Your wife, driving up the road, saw my wife and the boys in our Suburban. But when my wife slammed on her brakes, the car wouldn't stop. It skidded down the slick mountain road gathering speed. There was nothing she could do to stop it. Finally, at the last moment before the two vehicles were to crash into each other, she turned the wheel, slamming the front of the Suburban into the snow bank on one side of the road while the rear of the vehicle slammed into the bank on the other side . . . virtually blocking your wife from proceeding up the road. They tried for almost an hour to get the Suburban unstuck and finally had to get help from the ski resort."

"That's amazing," I said. "My wife never told me."

We chuckled about the "accident" and parted company. Then the force of what he had just revealed hit me.

If it hadn't been for this near "accident," my wife and son would most certainly have been killed in the avalanche!

I've often thought about that "accident" in the roadway. I imagine my wife sitting there in frustration as the Suburban blocked her way to the cabin. I can see my friend's wife at the scene, embarrassed by the whole situation. I see her boys upset and confused and wondering if God really hears prayers.

At the time, everyone viewed the situation as a complete disaster. And yet, with perspective, it was obvious that they had all unknowingly participated in a miracle.

Now I am slower to judge the "disasters" that occur from time to time in my life. Eventually, as more information becomes available, many of them turn out to be miracles in the making. When "accidents" happen, I try to ask myself, "What miracle is God fashioning out of this misfortune?"

Instead of wondering, "Why me, God?" I simply say "Thank you, God."

Then I wait until all of the evidence rolls in.

Robert G. Allen

You Very Good; You Very Fast

At the time, I was living in the Bay Area, and my mother had come to visit for a few days. On the last day of her stay, I was preparing to go out for a run. Working in a very negative environment, I found morning runs very beneficial. As I was going out the door, my mother said, "I don't think running is so hot—that famous runner died."

I started to recount what I had read about Jim Fixx, and how running had probably been the contributing factor to his living far longer than most of the other members of his family, but I knew there was absolutely no point.

As I started running on my favorite trail, I found I couldn't shake her statement. I was so discouraged I could barely run. I began thinking, "Why do I bother to run at all? Serious runners probably think I look ridiculous! I might have a heart attack on the trail—my dad had a fatal heart attack at 50 years old, and he was seemingly in better shape than I am."

My mother's statement hovered over me like a giant blanket. My jog slowed to a walk, and I felt extremely defeated. Here I was in my late 40s, still hoping for an encouraging word from my mother, and equally mad at myself for still seeking an approval that would never come.

Just as I was going to turn around at the two-mile mark and head for home—feeling more discouraged than I could recall in years—I saw an elderly Chinese gentleman walking toward me on the opposite side of the trail. I had seen him walking on other mornings; I had always said, "Good morning," and he had always smiled and nodded his head. This particular morning, he came over to my side of the trail and stood in my path, forcing me to stop. I was a little miffed. I had let my mother's comment (coupled with a lifetime of similar comments) ruin my day, and now this man was blocking my way.

I was wearing a T-shirt a friend had sent me from Hawaii for Chinese New Year's—it had three Chinese characters on the front, and a scene of Honolulu's Chinatown on the back. Seeing my shirt in the distance had prompted him to stop me. With limited English he pointed to the letters and excitedly said, "You speak?"

I told him I didn't speak Chinese, but that the shirt was a gift from a friend in Hawaii. I sensed he didn't understand all of what I was saying, and then, very enthusiastically he said, "Every time see you . . . you very good . . . you very fast."

Well, I am neither very good nor very fast, but that day I left with an unexplained bounce in my step. I didn't turn from the trail where my previous dark mood had intended, but continued for six more miles, and you know, for that morning I was very good. I was very fast in my spirit and in my heart.

Because of that little boost I continued to run, and I recently finished my fourth Honolulu Marathon. The New York Marathon is my goal for this year. I know I am never going to win a race, but now, when I get any negative feedback, I think of a kind gentleman who really believed, "You very good . . . you very fast."

Kathi M. Curry

Make a Wish

I'll never forget the day Momma *made* me go to a birthday party. I was in Mrs. Black's third grade class in Wichita Falls, Texas, and I brought home a slightly peanut-buttery invitation.

"I'm not going," I said. "She's a new girl named Ruth, and Berniece and Pat aren't going. She asked the whole class, all 36 of us."

As Momma studied the handmade invitation, she looked strangely sad. Then she announced, "Well, you are going! I'll pick up a present tomorrow."

I couldn't believe it. Momma had never made me go to a party! I was positive I'd just die if I had to go. But no amount of hysterics could sway Momma.

When Saturday arrived, Momma rushed me out of bed and made me wrap the pretty pink pearlized mirror-brush-and-comb set she'd bought for $2.98.

She drove me over in her yellow and white 1950 Oldsmobile. Ruth answered the door and motioned me to follow her up the steepest, scariest staircase I'd ever seen.

Stepping through the door brought great relief. The hardwood floors gleamed in the sun-filled parlor. Snow-white doilies covered the backs and arms of well-worn over-stuffed furniture.

The biggest cake I ever saw sat on one table. It was decorated with nine pink candles, a messily printed Happy Birthday Ruthey and what I think were supposed to be rosebuds.

Thirty-six Dixie cups filled with homemade fudge were near the cake—each one with a name on it.

This won't be too awful—once everyone gets here, I decided.

"Where's your mom?" I asked Ruth.

Looking down at the floor, she said, "Well she's sorta sick."

"Oh. Where's your dad?"

"He's gone."

Then there was a silence, except for a few raspy coughs from behind a closed door. Some 15 minutes passed . . . then 10 more. Suddenly the terrifying realization set in. *No one else was coming.* How could I get out of here? As I sank into self-pity, I heard muffled sobs. Looking up I saw Ruth's tear-streaked face. All at once my eight-year-old heart was overwhelmed with sympathy for Ruth and filled with rage at my 35 selfish classmates.

Springing to my white-patent leather feet, I proclaimed at the top of my lungs, "Who needs 'em?"

Ruth's startled look changed to excited agreement.

There we were—two small girls and a triple-decker cake, 36 candy-filled Dixie cups, ice cream, gallons of red Kool-Aid, three dozen party favors, games to play and prizes to win.

We started with the cake. We couldn't find any matches, and Ruthey (she was no longer just plain Ruth) wouldn't disturb her mom, so we just pretended to light them. I sang "Happy Birthday" while Ruthey made a wish and blew out the imaginary flames.

In a flash it was noon. Momma was honking out front. Gathering up all my goodies and thanking Ruthey repeatedly, I dashed to the car. I was bubbling over.

"I won *all* the games! Well, really, Ruthey won Pin the Tail on the Donkey, but she said it wasn't fair for the birthday girl to win a prize, so she gave it to me, and we split the party favors 50/50. Momma, she just loved the mirror set. I was the only one there—out of Mrs. Black's whole third-grade class. And I can't wait to tell every one of them what a great party they missed!"

Momma pulled over to the curb, stopped the car and hugged me tight. With tears in her eyes, she said, "I'm so proud of you!"

That was the day I learned that one person could really make a difference. I had made a big difference in Ruthey's ninth birthday, and Momma had made a big difference in my life.

LeAnne Reaves

The Accident

Our real blessings often appear to us in the shapes of pains, losses and disappointments; but let us have patience, and we soon shall see them in their proper figures.

Joseph Addison

Christmas Eve came on Sunday that year. As a result, the usual Sunday night youth group meeting at the church was going to be a big celebration. The mother of two teenage girls asked me after the morning service if I could find a ride for her girls that night. She was divorced. Her ex-husband had moved away. She hated to drive at night, especially since there was a possibility of freezing rain that night. I promised to get the girls to the meeting.

The girls were seated beside me as we drove to the church that night. We came up over a rise in the road, only to see that a multiple collision had just taken place on a railroad overpass just ahead. Because it had started to freeze and the road was very slick, we were unable to stop and slammed into the back of a car. I turned to see if the girls were okay when I heard the girl beside me scream, "O-o-oh, Donna!" I leaned forward to see what had happened to the girl seated by the window. This was before seat belts were installed in cars. She had been thrown face first through the windshield. When she fell back into the seat, the jagged edge of the broken windshield glass had gouged two deep gashes in her left cheek. Blood was streaming down. It was a horrible sight.

Fortunately, someone in one of the other cars had a first aid kit and applied a compress to Donna's cheek to stop the bleeding. The investigating police officer said the accident was unavoidable and there would be no charges made, but I still felt terrible that a beautiful 16-year-old girl would have to go through life with scars on her face. And it had happened when she was in my care.

At the hospital emergency room, Donna was taken immediately to the doctor to have her face stitched up. It seemed to take a long time. Afraid there were complications, I asked a nurse why the delay. She said the doctor on duty happened to be a plastic surgeon. He took many small time-consuming stitches. This also meant there would be minimal scar tissue. Perhaps God was at work in all this mess after all.

I dreaded visiting Donna in the hospital, fearful she would be angry and blame me. Since it was Christmas, the doctors in the hospital tried to send patients home and also postponed elective surgery. As a result, there were not many patients on Donna's floor. I asked a nurse how Donna was doing. The nurse smiled and said she was doing just fine. In fact, she was like a ray of sunshine. Donna seemed happy and kept asking questions about the medical procedures. The nurse confided that with so few patients on the floor, the nurses had time on their hands and made up excuses to go into Donna's room to chat with her!

I told Donna how sorry I was for what had happened. She brushed the apology aside, saying she would cover the scars with pancake make-up. Then she began to excitedly explain what the nurses had been doing and why. The nurses stood around the bed smiling. Donna seemed very happy. This was her first time in a hospital and she was intrigued.

Later at school, Donna was the center of attention as she described again and again the wreck and what happened in the hospital. Her mother and sister did not blame me for what happened and even went out of their way to thank me for taking care of the girls that night. As for Donna, her face was not disfigured and, surely enough, pancake make-up almost covered the scars. That made me feel better, but I still ached for the pretty girl with the scarred face. A year later, I moved to another city and lost touch with Donna and her family.

Fifteen years later, I was invited back to the church for a series of services. The last night, I noticed that Donna's mother stood in the line of people waiting to tell me good-bye. I shuddered as the memories of the wreck, the blood and the scars cascaded back. When Donna's mother stood before me she had a big smile on her face. She was almost laughing when she asked if I knew what had happened to Donna. No, I did not know what had happened. Well, did I remember how interested she was in what the nurses did? Yes, I remembered. Then her mother went on:

"Well, Donna decided to be a nurse. She went into training, graduated with honors, got a good job in a hospital, met a young doctor, they fell in love and are happily married and have two beautiful children. She told me to be sure to tell you that the accident was the best thing that ever happened to her!"

Robert J. McMullen Jr.

From the Mouth of a Small Boy

In 1992 my husband and I went on a Friendship Force exchange to Germany, where we stayed in the homes of three wonderful families. Recently, we were delighted when one of the couples we met in Germany came to visit us at our home in Iowa.

Our friends, Reimund and Toni, live in a city in the industrial Ruhr area of Germany, which suffered heavy bombing during World War II. One evening during their week-long stay with us, my husband, who is a history teacher, invited them to tell us what they remembered about being children in Germany during the war. Reimund proceeded to tell us a story that moved us to tears.

One day not long before the end of the war, Reimund saw two airmen parachuting out of an enemy plane that had been shot down. Like many other curious citizens who had seen the parachutists falling through the afternoon sky, 11-year-old Reimund went to the city's central square to wait for the police to arrive with the prisoners of war. Eventually two policemen arrived with two British prisoners in tow. They would wait there in the city square for a car that would take the British airmen to a prison in a neighboring city where prisoners of war were kept.

When the crowd saw the prisoners, there were angry shouts of "Kill them! Kill them!" No doubt they were thinking of the heavy bombings their city had suffered at the hands of the British and their allies. Nor did the crowd lack the means to carry out their intent. Many of the people had been gardening when they saw the enemy fall from the sky and had brought their pitchforks, shovels and other gardening implements with them.

Reimund looked at the faces of the British prisoners. They were very young, maybe 19 or 20 years old. He could see that they were extremely frightened. He could also see that the two policemen, whose duty it was to protect the prisoners of war, were no match for the angry crowd with its pitchforks and shovels.

Reimund knew he had to do something, and do it quickly. He ran to place himself between the prisoners and the crowd, turning to face the crowd and shouting to them to stop. Not wanting to hurt the little boy, the crowd held back for a moment, long enough for Reimund to tell them:

"Look at these prisoners. They are just young boys! They are no different from your own sons. They are only doing what your own sons are doing—fighting for their country. If your sons were shot down in a foreign country and became prisoners of war, you wouldn't want the people there to kill your sons. So please don't hurt these boys."

Reimund's fellow townspeople listened in amazement, and then shame. Finally, a woman said, "It took a little boy to tell us what is right and what is wrong." The crowd began to disperse.

Reimund will never forget the look of tremendous relief and gratitude he then saw on the faces of the young British airmen. He hopes they have had long, happy lives, and that they haven't forgotten the little boy who saved them.

Elaine McDonald

I Won Because I Lost

*I have lived to thank God that all my prayers
have not been answered.*

Jean Ingelow

It started as a dream, some 25 years before. I watched
my heroes with names like Shepard, Glenn and Grissom
climb into phone-booth size capsules and then launch
into space atop blazing rockets. The astronauts set out to
explore a new frontier; I began to explore a new dream.

I knew I wanted to do that—I wanted to be an astro-
naut, I wanted to fly in space. But I didn't have "the right
stuff"—I didn't have a college degree, nor was I an accomplished test pilot. To make matters worse, I was only 13
years old! But that didn't stop me from dreaming.

Coming from a small, conservative coal mining town
and having a very limited view of the world, I did what
many other young people did. I graduated from high
school and college and began to work as a science teacher
only eight miles from where I was born. But my dream of
flying in space never died. New heroes and new manned
missions kept me glued to the TV set during every space
flight. I always envisioned myself in those capsules soaring into space. Maybe . . . maybe someday.

But as the years went by, my realistic side told me that my dream of flying in space would not be fulfilled. As a science teacher, I then took on a new goal of sparking interest in space exploration in my students. Maybe one of them would someday fly in space because I inspired them with my dream.

Then it happened! In early 1985, like a lightning bolt from the sky, the White House announced that President Reagan was directing NASA to begin the search for an ordinary citizen to fly into space on board a space shuttle mission. The President further specified that this citizen would be a teacher. I was a teacher and I was an ordinary citizen! Did this mean that I had "the right stuff"? Would this be my chance to fulfill my lifelong dream?

Two weeks later, NASA announced that any teacher interested in competing for the honor of being the first ordinary citizen and teacher in space should write to them to request an application. That very same day, I sent my request to Washington . . . Express Mail! I wondered if other teachers had the same dream.

Filling out the application was a long, thought-provoking process. Even for a teacher, who was used to giving rather than taking tests, completing the 25-page application was not an easy task. I spent days and nights trying to think of what answers NASA would be looking for. I answered every question as if my life depended on it—little did I know that it did.

After I dropped my completed application into the mailbox, I learned that many other teachers were hoping to live out their dream by being chosen to be part of the crew of flight 51-L—the Space Shuttle Challenger. More than 43,000 application requests were received by NASA. What were my chances?

Every day, I ran to the mailbox to see if I had survived the space agency's scrutiny. NASA took several weeks to review the 11,000 submitted applications, but then it came . . . an official-looking envelope with NASA's logo in the upper left-hand corner. I'd waited so long for this news, and now that I had it, I was afraid to open the envelope. What if it was bad news? I prayed that the news would be good as I excitedly read the letter.

My prayers were answered! I survived the first cut! NASA wanted to know more about me. My confidence soared, and so did the support from my family, my students and the people in my community. This was really happening to me!

During the next few weeks the realization of my dreams came closer and closer as NASA put me through a series of physical and psychological tests. When they were completed, there was more waiting, more praying. I knew that I was getting closer to my dream. I could now clearly see my name written next to those of Dick Scobee, Judy Resnik, Michael Smith and the other astronauts assigned to the Challenger flight.

Each step of the way, I shared my experiences with my family, my students and my community. The closer I got to being chosen, the more people shared in my excitement. People envisioned me as the one who would put my small community of 2,000 people on the map. My dream also became their dream. I couldn't let them down now.

I finally received the call that I had prayed for. NASA informed me that they had chosen me to attend their special astronautics training program at the Kennedy Space Center! This was it; this was the final step toward being chosen! My confidence soared as I knew that I would be the one who would be the first teacher in space.

An elite group it was, from 11,000 applicants to fewer than 100 men and women with the same dream, gathered for the final evaluation. Only one of us would have our dream fulfilled. It had to be me. Not only was this *my* dream; it was the dream of my students, my family and my community.

Friendly but fiercely competitive is the way I would describe these chosen few. We never knew when we were being tested and evaluated by NASA, so we were always on guard. The smallest task became a competitive challenge to each one of us. Then there were the simulators, the claustrophobia tests, the dexterity exercises and the motion sickness experiments, all designed to see which one of us had "the right stuff." Which one of us would best endure these final tests? God, please let it be me, I prayed. I want this so badly!

When our training was over, we said good-bye to each other, wished each other luck and began the final wait to see who would be chosen. This select few shared an experience that few people will ever get to share. We shared a special bonding, a special caring for each other, but deep down, each of us prayed that we would be the one to be chosen to fly the Challenger mission. I was sure that no one prayed for that dream more than I did. We all went home to wait.

Then came the devastating news. I would not be the first teacher to fly in space. NASA had chosen a teacher from Concord, New Hampshire, by the name of Christa McAuliffe. I had lost. My lifelong dream was over.

Depression, loss of confidence and anger replaced my euphoria as I questioned everything: Why God, why not me? What part of the right stuff did I lack? Why had life dealt me such a cruel blow? How could I face my students, my family and my community? Why did my dream have to end when I was so close?

As I had done so many times when I was a child, I turned to my family to ease my pain. As I told my father my devastating news, he looked at me, as a loving father does, and said, "Everything happens for a reason."

What kind of help was this? How could he be so matter-of-fact about my dream when I was dying inside? Why couldn't he do better than that? Why couldn't he take this pain away? I just didn't understand.

Tuesday, January 28, 1986, the day I had dreamed about for 25 years, found me gathered with those that I had shared my failed dream with: my students, my family and people from the community, along with members of the media. We all came to witness history and watch the historic flight of teacher Christa McAuliffe. We watched as the space shuttle Challenger lifted off the launch pad on what seemed like a perfect launch. As it cleared that launch tower, I challenged my dream one final time. God, I would do anything to be in that shuttle. Why can't that be me?

Seventy-three seconds later, God answered all of my questions and invalidated all of my doubts as the Challenger exploded, killing all on board, including teacher Christa McAuliffe. My father's words, "Everything happens for a reason," instantly came back to me. I was not chosen for that flight no matter how much I wanted it or prayed for it, because the Divine Plan included another reason for my presence on this earth. I had another mission in life. I was not a loser; I was a winner! I had won because I had lost.

Today, I travel throughout the world speaking to adult and youth audiences about life's lessons inspired by losing my dream. As a result of the Challenger experience, my life changed forever. The pain and disappointment that I endured inspired me to help people find their own strengths in the midst of life's challenges. The loss of seven friends in that disaster has driven me to continue the inspirational good that can come out of what appears to be failure.

Frank Slazak

6

A
MATTER
OF
ATTITUDE

*The meaning of things lies not in the
things themselves, but in our attitude
towards them.*

Antoine de Saint Exupéry

Our Deepest Fear

Our deepest fear is not that we are inadequate.
Our deepest fear is that we are powerful beyond measure.
It is our Light, not our Darkness, that most frightens us.
We ask ourselves, who am I to be brilliant,
    gorgeous, talented, fabulous?
Actually, who are you NOT to be?
You are a child of God. Your playing small
    does not serve the World.
There is nothing enlightening about shrinking so that
    other people won't feel unsure around you.
We were born to make manifest the glory of God
    that is within us.
It is not just in some of us;
    it is in everyone.
As we let our own Light shine, we unconsciously
    give other people permission to do the same.
As we are liberated from our own fear,
    our presence automatically liberates others.

Nelson Mandela
From his 1994 inaugural speech

Whiners

Fear less, hope more;
Whine less, breathe more;
Talk less, say more;
Hate less, love more;
And all good things are yours.

Anonymous

When my grandmother was raising me in Stamps, Arkansas, she had a particular routine when people who were known to be whiners entered her store. Whenever she saw a known complainer coming, she would call me from whatever I was doing and say conspiratorially, "Sister, come inside. Come." Of course I would obey.

My grandmother would ask the customer, "How are you doing today, Brother Thomas?"

And the person would reply, "Not so good." There would be a distinct whine in the voice. "Not so good today, Sister Henderson. You see, it's this summer. It's this summer heat. I just hate it. Oh, I hate it so much. It just frazzles me up and frazzles me down. I just hate the heat. It's almost killing me." Then my grandmother would stand stoically, her arms folded, and mumble, "Uh-huh, uh-huh." And she would cut her eyes at me to make certain that I had heard the lamentation.

At another time a whiner would mewl, "I hate plowing. That packed-down dirt ain't got no reasoning, and mules ain't got good sense. Sure ain't. It's killing me. I can't ever seem to get done. My feet and my hands stay sore, and I get dirt in my eyes and up my nose. I just can't stand it." And my grandmother, again stoically, with her arms folded, would say, "Uh-huh, uh-huh," and then look at me and nod.

As soon as the complainer was out of the store, my grandmother would call me to stand in front of her. And then she would say the same thing she had said at least a thousand times, it seemed to me. "Sister, did you hear what Brother So-and-So or Sister Much-to-Do complained about? You heard that?" And I would nod. Mamma would continue, "Sister, there are people who went to sleep all over the world last night, poor and rich and white and black, but they will never wake again. Sister, those who expected to rise did not, their beds became their cooling boards, and their blankets became their winding sheets. And those dead folks would give anything, anything at all for just five minutes of this weather or 10 minutes of that plowing that person was grumbling about. So you watch yourself about complaining, Sister. What you're supposed to do when you don't like a thing is change it. If you can't change it, change the way you think about it. Don't complain."

It is said that persons have few teachable moments in their lives. Mamma seemed to have caught me at each one I had between the ages of three and 13. Whining is not only graceless, but can be dangerous. It can alert a brute that a victim is in the neighborhood.

Maya Angelou

Great Value in Disaster

If your house is on fire, warm yourself by it.

Spanish Proverb

Thomas Edison's laboratory was virtually destroyed by fire in December, 1914. Although the damage exceeded 2 million dollars, the buildings were only insured for $238,000 because they were made of concrete and thought to be fireproof. Much of Edison's life's work went up in spectacular flames that December night.

At the height of the fire, Edison's 24-year-old son, Charles, frantically searched for his father among the smoke and debris. He finally found him, calmly watching the scene, his face glowing in the reflection, his white hair blowing in the wind.

"My heart ached for him," said Charles. "He was 67—no longer a young man—and everything was going up in flames. When he saw me, he shouted, 'Charles, where's your mother?' When I told him I didn't know, he said, 'Find her. Bring her here. She will never see anything like this as long as she lives.'"

The next morning, Edison looked at the ruins and said, "There is great value in disaster. All our mistakes are burned up. Thank God we can start anew."

Three weeks after the fire, Edison managed to deliver his first phonograph.

The Sower's Seeds

Good News

Robert De Vincenzo, the great Argentine golfer, once won a tournament and, after receiving the check and smiling for the cameras, he went to the clubhouse and prepared to leave. Some time later, he walked alone to his car in the parking lot and was approached by a young woman. She congratulated him on his victory and then told him that her child was seriously ill and near death. She did not know how she could pay the doctor's bills and hospital expenses.

De Vincenzo was touched by her story, and he took out a pen and endorsed his winning check for payment to the woman. "Make some good days for the baby," he said as he pressed the check into her hand.

The next week he was having lunch in a country club when a Professional Golf Association official came to his table. "Some of the boys in the parking lot last week told me you met a young woman there after you won that tournament." De Vincenzo nodded. "Well," said the official, "I have news for you. She's a phony. She has no sick baby. She's not even married. She fleeced you, my friend."

"You mean there is no baby who is dying?" said De Vincenzo.

"That's right," said the official.

"That's the best news I've heard all week," De Vincenzo said.

The Best of Bits & Pieces

©1995 Joe Martin, Inc./Dist. by Universal Press Syndicate

Roles—and How We Play Them

Whenever I'm disappointed with my spot in life, I stop and think about little Jamie Scott. Jamie was trying out for a part in a school play. His mother told me that he had his heart set on being in it, though she feared he would not be chosen. On the day the parts were announced, I went with her to collect him after school. Jamie rushed up to her, eyes shining with pride and excitement. "Guess what, Mum," he shouted, and then said those words that remain a lesson to me: "I've been chosen to clap and cheer."

Marie Curling

When We're Alone, We Can Dance

The little cruise ship was crowded with people, many of them retired, all of them off for three days of pleasure.

Ahead of me in the carpeted passageway was a tiny woman in brown polyester slacks, her shoulders hunched, her white hair cut in a short, straight bob.

From the ship's intercom came a familiar tune—"Begin the Beguine" by Artie Shaw. And suddenly, a wonderful thing happened.

The woman, unaware that anyone was behind her, began to shimmy and shake. She snapped her fingers. She swiveled her hips. She did a quick and graceful Lindy step—back, shuffle, slide.

Then, as she reached the door to the dining salon, she paused, assembled her dignity, and stepped soberly through.

She became a hunched old lady again.

That visual fragment has returned to mind many times. I think of it now as I reach another birthday—and an age where most people would not believe that I still shimmy, too.

Younger people think folks of my years are beyond music, romance, dancing, or dreams.

They see us as age has shaped us: camouflaged by wrinkles, with thick waists and graying hair.

They don't see all the other people who live inside.

We present a certain face to the world because custom dictates it. We are the wise old codgers, the dignified matrons.

We have no leeway to act our other selves—or use our other lives.

No one would ever know, for instance, that I am still the skinny girl who grew up in a leafy suburb of Boston.

Inside, I still think of myself as the youngest of four children in a vivacious family, headed by a mother of great beauty and a dad of unfailing good cheer. It doesn't matter that my parents are long gone, and that the four children are now three.

I am still the faintly snobbish child accustomed to long cars and maids—though my dad lost his money in the Depression and I live these days from paycheck to paycheck.

Beth Ashley

Johnny

We are challenged on every hand to work untiringly to achieve excellence in our lifework. Not all men are called to specialized or professional jobs; even fewer rise to the heights of genius in the arts and sciences; many are called to be laborers in factories, fields, and streets. But no work is insignificant. All labor that uplifts humanity has dignity and importance and should be undertaken with painstaking excellence. If a man is called to be a street sweeper, he should sweep even as Michelangelo painted, or Beethoven composed music, or Shakespeare wrote poetry. He should sweep streets so well that all the host of heaven and earth will pause to say, "Here lived a great street sweeper who did his job well."

Martin Luther King Jr.

Last fall I was asked to speak to 3,000 employees of a large supermarket chain in the Midwest on building customer loyalty and regenerating the spirit in your workplace.

One of the ideas I stressed was the importance of adding a personal "signature" to your work. With all the downsizing, re-engineering, overwhelming technological changes and stress in the workplace, I think it is essential for each of us to find a way we can really feel good about ourselves and our jobs. One of the most powerful ways to do this is to do something that differentiates you from all the other people that do the same thing you do.

I shared the example of a United Airlines pilot who, after everything is under control in the cockpit, goes to the computer and randomly selects several people on board the flight and handwrites them a thank-you note for their business. A graphic artist I work with always encloses a piece of sugarless gum in everything he sends his customers, so you never throw away any mail from him!

A Northwest Airlines baggage attendant decided that his personal signature would be to collect all the luggage tags that fall off customers' suitcases, which in the past have been simply tossed in the garbage, and in his free time send them back with a note thanking them for flying Northwest. A senior manager with whom I worked decided that his personal signature would be to attach Kleenex to memos that he knows his employees won't like very much.

After sharing several other examples of how people add their unique spirit to their jobs, I challenged the audience to get their creative juices flowing and to come up with their own creative personal signature.

About three weeks after I had spoken to the supermarket employees, my phone rang late one afternoon. The person on the line told me that his name was Johnny and that he was a bagger in one of the stores. He also told me that he was a person with Down's syndrome. He said, "Barbara, I liked what you said!" Then he went on to tell me that when he'd gone home that night, he asked his dad to teach him to use the computer.

He said they set up a program using three columns,

and each night now when he goes home, he finds a "thought for the day." He said when he can't find one he likes, he "thinks one up!" Then he types it into the computer, prints out multiple copies, cuts them out, and signs his name on the back of each one. The next day, as he bags customers' groceries—"with flourish"—*he puts a thought for the day in each person's groceries,* adding his own personal signature in a heartwarming, fun and creative way.

One month later the manager of the store called me. He said, "Barbara, you won't believe what happened today. When I went out on the floor this morning, the line at Johnny's checkout was *three times longer* than any other line! I went ballistic yelling, 'Get more lanes open! Get more people out here,' but the customers said, 'No no! We want to be in Johnny's lane—we want the thought for the day!'"

The manager said one woman approached him and said, "I only used to shop once a week. Now I come here every time I go by because I want the thought for the day!" (Imagine what that does to the bottom line!) He ended by saying, "Who do you think is the *most important person* in our whole store? Johnny, of course!"

Three months later he called me again. "You and Johnny have transformed our store! Now in the floral department, when they have a broken flower or an unused corsage, they go out on the floor and find an elderly woman or a little girl and pin it on them. One of our meat packers loves Snoopy, so he bought 50,000 Snoopy stickers, and each time he packages a piece of meat, he puts a Snoopy sticker on it. We are having so much fun, and so are our customers!"

That is spirit in the workplace!

Barbara A. Glanz

I Can't Accept Not Trying

I visualized where I wanted to be, what kind of player I wanted to become. I knew exactly where I wanted to go, and I focused on getting there.

Michael Jordan

On Fears

I never looked at the consequences of missing a big shot. Why? Because when you think about the consequences you always think of a negative result.

Some people get frozen by that fear of failure. They get it from peers or from just thinking about the possibility of a negative result. They might be afraid of looking bad or being embarrassed. I realized that if I was going to achieve anything in life I had to be aggressive. I had to get out there and go for it. I don't believe you can achieve anything by being passive. I'm not thinking about anything except what I'm trying to accomplish. Any fear is an illusion. You think something is standing in your way, but nothing is really there. What *is* there is an opportunity to do your best and gain some success. If it turns out my best isn't good enough, then at least I'll never be able to look back and say I was too afraid to try. Failure always made me try harder the next time.

That's why my advice has always been to "think positive" and find fuel in any failure. Sometimes failure actually just gets you closer to where you want to be. If I'm trying to fix a car, every time I try something that doesn't work, I'm getting closer to finding the answer. The greatest inventions in the world had hundreds of failures before the answers were found.

I think fear sometimes comes from a lack of focus or concentration. If I had stood at the free-throw line and thought about 10 million people watching me on the other side of the camera lens, I couldn't have made anything. So I mentally tried to put myself in a familiar place. I thought about all those times I shot free throws in practice and went through the same motion, the same technique that I had used thousands of times. You forget about the outcome. You know you are doing the right things. So you relax and perform. After that you can't control anything anyway. It's out of your hands, so don't worry about it.

On Commitment

I approached practices the same way I approached games. You can't turn it on and off like a faucet. I couldn't dog it during practice and then, when I needed that extra push late in the game, expect it to be there. But that's how a lot of people approach things. And that's why a lot of people fail. They sound like they're committed to being the best they can be. They say all the right things, make all the proper appearances. But when it comes right down to it, they're looking for reasons instead of answers. If you're trying to achieve, there will be roadblocks. I've had them; everybody has had them.

But obstacles don't have to stop you. If you run into a wall, don't turn around and give up. Figure out how to climb it, go through it, or work around it.

Michael Jordan

7

OVERCOMING OBSTACLES

Obstacles cannot crush me; every obstacle yields to stern resolve.

Leonardo da Vinci

The Passionate Pursuit of Possibility

Cherish your visions and your dreams, as they are the children of your soul; the blueprints of your ultimate achievements.

Napolean Hill

Years ago, while unearthing an ancient Egyptian tomb, an archaeologist came upon seeds buried in a piece of wood. Planted, the seeds realized their potential after more than 3,000 years! Are there conditions in the lives of people so discouraging, so defeating, that human beings—regardless of inherent potentiality—are doomed to lives of failure and quiet desperation? Or are there also seeds of possibility in people, an urge for becoming that is so strong that the hard crust of adversity is breached? Consider this story that came over the wires of the Associated Press on May 23, 1984:

As a child, Mary Groda did not learn to read and write. Experts labeled her retarded. As an adolescent, she "earned" an additional label, "incorrigible," and was sentenced to two years in a reformatory. It was here, ironically, in this closed-in place, that Mary—bending to the challenge to learn—worked at her task for as long as 16 hours a day. Her hard work paid off: She was awarded her (GED) high school diploma.

But more misfortune was to visit Mary Groda. After leaving the reformatory, she became pregnant without benefit of marriage. Then, two years later a second pregnancy resulted in a stroke, erasing her hard-earned powers of reading and writing. With the help and support of her father, Mary battled back, regaining what she had lost.

In dire financial straits, Mary went on welfare. Finally, to make ends meet, she took in seven foster children. It was during this period that she started taking courses at a community college. Upon completion of her course work, she applied to and was accepted by the Albany Medical School to study medicine.

In the spring of 1984 in Oregon, Mary Groda Lewis— she's married now—paraded in full academic regalia across the graduation stage. No one can know what private thoughts went through Mary's mind as she reached out to grasp this eloquent testimony to her self-belief and perseverance, her diploma that announced to all the world: Here stands on this small point of Planet Earth a person who dared to dream the impossible dream, a person who confirms for all of us our human divineness. Here stands Mary Groda Lewis, M.D.

James E. Conner

Player of the Game

Pain is inevitable. Suffering is optional.

Source Unknown

Senior Byron Houston, star forward on the Oklahoma State University basketball team, threw a final pass to Bryant Reeves and watched the gawky blond freshman slam the ball through the hoop. The two OSU Cowboys were winding up practice for that night's home game against the University of California, Berkeley. Just then, they saw Cowboys coach Eddie Sutton walk toward the court with a man pushing a kid in a wheelchair.

"I want you to meet Scott Carter and his father, Mike," the coach said, after calling the whole team over.

"Hi, guys," the soon to be 12-year-old said brightly, waving a bony arm. He wore black horn-rimmed glasses too large for his pale, sunken face, and a baseball cap that covered his bald head. From beneath the sweatpant on his left leg jutted the plastic shank of an artificial limb.

Sutton explained that Scott had lost part of his leg to bone cancer. Then the coach asked Scott if he wanted to say anything to the team.

The players expected him to speak about his illness. Instead, Scott shrugged. "Well, I don't know, Coach," he said wryly. "My speech to the football team didn't do them much good. They didn't win a game all season!"

At first there was silence; then all the players roared with laughter. *That is one gutsy kid,* Houston thought.

Freshman Reeves, especially, was awed by Scott's poise. The shy center had taken several minutes to stammer a reply to a question during his first press conference. He turned red-faced just thinking about the courage it took to talk in front of these athletes.

The youngest of three children, Scott had always loved sports, even though he wasn't a natural athlete. He also adored fishing with his Grandfather Bo and Uncle Tom, both of whom had died. He lived in Tulsa with his father, who was a lawyer, and his mother, Paula.

When Scott first complained of pain in his left knee, the Carters assumed it was a sports injury. Later, when told their son had a malignant tumor and would need a complex operation to remove it, Mike and Paula began weeping. Scott looked at his parents, then turned to the doctor. "What I don't understand," he said in mock annoyance, "is why they're doing all the crying. I'm the one with the bad leg."

Scott's irreverence continued through 10 months of stomach-wrenching chemotherapy. When asked how he felt after he awoke from the leg surgery, he responded: "Help! I've fallen and I can't get up!"

A week after the Cowboys beat Berkeley that December night in 1991, the team was slated to play Wichita State University before a sellout crowd in the Cowboys' stadium in Stillwater. Just before the tip-off, assistant coach Bill Self caught a glimpse of Mike Carter trying to squeeze his son into a crowded row. "Look," he whispered to Sutton.

"If the kid wants to sit at the end of the players' bench," the coach said, "it's okay by me."

When Self relayed Sutton's invitation, Scott bobbed up and down excitedly. Seated beside the team, the 12-year-old cheered boisterously. Then Byron Houston came off the court for a rest.

Growing up, Houston had spent his younger years on the tough streets of Kansas City, Kansas. Now a top-billed athlete, he kept his distance from fans and often from his teammates.

Scott began to needle Houston about having elbowed an opposing center. "You think you're a bruiser, but you're playing like a teddy bear."

The young athlete tightened his jaw. Who was this sickly kid to judge his prowess? But then Houston caught Scott's ironic grin.

"Watch out," said Houston, kidding back. "You're going to hate holding this teddy bear."

After the game, OSU's ninth straight victory, Sutton invited Scott to follow the athletes into the locker room. Running his hand across one player's shaved head, Scott joked, "We must have the same barber."

As Sutton watched how easily his Cowboys accepted Scott, a thought struck him. "You just may be our good-luck charm," the trim, graying coach drawled. "How about sitting on the bench at all our home games?"

Scott's eyes widened. For once, he was speechless.

"I'll take that as a yes," the coach said.

Soon a ritual was born. During one game, as Scott sat on the bench, a Cowboy leaving the court high-fived him. Then another player did. By early January, no Cowboy ever left without high-fiving Scott.

One night Scott and his father caught a post-game radio show. The sponsor named one of the Cowboys its "player of the game."

"Dad, how about if we give out our own award?" Scott suggested. The two fashioned a certificate with the words

"Scott's Player of the Game" printed across the top. The award would go to the person who gave his team the best he could muster in a game. In the February loss to the University of Colorado, Scott watched sixth-man Cornell Hatcher make three steals and dubbed him the "Cowboy Burglar." Another player was given the "Pine Time Award" for good humor on the bench. Players loved these awards, taping them up in their lockers and dormitory rooms.

By early February 1992, the Cowboys were ranked the No. 2 college basketball team in the country. Then scoring leader Byron Houston suffered a severe sprain. With Houston sidelined, the University of Missouri overran the Cowboys 66-52, handing them their fourth straight loss.

Sutton knew that without Houston in the upcoming match against the University of Nebraska, the team would have a tough time. He sat Houston down before the game. "Do you think you're up to playing?" he asked him.

"No," the young athlete mumbled, fingering his swollen left ankle.

Scott wheeled his chair over to Houston, joking, "I guess I've got to suit up if you don't play." Houston chuckled, and then the irony hit him. His ankle was only sprained. This child was missing half a leg. He gave the boy a playful jab. "I'm going to play the greatest game— for you."

When the final buzzer sounded that evening, OSU had whipped Nebraska 72-51. Few would have guessed by the 17 points he scored that Byron Houston was in constant pain.

Scott Carter wheeled himself into the post-game locker room. "Tonight's Player of the Game award goes to a guy who doesn't quit, no matter how hard things get," Scott said. "I admire him because he cares about his team and he's my friend." On the certificate, in a 12-year-old's scrawl, was the name Byron Houston.

Tears in his eyes, Houston walked up to the boy. "Thank you," he mumbled, then retreated quickly from the limelight.

A week later, after the Cowboys' last home game of the season, as Houston jogged off the court to a standing ovation, the graduating senior finally uttered what he had not been able to say in the locker room. Wrapping a long, muscular arm around the frail boy and weeping openly, he whispered in Scott's ear, "I love you, buddy." Scott responded, "I love you too."

It was a hopeful time for Scott. He was getting around on crutches. Lung and bone scans had revealed no new tumors, although he did appear to have a small spinal fracture. If Scott remained tumor-free, doctors promised, he could quit chemotherapy, even go swimming and fishing again.

Then Scott's doctor called Paula. "That area on your son's spine isn't a fracture but a malignant tumor." Scott would need a painful operation, followed by six months in a neck-to-hip body brace, and more chemotherapy and radiation.

Paula had always tried to urge Scott to be upbeat about his condition. He took the news with a simple nod of the head. But when Paula continued to cry, he hugged her and then shook a finger in motherly imitation. "Now, Mom, we can't be un-positive about this."

Scott took refuge in the plight of others. One day, seeing a trembling boy being lifted into a wheelchair at the hospital entrance, he said to Paula, "Next time somebody says they will pray for me, I'm going to tell them to pray for him. I'll be all right."

Paula and Mike often talked to their children about God and heaven. At every turn, Scott demonstrated a kindness and concern for others that convinced the Carters he understood there was more to life than fulfilling one's selfish needs.

The news of Scott's latest tumor hit the Cowboys hard. Their sadness deepened when they learned that surgeons hadn't been able to remove all of it, since doing so would have risked leaving Scott paraplegic.

Coach Sutton longed to do something special for Scott. One day an idea struck him. He ordered a Cowboy practice uniform, in Scott's size, to be shipped to the boy.

"I guess this means I'm really a Cowboy!" Scott said when he called Sutton.

"You'll always be a Cowboy, Son," Sutton assured him. "You've got a warrior's spirit."

No one was more dazzled by Scott's continued good humor than Bryant Reeves. Now that Houston had graduated, the shy blond center had become the Cowboys' star player. But as confident as he was on the court, the sophomore was still agonizingly reticent elsewhere.

On a frosty night in late February 1993, the Cowboys played Missouri. Back in the hospital, Scott was watching the game on TV. With the team trailing 64-61 with two seconds left, Reeves had been told to tip the ball to either wing, where guards would try for a long three-pointer. Instead, Reeves reached for the ball and turned toward the hoop. Just as the buzzer sounded, the ball swished through the net. Reeves' incredible 45-foot shot sent the game into overtime, and the Cowboys won 77-73.

In that giddy moment, Reeves felt possessed of the same courage and confidence he'd seen in Scott. He wished he could tell him how he felt, but of course the boy wasn't there.

Weeks later, Reeves sat quietly at the head table in the student union center as the annual basketball banquet—with 600 fans, reporters and players' families—was coming to a close. The task before him was perhaps the hardest of his life.

Sutton stepped to the podium and announced, "Bryant

Reeves has something he'd like to say."

Standing at the podium, hearing nothing in the terrifying silence but an occasional tinkling of glasses, the shy athlete took a deep breath and tried to focus his mind. Then, as he looked beyond the spotlights, he saw Scott, with his family, smiling up at him.

"Scott Carter is an inspiration to every player on this team," said Reeves, his voice trembling. "I'd like to thank him for showing me what determination is all about."

Reeves beckoned the boy to the dais. As Scott slipped his crutches under his arms and began to walk, Reeves lifted a basketball from underneath the podium. Scribbled across it were Reeves' autograph and the words "Oklahoma State versus Missouri, Feb. 24, 1993, the Big Shot.'"

"I want you to have the ball I used to make that shot against Missouri," the athlete said. "Nobody deserves it more."

Scott, balanced on his crutches, fell into the huge athlete's arms. As Reeves fought back tears, the room erupted into a standing ovation.

In early October 1993, a bone scan revealed new tumors growing around Scott's spine, threatening to choke off his spinal cord. This would end his intense pain, but also destroy all sensation from the waist down. More tumors were found in his lungs and brain.

"It's over," the doctors told his parents. "He's likely to die before Thanksgiving."

The fear that had beat in Mike's and Paula's hearts from the moment they first heard the word cancer had now come to pass. They were being asked to summon the strength to say good-bye.

As Mike and Paula broke the news to Scott, the frail teenager listened quietly. When he finally spoke, he didn't mention all the things he wouldn't be able to do—graduate from high school, marry, become a father—but the one thing he would do. "I'll get to see Uncle Tom again in heaven," he said. "I'll get to fish with him and Grandfather Bo."

On Thanksgiving Day, vans started pulling up in front of the Carters' house in Tulsa. "You won't believe who's at the door!" Paula called out to her son, now confined to a bed in the family room. Scott smiled as one by one the Cowboys, their coaches and their families filed through the Carters' hallway.

Permanently paralyzed from the waist down, Scott's body was bloated from heavy doses of steroids. Drugs to control brain tumor seizures slowed his speech. Yet the old Scott shone through. "You'd better win tomorrow night," he told Reeves, "because I'm going to be there to make sure you do."

The next evening, despite a packed house, one seat remained empty—at the end of the Cowboys' bench. Throughout the first half of their game against Providence College, the Cowboys played mechanically.

Sutton shook his head. It had been foolish to hope that Scott could make the game. Still, he wished he could share one more win with the kid.

Then, beneath the crowd's roar, Sutton detected the squeak of a wheelchair. He turned and saw Mike Carter pushing Scott toward the court. Scott, no longer able to sit up, was stretched out in a reclining wheelchair, his head propped to view the game. The Cowboys on the court sensed it immediately: Scott's here. Now they would be playing for him. OSU beat Providence 113-102. Senior guard Brooks Thompson scored a career-high 33 points. And Scott got in a final barb. "Pretty good game," he said to Thompson. "But why'd you miss that last shot?"

Then Scott did something he'd been doing for more than two seasons, though now it took every ounce of his energy. As each player passed him on the way to the shower, the boy lifted his pale, bony hand high in the air. One by one, every Cowboy spread open a sweaty palm and high-fived him.

It would be their last time. On December 2, 1993, minutes before the tip-off against Arizona State, Scott, surrounded by his parents and brother and sister, stopped breathing. At his side was a plaque with a Biblical verse from 2 Timothy 4:7. "I have fought the good fight, I have finished the race, I have kept the faith. Now there is in store for me the crown of righteousness, which the Lord . . . will award to me on that day."

Scott was buried in a black OSU warm-up uniform beside a creek like the one he had fished with his uncle and grandfather. "He's in a better place," Paula and Mike Carter told a red-eyed Coach Sutton and the Cowboys— Scott's honorary pallbearers.

In the months to come, when Coach Sutton became depressed thinking about the empty spot on his bench, when he caught a player looking glum, he reminded the team of Scott's awards. The Player of the Game, he told them, was the person who offered up his last ounce of breath no matter how defeating the odds. He was the player who valued his team, his fans and his faith in God too much to quit.

Scott Carter, he told them, would forever be his model for Player of the Game.

Suzanne Chazin

We Never Told Him He Couldn't Do It

They can because they think they can.

Virgil

When my son Joey was born, his feet were twisted upward with the bottoms resting on his tummy. As a first-time mother, I thought this looked odd, but I didn't really know what it meant. It meant that Joey had been born with club feet. The doctors assured us that with treatment he would be able to walk normally, but would probably never run very well. The first three years of his life, Joey spent in surgery, casts and braces. His legs were massaged, worked and exercised and, yes, by the time he was seven or eight you wouldn't even know he'd had a problem if you watched him walk.

If he walked great distances, like at the amusement parks or on a visit to the zoo, he complained that his legs were tired and that they hurt. We would stop walking, take a break with a soda or ice cream cone and talk about what we had seen and what we had to see. We didn't tell him why his legs hurt and why they were weak. We didn't tell him this was expected due to his deformity at birth. We didn't tell him, so he didn't know.

The children in our neighborhood ran around as most

children do during play. Joey would watch them play and, of course, would jump right in and run and play too. We never told him that he probably wouldn't be able to run as well as the other children. We didn't tell him he was different. We didn't tell him. So he didn't know.

In seventh grade he decided to go out for the cross-country team. Every day he trained with the team. He seemed to work harder and run more than any of the others. Perhaps he sensed that the abilities that seemed to come naturally to so many others did not come naturally to him. We didn't tell him that although he could run, he probably would always remain in the back of the pack. We didn't tell him that he shouldn't expect to make the "team." The team runners are the top seven runners of the school. Although the entire team runs, it is only these seven who will have potential to score points for the school. We didn't tell him he probably would never make the "team," so he didn't know.

He continued to run four to five miles a day, every day. I'll never forget the time he had a 103-degree fever. He couldn't stay home because he had cross-country practice. I worried about him all day. I expected to get a call from the school asking me to come get him and take him home. No one called.

I went out to the cross-country training area after school, thinking that if I were there, he might decide to skip practice that evening. When I got to the school, he was running along the side of a long tree-lined street, all alone. I pulled up alongside of him and drove slowly to keep pace with him as he ran. I asked how he felt. "Okay," he said. He only had two more miles to go. As the sweat rolled down his face, his eyes were glassy from his fever. Yet he looked straight ahead and kept running. We never told him he couldn't run four miles with a 103-degree fever. We never told him. So he didn't know.

Two weeks later, the day before the second to the last race of the season, the names of the "team" runners were called. Joey was number 6 on the list. Joey had made the "team." He was in seventh grade. The other six team members were all eighth-graders. We never told him he probably shouldn't expect to make the "team." We never told him he couldn't do it. We never told him he couldn't do it . . . so he didn't know. He just did it.

Kathy Lamancusa

A Lesson in Heart

A lesson in "heart" is my little 10-year-old daughter, Sarah, who was born with a muscle missing in her foot and wears a brace all the time. She came home one beautiful spring day to tell me she had competed in "field day"—that's where they have lots of races and other competitive events.

Because of her leg support, my mind raced as I tried to think of words of encouragement for my Sarah, things I could say to her about not letting this get her down—things I have heard many famous coaches tell the players when they were faced with defeat—but before I could get a word out, she looked up and said, "Daddy, I won two of the races!"

I couldn't believe it! And then Sarah said, "I had an advantage."

Ahh. I knew it. I thought she must have been given a head start . . . some kind of physical advantage. But again, before I could say anything, she said, "Daddy, I didn't get a head start . . . my advantage was I had to try harder!"

That's heart! That's my Sarah.

Stan Frager

Fourteen Steps

Adversity introduces a man to himself.

Anonymous

They say a cat has nine lives, and I am inclined to think that possible since I am now living my third life and I'm not even a cat.

My first life began on a clear, cold day in November, 1904, when I arrived as the sixth of eight children of a farming family. My father died when I was 15, and we had a hard struggle to make a living. Mother stayed home and cooked the potatoes and beans and cornbread and greens, while the rest of us worked for whatever we could get—a small amount at best.

As the children grew up, they married, leaving only one sister and myself to support and care for Mother, who became paralyzed in her last years and died while still in her 60s. My sister married soon after, and I followed her example within the year.

This was when I began to enjoy my first life. I was very happy, in excellent health, and quite a good athlete. My wife and I became the parents of two lovely girls. I had a good job in San Jose and a beautiful home up the peninsula in San Carlos.

Life was a pleasant dream.

Then the dream ended and became one of those horrible nightmares that cause you to wake in a cold sweat in the middle of the night. I became afflicted with a slowly progressive disease of the motor nerves, affecting first my right arm and leg, and then my other side.

Thus began my second life. . . .

In spite of my disease I still drove to and from work each day, with the aid of special equipment installed in my car. And I managed to keep my health and optimism, to a degree, because of 14 steps.

Crazy? Not at all.

Our home was a split-level affair with 14 steps leading up from the garage to the kitchen door. Those steps were a gauge of life. They were my yardstick, my challenge to continue living. I felt that if the day arrived when I was unable to lift one foot up one step and then drag the other painfully after it—repeating the process 14 times until, utterly spent, I would be through—I could then admit defeat and lie down and die.

So I kept on working, kept on climbing those steps. And time passed. The girls went to college and were happily married, and my wife and I were alone in our beautiful home with the 14 steps.

You might think that here walked a man of courage and strength. Not so. Here hobbled a bitterly disillusioned cripple, a man who held on to his sanity and his wife and his home and his job because of 14 miserable steps leading up to the back door from his garage.

As I dragged one foot after another up those steps—slowly, painfully, often stopping to rest—I would sometimes let my thoughts wander back to the years when I was playing ball, golfing, working out at the gym, hiking, swimming, running, jumping. And now I could barely manage to climb feebly up a set of steps.

As I became older, I became more disillusioned and frustrated. I'm sure that my wife and friends had some unhappy times when I chose to expound to them my phi-losophy of life. I believed that in this whole world I alone had been chosen to suffer. I had carried my cross now for nine years and probably would bear it for as long as I could climb those 14 steps.

I chose to ignore the comforting words from 1 Cor. 15:52: "In a moment, in the twinkling of an eye . . . we shall be changed." And so it was that I lived my first and sec-ond lives here on earth.

Then on a dark night in August, 1971, I began my third life. I had no idea when I left home that morning that so dramatic a change was to occur. I knew only that it had been rougher than usual even getting *down* the steps that morning. I dreaded the thought of having to climb them when I arrived home.

It was raining when I started home that night; gusty winds and slashing rain beat down on the car as I drove slowly down one of the less-traveled roads. Suddenly the steering wheel jerked in my hands and the car swerved violently to the right. In the same instant I heard the dreaded bang of a blowout. I fought the car to a stop on the rain-slick shoulder of the road and sat there as the enormity of the situation swept over me. It was impos-sible for me to change that tire! Utterly impossible!

A thought that a passing motorist might stop was dis-missed at once. Why should anyone? I knew I wouldn't! Then I remembered that a short distance up a little side road was a house. I started the engine and thumped slowly along, keeping well over on the shoulder until I came to the dirt road, where I turned in—thankfully. Lighted windows welcomed me to the house and I pulled into the driveway and honked the horn.

The door opened and a little girl stood there, peering at

me. I rolled down the window and called out that I had a flat and needed someone to change it for me because I had a crutch and couldn't do it myself.

She went into the house and a moment later came out bundled in raincoat and hat, followed by a man who called a cheerful greeting.

I sat there comfortable and dry, and felt a bit sorry for the man and the little girl working so hard in the storm. Well, I would pay them for it. The rain seemed to be slackening a bit now, and I rolled down the window all the way to watch. It seemed to me that they were awfully slow and I was beginning to become impatient. I heard the clank of metal from the back of the car and the little girl's voice came clearly to me. "Here's the jack-handle, Grandpa." She was answered by the murmur of the man's lower voice and the slow tilting of the car as it was jacked up.

There followed a long interval of noises, jolts and low conversation from the back of the car, but finally it was done. I felt the car bump as the jack was removed, and I heard the slam of the trunk lid, and then they were standing at my car window.

He was an old man, stooped and frail-looking under his slicker. The little girl was about eight or 10, I judged, with a merry face and a wide smile as she looked up at me.

He said, "This is a bad night for car trouble, but you're all set now."

"Thanks," I said, "thanks. How much do I owe you?"

He shook his head. "Nothing. Cynthia told me you were a cripple—on crutches. Glad to be of help. I know you'd do the same for me. There's no charge, friend."

I held out a five-dollar bill. "No! I like to pay my way."

He made no effort to take it and the little girl stepped closer to the window and said quietly, "Grandpa can't see it."

In the next few frozen seconds the shame and horror of that moment penetrated, and I was sick with an intensity

I had never felt before. A blind man and a child! Fumbling, feeling with cold, wet fingers for bolts and tools in the dark—a darkness that for him would probably never end until death.

They changed a tire for me—changed it in the rain and wind, with me sitting in snug comfort in the car with my crutch. My handicap. I don't remember how long I sat there after they said good night and left me, but it was long enough for me to search deep within myself and find some disturbing traits.

I realized that I was filled to overflowing with self-pity, selfishness, indifference to the needs of others and thoughtlessness.

I sat there and said a prayer. In humility I prayed for strength, for a greater understanding, for keener awareness of my shortcomings and for faith to continue asking in daily prayer for spiritual help to overcome them.

I prayed for blessings upon the blind man and his granddaughter. Finally I drove away, shaken in mind, humbled in spirit.

"Therefore all things whatsoever ye would that men should do to you, do ye even so to them: for this is the law and the prophets." (Matt. 7:12.)

To me now, months later, this scriptural admonition is more than just a passage in the Bible. It is a way of life, one that I am trying to follow. It isn't always easy. Sometimes it is frustrating, sometimes expensive in both time and money, but the value is there.

I am trying now not only to climb 14 steps each day, but in my small way to help others. Someday, perhaps, I will change a tire for a blind man in a car—someone as blind as I had been.

Hal Manwaring

My Body Was
Turning to Stone

*In the depth of winter I finally learned there
was in me invincible summer.*
Albert Camus

By 1984, at age 30, I had been happily married for seven years, was enjoying a challenging career as a management consultant in San Francisco and until two years before, had always been active and healthy. So when my doctors told me that I had as little as three years to live, I was stunned. Like millions of people, I'd never even heard of scleroderma—the incurable disease that was hardening my tissues, from my skin to my internal organs.

My body was turning to stone. I went to the library to find out all that I could about the illness, and what I learned astonished me. Scleroderma (literally, hard skin) causes overproduction of collagen, the fibrous protein in the body's connective tissues. Though scleroderma is more common than multiple sclerosis, muscular dystrophy and cystic fibrosis, little research had been done on it and almost nothing was known about how or why it develops. "You're telling me I am going to die in a couple years and nobody knows anything about the disease?"

I remember saying to my doctors. Though I was shocked, I didn't want to waste time on self-pity.

My choice was simple: I could quit or I could live my life the way I chose to. Faced with what would many times be an anguished battle against a debilitating, disfiguring and often deadly disease, I was also given a remarkable opportunity to make a meaningful contribution. Scleroderma is a solvable problem that had never before received attention or resources. What I would do was launch an exciting, innovative search for a cure.

I've always considered myself small but determined: I'm 5 feet tall and have never weighed more than 100 pounds. While growing up in Omaha, I spent much of my adolescence traveling as a competitive figure skater. But at 17, I realized I wanted a more well-rounded life, so I retired from competitive skating and enrolled at Pitzer College, in Claremont, California. My first day there I met Mark Scher. I thought of him as my very best friend all through college, but it was my father who said five years later, "You're in love with Mark—and he is in love with you." He was right. Mark and I married in 1977. Not long after, I got my master's degree in business administration from Stanford University and joined McKinsey & Co., one of the premier management consulting firms in the world.

Then in early 1982 I suddenly ran out of energy. Some days I literally couldn't get out of bed. My joints were swollen and painful; my hands turned blue in the cold. My fingers could barley grasp a pen. During the next two years I was evaluated by internists, dermatologists, rheumatologists and infectious disease and pulmonary specialists. No one could figure out what was wrong. Eventually the skin on my face tightened until it became so taut I could barely close my lips over my teeth. But it wasn't until 1984, when I was hospitalized with intense pain and breathing difficulty, that I was diagnosed with severe scleroderma. By that time, I'd deteriorated so much that the disease was unmistakable.

Within a year I was too disabled to work, but Mark and I were determined to start a family. From what I read, if I lived through the pregnancy I'd have the same chance as any other woman of having a healthy infant. But my physicians told me I shouldn't risk it, even though they couldn't say why. When I became pregnant, problems arose from the start. I began having contractions in the fourth month and had to take medication to prevent preterm labor. I was in and out of the hospital throughout the pregnancy. When Max was born on March 9, 1985, six weeks early and just around 5 pounds 9 ounces, my obstetrician said, "This is a miracle." For me the pregnancy was a real turning point. I decided that I no longer wanted to hear that nothing could be done about this disease. I knew my illness and my body better than anyone.

It took me a long time to recover, but I was so in love with Max that nothing else mattered. And I had a new goal as well as a new baby: In 1986, mobilizing my business and management skills, I organized the Scleroderma Research Foundation to bring together the best minds in science, medicine and business to battle this devastating disease. The idea behind the foundation is to develop a fast track, collaborative approach to finding a cure and raising the money to fund the research. Once the foundation was on its feet, when Max was three-and-a-half years old, Mark and I began thinking of another child. This time my obstetrician reassured us: Whatever you decide, don't base it on your last pregnancy. We've learned a great deal about how to take care of you. With my second pregnancy we were able to prevent most complications; Samantha was born, full term, on November 7, 1988.

Dealing with the foundation, two small babies and scleroderma day in and day out was more than a full-time commitment. I've struggled to pace myself. My lungs have lost much of their elasticity, and I have only 38 percent of my normal lung capacity, which affects my stamina. Everything that requires finger flexibility—turning a door-knob, buttoning a blouse—is a nightmare. It's taken me years to figure out how to cope, and the obstacles never end. I can drive, for instance, but only in cars with certain types of handles and locks. Just getting dressed in a busi-ness suit and putting my hair in a bun are real challenges.

Since scleroderma has disfigured my face, I've had to get used to people staring at me. I've learned to separate myself from my body. The real me, the person inside, doesn't look like the face in the mirror. My life is not deter-mined by the way my body functions or looks. In 1990, Mark and I decided to try for a third miracle. I was preg-nant again when we moved to Santa Barbara, California, for Mark's business. Relocating my family and the founda-tion, and renovating a home, I was experiencing one of the most stressful times in my life. I think that is why Montana was born a month early, on October 28, 1990. Yet at 6 pounds, 4 ounces, she was the biggest of my babies.

Regardless of what the future holds, having children is the best thing we could have done. Max is 10 years old; Samantha, six; and Montana, four. They are the joys of my life—24-hour, high-maintenance joys, but joys nonethe-less. They keep me alive because I know they need me. I want to make them feel loved and secure. If I can give them enough confidence in themselves now, I know they're going to make it whether I'm here or not. I don't try to hide my disease from the children. I want them to feel that even if I'm sick, they can come talk to me. I've told them that I have a serious illness, that they have to be careful around me because I can be injured easily. I let them learn about my scleroderma little by little over time, as they wanted to know.

Of course, my disease has affected them. Once when I went to Max's school, some kids pointed at me and started laughing. But I heard Max say, "Don't laugh at my mother; she has scleroderma." I was so proud he could handle it. I try to do as many normal things as I can with the children. When Max took up in-line skating, I tried it, too, even though I had to be careful. I also encouraged my children to bring their friends home, so there are always tons of kids around. Sure, the house is messy, but I've learned that it's so unimportant in the scheme of things.

The hardest thing about this illness is the day-to-day physical suffering. Not a week goes by that I don't need to see one or more doctors. I'm in constant pain, and it can be excruciating. My joints freeze up when I lie down too long. Some mornings I look down the hallway from the bedroom to the kitchen and I think, *That's just too far.* But then I say to myself, *Okay, put one foot in front of the other. You can do it.* I've found ways to cut corners. I buy my kids slip-on shoes because I can't tie laces. We have simple meals. Snacks are kept in reach of the children, who set the table and do chores. But it's important to me to have breakfast with the children, make their lunches, brush their hair and take them to school.

My family, my friends and my doctors look at every day I have not as a gift, but as an achievement. I've lived years longer than anyone had predicted. I believe the reason is that I made a decision: I'm going to live and beat this disease. I go to physical therapy regularly to strengthen and stretch my muscles. Acupuncture helps relieve the pain. I follow a special diet I put together with a nutritionist; by trial and error, I've discovered that I feel best if I avoid beef, chocolate and acidic foods. Over the years, I've tried several experimental treatments; they have not been cures but, once thoroughly tested, may eventually improve the quality of life for many sufferers.

At times I take other medications, such as antibiotics and anti-inflammatory agents, for special symptoms.

What's important to me is to function at as high a level as I can for as long as I can. I want to be independent. I have chosen not to make my disease central to my family, and I've succeeded, though our life is not easy. I am so fortunate to have Mark as my husband. I know it's hard for him to see me suffer. It took me years to believe that he truly wants to be with me. I used to think he deserved a healthy wife who could go skiing with him and do all the things we loved. But after everything we've shared, I can see that I bring something to his life too. He's proud of me and the foundation's incredible success. He tells everyone about the time we met with the director of the National Institutes of Health (which allocates billions in funding), who said, "Sharon, I know all about the work you've been doing, and I think it's the future for scientific research."

The Scleroderma Research Foundation's two research centers—one in San Francisco and one near Washington, D.C.—have made more progress in developing a diagnostic test and identifying the cells involved in the disease. Nearly every dollar the foundation raises—more than three million so far—goes to research. (Muscular dystrophy research receives $80 million in federal funds each year; by contrast, scleroderma, with twice the number of victims, gets only 1.6 million.) Our biggest annual fund-raising event—Cool Comedy, Hot Cuisine—is held in Los Angeles with top comics such as Robin Williams, Gary Shandling and Bob Saget. How do I get such great talent? The same way I got top-notch scientists from many disciplines to concentrate on scleroderma: I don't take no for an answer. When I learned that Lily Tomlin had an aunt who died from scleroderma, I wrote and called and faxed the performer for five years until she agreed to see me for 10 minutes; we talked for hours, and now she's become a great supporter.

Stars like Lesley Ann Warren, Linda Gray, Marilu Henner and Dana Delany have responded generously to battle an illness that primarily targets women of child-bearing age. The truth is, if scleroderma were a disease that more often affected children or men, we'd be light years ahead of where we are now. The illness had never before had anyone come forward to lead a fund-raising and publicity effort. The public must know that scleroderma leaves children without their mothers. As chairman of the foundation, I've appeared on television and before Congress, the National Institutes of Health and other federal agencies to put a human face on the disease. Even though I'm a very private person, I've become a public figure. My efforts have earned a $5,000 American Award, given by the Positive Thinking Foundation to honor "unsung heroes who personify the American Spirit." But what's most gratifying is offering people who may be terrified and in pain something they really need: hope. They can look at me and see someone just like them who's making things happen that will affect hundreds of thousands of people. Maybe that can get them through the day.

My goal is a cure. Will it happen in my lifetime? I don't know because we're racing against time. But I'm optimistic that our trailblazing path will be successful. Even if a cure is found too late to help me, at least I will have accomplished this: My children will know who I was and what I stood for. I just wish there were more hours in the day. I have a lot of living to do.

Sharon Monsky, as told to Dianne Hales

The Beauty Remains;
the Pain Passes

Although Henri Matisse was nearly 28 years younger than Auguste Renoir, the two great artists were dear friends and frequent companions. When Renoir was confined to his home during the last decade of his life, Matisse visited him daily. Renoir, almost paralyzed by arthritis, continued to paint in spite of his infirmities. One day as Matisse watched the elder painter working in his studio, fighting tortuous pain with each brush stroke, he blurted out: "Auguste, why do you continue to paint when you are in such agony?"

Renoir answered simply: "The beauty remains; the pain passes." And so, almost to his dying day, Renoir put paint to canvas. One of his most famous paintings, *The Bathers*, was completed just two years before his passing, 14 years after he was stricken by this disabling disease.

The Best of Bits & Pieces

The Miracle Bridge

The Brooklyn Bridge that spans the river between Manhattan and Brooklyn is simply an engineering miracle. In 1883, a creative engineer, John Roebling, was inspired by an idea for this spectacular bridge project. However, bridge-building experts told him to forget it, it just was not possible. Roebling convinced his son, Washington, an up-and-coming engineer, that the bridge could be built. The two of them conceived the concept of how it could be accomplished and how to overcome the obstacles. Somehow they convinced bankers to finance the project. Then, with unharnessed excitement and energy, they hired their crew and began to build their dream bridge.

The project was only a few months under way when a tragic on-site accident killed John Roebling and severely injured his son. Washington was severely brain-damaged, unable to talk or walk. Everyone thought the project would have to be scrapped, since the Roeblings were the only ones who understood how the bridge could be built.

Though Washington Roebling was unable to move or talk, his mind was as sharp as ever. One day as he lay in his hospital bed, an idea flashed in his mind as to how to develop a communication code. All he could move was one finger, so he touched the arm of his wife with that finger. He tapped out the code to communicate to her what she was to tell the engineers who continued building the bridge. For 13 years, Washington tapped out his instructions with one finger until the spectacular Brooklyn Bridge was finally completed.

A Fresh Packet of Sower's Seeds

True Height

The greater the obstacle, the more glory in overcoming it.

Molière

When it is dark enough, you can see the stars.

Charles A. Beard

His palms were sweating. He needed a towel to dry his grip. A glass of ice water quenched his thirst but hardly cooled his intensity. The Astroturf he sat on was as hot as the competition he faced today at the National Junior Olympics. The pole was set at 17 feet. That was three inches higher than his personal best. Michael Stone confronted the most challenging day of his pole-vaulting career.

The stands were still filled with about 20,000 people, even though the final race had ended an hour earlier. The pole vault is truly the glamour event of any track and field competition. It combines the grace of a gymnast with the strength of a body builder. It also has the element of flying, and the thought of flying as high as a two-story building is a mere fantasy to anyone watching such an event. Today and now, it is not only Michael Stone's reality and dream—it is his quest.

As long as Michael could remember he had always dreamed of flying. Michael's mother read him numerous stories about flying when he was growing up. Her stories were always ones that described the land from a bird's-eye view. Her excitement and passion for details made Michael's dreams full of color and beauty. Michael had this one recurring dream. He would be running down a country road. He could feel the rocks and chunks of dirt at his feet. As he raced down the golden-lined wheat fields, he would always outrun the locomotives passing by. It was at the exact moment he took a deep breath that he began to lift off the ground. He would begin soaring like an eagle.

Where he flew would always coincide with his mother's stories. Wherever he flew was with a keen eye for detail and the free spirit of his mother's love. His dad, on the other hand, was not a dreamer. Bert Stone was a hard-core realist. He believed in hard work and sweat. His motto: *If you want something, work for it!*

From the age of 14, Michael did just that. He began a very careful and regimented weightlifting program. He worked out every other day with weights, with some kind of running work on alternate days. The program was carefully monitored by Michael's coach, trainer and father. Michael's dedication, determination and discipline was a coach's dream. Besides being an honor student and only child, Michael Stone continued to help his parents with their farm chores. Michael's persistence in striving for perfection was not only his obsession but his passion.

Mildred Stone, Michael's mother, wished he could relax a bit more and be that "free dreaming" little boy. On one occasion she attempted to talk to him and his father about this, but his dad quickly interrupted, smiled and said, *"You want something, work for it!"*

All of Michael's vaults today seemed to be the reward for his hard work. If Michael Stone was surprised, thrilled or arrogant about clearing the bar at 17 feet, you couldn't tell. As soon as he landed on the inflated landing mat, and with the crowd on its feet, Michael immediately began preparing for his next attempt at flight. He seemed oblivious of the fact he had just surpassed his personal best by one foot and that he was one of the final two competitors in the pole-vaulting event at the National Junior Olympics.

When Michael cleared the bar at 17 feet 2 inches and 17 feet 4 inches, again he showed no emotion. Constant preparation and determination were his vision. As he lay on his back and heard the crowd groan, he knew the other vaulter had missed his final jump. He knew it was time for his final jump. Since the other vaulter had fewer misses, Michael needed to clear this vault to win. A miss would get him second place. Nothing to be ashamed of, but Michael would not allow himself the thought of not winning first place.

He rolled over and did his ritual of three finger-tipped pushups along with three Marine-style push-ups. He found his pole, stood and stepped on the runway that led to the most challenging event of his 17-year-old life.

The runway felt different this time. It startled him for a brief moment. Then it all hit him like a wet bale of hay. The bar was set at 18 inches higher than his personal best. That's only one inch off the National record, he thought. The intensity of the moment filled his mind with anxiety. He began shaking the tension from his body. It wasn't working. He became more tense. Why was this happening to him now, he thought. He began to get nervous. Afraid would be a more accurate description. What was he going to do? He had never experienced these feelings. Then out of nowhere, and from the deepest depths of his soul, he envisioned his mother. Why now? What was his mother doing in his thoughts at a time like this? It was simple. His mother always used to tell him when you felt tense, anxious or even scared, take deep breaths.

So he did. Along with shaking the tension from his legs, he gently laid his pole at his feet. He began to stretch out his arms and upper body. The light breeze that was once there was now gone. He could feel a trickle of cold sweat running down his back. He carefully picked up his pole. He felt his heart pounding. He was sure the crowd did, too. The silence was deafening. When he heard the singing of some distant robins in flight, he knew it was his time to fly.

As he began sprinting down the runway, something felt wonderfully different, yet familiar. The surface below him felt like the country road he used to dream about. The rocks and chunks of dirt, the visions of the golden wheat fields seemed to fill his thoughts. When he took a deep breath, it happened. He began to fly. His take-off was effortless. Michael Stone was now flying, just like in his childhood dreams. Only this time he knew he wasn't dreaming. This was real. Everything seemed to be moving in slow motion. The air around him was the purest and freshest he had ever sensed. Michael was soaring with the majesty of an eagle.

It was either the eruption of the people in the stands or the thump of his landing that brought Michael back to earth. On his back with that wonderful hot sun on his face, he knew he could only envision the smile on his mother's face. He knew his dad was probably smiling too, even laughing. Bert would always do that when he got excited, smile and then sort of giggle. What he didn't know was that his dad was hugging his wife and crying. That's right: Bert "If You Want It, Work For It" Stone was crying like a baby in his wife's arms. He was crying harder than Mildred had ever seen before. She also knew he was crying the greatest tears of all: tears of pride. Michael was immediately swarmed with people hugging and congratulating him on the greatest accomplishment of his life. He later went on that day to clear 17 feet 6½ inches: a National and International Junior Olympics record.

With all the media attention, endorsement possibilities and swarming herds of heartfelt congratulations, Michael's life would never be the same. It wasn't just because he won the National Junior Olympics and set a new world record. And it wasn't because he had just increased his personal best by 9½ inches. It was simply because Michael Stone is blind.

David Naster

Consider This

The marvelous richness of human experience would lose something of rewarding joy if there were not limitations to overcome. The hilltop hour would not be half so wonderful if there were no dark valleys to traverse.

Helen Keller

Consider this:

- Ski instructor Pete Seibert was considered crazy when he first disclosed his dream to start a ski resort. Standing on the summit of a mountain in the Gore Range in Colorado, Seibert described a dream he had carried with him since age 12, and began the challenge of convincing others that it was possible. Seibert's dream is now a reality called Vail.
- Young Dr. Ignatius Piazza, fresh out of chiropractic school, wanted to open a practice in the beautiful Monterey Bay area of California. He was told by the local chiropractic community that the area was already overrun with chiropractors and there were not enough potential patients to support another practice. For the next four months, Piazza spent 10 hours a day

going door to door and introducing himself as a new chiropractic doctor in town. He knocked on 12,500 doors, spoke to 6,500 people and invited them to come to his future open house. As a result of his perseverance and commitment, during his first month in practice, he saw 233 new patients and earned a record income for that time of $72,000 in one month!

- During its first year of business, the Coca-Cola Company sold only 400 Cokes.
- Basketball superstar Michael Jordan was cut from his high school basketball team.
- At age 17, Wayne Gretzky was an outstanding athlete intent on pursuing a career in either soccer or hockey. His first love was hockey, but when he tried out for the pros, he was told, "You don't weigh enough. At 172 pounds, you're over 50 pounds lighter than the average player. You won't be able to survive on the rink."
- Sheila Holzworth lost her sight when she was only 10 years old. The orthodontic headgear that was attached to her braces snapped and gouged her eyes. Despite her lack of sight, she went on to become an internationally known athlete whose accomplishments included climbing to the icy summit of Mount Ranier in 1981.
- Rafer Johnson, the decathlon champion, was born with a club foot.
- Dr. Seuss's first children's book, *And to Think that I Saw It on Mulberry Street*, was rejected by 27 publishers. The 28th publisher, Vanguard Press, sold 6 million copies of the book.
- Richard Bach completed only one year of college, then trained to become an Air Force jet-fighter pilot. Twenty months after earning his wings, he resigned. Then he became an editor of an aviation magazine that went bankrupt. Life became one failure after

another. Even when he wrote *Jonathan Livingston Seagull*, he couldn't think of an ending. The manuscript lay dormant for eight years before he decided how to finish it—only to have 18 publishers reject it. However, once it was published, the book went on to sell 7 million copies in numerous languages and make Richard Bach an internationally known and respected author.

* The author William Kennedy had written several manuscripts, all of them rejected by numerous publishers, before his "sudden success" with his novel *Ironweed*, which was rejected by 13 publishers before it was finally accepted for publication.

* When we wrote *Chicken Soup for the Soul*, it was turned down by 33 publishers before Health Communications agreed to publish it. All the major New York publishers said, "It is too nicey-nice" and "Nobody wants to read a book of short little stories." Since that time over 7 million copies of *Chicken Soup for the Soul, A 2nd Helping of Chicken Soup for the Soul* and the *Chicken Soup for the Soul Cookbook* have been sold worldwide, with the books translated into 20 languages.

* In 1935, the *New York Herald Tribune's* review of George Gershwin's classic *Porgy and Bess* stated that it was "Sure-fire rubbish."

* In 1902, the poetry editor of the *Atlantic Monthly* returned the poems of a 28-year-old poet with the following note: "Our magazine has no room for your vigorous verse." The poet was Robert Frost.

* In 1889, Rudyard Kipling received the following rejection letter from the *San Francisco Examiner:* "I'm sorry, Mr. Kipling, but you just don't know how to use the English language."

* Alex Haley got a rejection letter once a week for four years as a budding writer. Later in his career, Alex was

ready to give up on the book *Roots* and himself. After nine years on the project, he felt inadequate to the task and was ready to throw himself off a freighter in the middle of the Pacific Ocean. As he was standing at the back of the freighter, looking at the wake and preparing to throw himself into the ocean, he heard the voices of all his ancestors saying, "You go do what you got to do because they are all up there watching. Don't give up. You can do it. We're counting on you!" In the subsequent weeks the final draft of *Roots* poured out of him.

• John Bunyan wrote *Pilgrim's Progress* while confined to a Bedford prison cell for his views on religion; Sir Walter Raleigh wrote the *History of the World* during a 13-year imprisonment; and Martin Luther translated the Bible while confined in the Castle of Wartburg.

One of the secrets of success is to refuse to let temporary setbacks defeat us.

Mary Kay

• After Thomas Carlyle lent the manuscript of *The French Revolution* to a friend whose servant carelessly used it to kindle a fire, he calmly went to work and re-wrote it.

• In 1962, four young women wanted to start a professional singing career. They began performing in their church and doing small concerts. Then came their time to cut a record. It was a flop. Later, another record was recorded. The sales were a fiasco. The third, fourth, fifth and on through their ninth recordings were all failures. Early in 1964, they were booked for *The Dick*

Clark Show. He barely paid enough to meet expenses, and no great contracts resulted from their national exposure. Later that summer, they recorded "Where Did Our Love Go?" This song raced to the top of the charts, and Diana Ross and the Supremes gained national recognition and prominence as a musical sensation.

- Winston Churchill was unable to gain admittance to the prestigious Oxford or Cambridge universities because he "was weak in the classics."
- James Whistler, one of America's greatest painters, was expelled from West Point for failing chemistry.
- In 1905, the University of Bern turned down a doctoral dissertation as being irrelevant and fanciful. The young physics student who wrote the dissertation was Albert Einstein, who was disappointed but not defeated.

Jack Canfield and Mark Victor Hansen

Opportunity

If you don't hear opportunity knocking, find another door.

—Author Unknown

Every fiber of my small, seven-year-old body was fearfully shaking as we walked through Customs and explained the purpose of our trip: "We're vacationing in Miami," I heard my pregnant mother say as I clung to her dress. Even though I heard those words, I knew we would never be going home again.

Communism was quickly tightening the noose around the free enterprise system in Cuba, and my father, a successful entrepreneur, decided it was time to take his family and flee to a land where freedom, promise and opportunity still thrived. Looking back now, it was the most courageous decision I've ever seen anybody make.

Castro's regime was watching my father very carefully, making it necessary for my mother to bring my brother and me over first. My father met us a few weeks later. Miami International Airport overwhelmed me. Everybody was speaking in strange words that didn't make sense to me. We had no money, no family—nothing but the clothes on our backs.

Within a few months, we were on a church-sponsored flight to Joliet, Illinois, via Chicago's O'Hare International Airport. A burst of cold air greeted us as we walked out of the terminal into the still talked-about winter of 1961. It had snowed nearly four feet, and amidst the blowing drifts stood a young priest by a large International Suburban, waiting to take us to our new home. This was absolutely amazing for a Cuban boy who had never seen snow.

My father was an educated man and owned a chain of gas stations and a car dealership in Cuba. Unable to speak English, he adapted quickly by finding work as a mechanic; and thanks to St. Patrick's church, we were able to find a comfortable although small apartment in a middle-class neighborhood. We didn't have a lot, but we had each other, a whole lot of love and my father's burning desire to succeed.

It was during this time that my father, with his tattered Spanish copy of Dale Carnegie's book, *How to Win Friends and Influence People,* taught me one of the greatest lessons in life. He told me over and over again: "It doesn't matter who you are, where you're from or what color you are. You can do anything you put your mind to." These words gave me comfort and inspiration as my brother and I mixed into the great Chicago melting pot.

My brother Ed and I struggled in school because we couldn't speak English. It wasn't uncommon to be called a "spic," not to be chosen to be on a team or have our hand-me-down bikes stolen, but my father's words continued to burn inside of me. We also met some truly wonderful people who helped us overcome the obstacles of adjusting to our new surroundings. Many of these people are still my best friends today.

When I was 14, my father was already teaching me about the great principle of free enterprise. He gave me $18 for every set of valves and engine heads I would clean and grind (what we called a valve job). Later he taught me how to hire other people to do the work for me, and I went out and found new customers and collected money—basically ran the business. Little did I know he was teaching me how to be an entrepreneur. America was truly a land of promise.

I was also fortunate to be born into a musically talented family, and I remember listening to my mother sing beautiful Spanish songs to me as I was growing up. These songs inspired me to sing in the church choir as a boy soprano, and because of this same influence, my brother Ed started a contemporary rock band. I attended every band rehearsal and at night harmonized with him and my mother. Later, through working as a laborer in a stone quarry and a scholarship, I studied opera and music at Southern Illinois University. After two years of college, I went back to work in the stone quarry and saved the money I earned for my move west to California.

My goal in moving to California was to break into the music business and cut my own records. It didn't take very long for reality to set in. I had to take a job selling health club memberships to support myself. Depression set in. I was broke and didn't know where to turn. Then I met Tom Murphy, one of the owners of the health club.

My father always told me that if you want to be wealthy, you have to do what wealthy people do, so I asked Mr. Murphy if we could talk over coffee to find out what made him so successful. It just so happened that Mr. Murphy was the business partner of Tom Hopkins, one of the country's top sales trainers. So, of course, he recommended that I start attending sales training seminars, reading self-improvement books and listening to sales tapes. He also introduced me to many successful business men and women and their published materials. I was so hungry for success that it didn't take long before I was the top salesperson in the company. But that wasn't good enough. After saving every penny I could, I invested in my own health club. By the time I was finished, I owned nine of the most successful health clubs and sports medicine facilities in the United States, but I still hadn't achieved my goal—to cut my own record.

Recording my first demo was exciting yet discouraging, as I presented it to record company after record company. Each time I heard the word "no." Not to be defeated, I recorded the demo in Spanish and took it back to the same record companies—all with the same results. On the verge of giving up, I called my father to discuss what had happened. He said, "Omar, you're doing very well financially, aren't you?" I replied that I was. "Well, why don't you just buy a record company and record your music!"

When I went back to the record company I intended to buy, hoping to save my ego, I asked the company executives one more time to record my music. They said, "Omar, we can't help you. Go to Broadway. You'll be great there." You should have seen their faces when I told them I was going to be the new owner.

I then set out to finance, record and produce my first album in Spanish. From there I went on to be named "Best Latin Male Vocalist" and "Entertainer of the Year" in 1986, 1987 and 1988 "CHIN de PLATA" and "OTTO."

Today I am enjoying success as a public speaker and trainer with Tom Hopkins International. It's such a thrill for me now to help others learn how to find the right opportunities to achieve their career goals. Take it from me, my father was right: you can achieve anything you want in life when you set your mind to it.

Omar Periu

Crusader Could Close Her Eyes to Trouble No More

God helps them that help themselves.

Benjamin Franklin

It was one ordinary woman with an extraordinarily simple request of city hall that helped turn around a blighted block and troubled neighborhood, and changed how the city of Roanoke, Virginia, interacts with its citizens—and possibly, how America will reconnect with its government.

Florine Thornhill, 73, had no intention of causing such a stir. She just decided to do something small to make her block better.

So she marched down to city hall and asked a suspicious official if she could borrow a lawn mower to clean up one abandoned and overgrown lot.

For years, she had walked her neighborhood with blinders to the blight, stepping past the decaying homes, drug deals and derelicts. One Sunday in 1979, on her way to church choir, she passed an unconscious woman in the overgrowth of a nearby lot. Thornhill assumed it was a drug addict and walked on. But she couldn't dismiss the woman from her mind.

What, she found herself wondering, would Jesus have her do? So she turned back home and got her son to help her get the woman to safety. Thornhill never learned the woman's name or why she was unconscious. But the encounter opened her eyes to the sadness and poverty she had spent so much time blocking out.

The mother of nine—including one child with mental disabilities—decided to do what she could. She borrowed that mower and cleaned one lot.

Her neighbors became curious, then joined in. On weekends, 15 middle-aged and elderly residents soon were picking up the trash and mowing vacant lots.

In city hall, officials noticed that the once-decrepit neighborhood had begun to shine. In 1980, Roanoke city officials asked Thornhill and her Gilmer neighbors to join in a pilot project with three other city neighborhoods. It would allow them to help set goals for the city, to show the officials how to turn their poor, urban areas around.

The experiment was successful, thanks to Thornhill and the other ordinary people like her. Today, 25 neighborhoods are working in the system to improve Roanoke. Other Virginia cities have followed Roanoke's lead. The Roanoke model is being studied across America, as government officials try to involve the people they serve. Thornhill and her group, the Northwest Neighborhood Environmental Organization, won the 1994 President's Volunteer Action Award, presented by President Clinton for volunteer efforts that changed a community.

But Thornhill said her real measure of success is not in the White House recognition. It is in the children playing at a fully equipped park that was once an open-air market for drug dealers. It is in the homes that her group has been able to buy and rebuild with housing grants they tracked down and won with some city help.

It is in the professionals they have been able to entice

back to Gilmer with low-interest loans, and it is in the part-time worker they have been able to hire to help organize neighborhood activities and get more grant money. "It's just so wonderful to see the children coming home," Thornhill said. "I know they care; they will keep this neighborhood going long after I'm gone."

Toni Whitt

Ask, Affirm, Take Action

Many things are lost for want of asking.

English Proverb

When my daughter, Janna, was a junior in high school, she was accepted as a foreign exchange student to Germany. We were delighted that she had been chosen for such a special experience. Then the exchange organization informed us that we had to pay $4,000 in costs—and the money was due on June 5; two months away.

At the time I was divorced with three teenage children. The idea of raising $4,000 was completely overwhelming to me. Financially, I was barely making ends meet as it was. I had no savings, no credit for a loan and no relatives who could lend me the money. At first it felt as hopeless as if I had to raise $4 million!

Luckily, I had recently attended one of Jack Canfield's Self-Esteem Seminars in Los Angeles. Three of the things I learned at the seminar were to ask for what you want, affirm for what you want and take action for what you want.

I decided to put these new-found principles to work. First, I wrote an affirmation that stated, "I am joyfully receiving $4,000 by June 1 for Janna's trip to Germany." I put the affirmation on my bathroom mirror and carried a copy in my purse so I could look at it every day. Then I wrote out an actual check for $4,000 and put it on the dashboard of my car. I spent a lot of time driving each day and this was a visible reminder. I took a picture of a hundred-dollar bill, enlarged it and put it on the ceiling over Janna's bed so it was the first thing she saw in the morning and the last thing at night.

Janna was a typical 15-year-old Southern California teenager and wasn't too thrilled with these rather "weird" ideas. I explained them all to her and suggested that she write her own affirmation.

Now that I was affirming what I wanted, l needed to take some action and to ask for what I wanted. I have always been a very self-sufficient and independent person who didn't need anyone else's help. It was very difficult for me to ask for money from family and friends that I knew, and even more so from strangers. But I decided to go for it anyway. What did I have to lose?

I made up a flier with Janna's photo and her statement of why she wanted to go to Germany. At the bottom was a coupon for people to tear off and mail back with their check to us by June 1st. Then I asked for a $5, $20, $50 or $100 contribution. I even left a blank space for them to fill in their own amount. Then I mailed this flier to every single friend, family member and person that I knew or even slightly knew. I distributed fliers at the corporate office where I worked, and sent them to the local newspapers and radio station. I researched the addresses of 30 of the service organizations in our valley and mailed them fliers. I even wrote the airlines asking for free travel to Germany.

The newspaper didn't run an article, the radio station didn't do a story, the airline said no to my request, but I kept on asking and continued to mail out fliers. Janna began having dreams of strangers giving her money. In the weeks that followed, the money began to come in. The first gift was for $5. The largest single gift was for $800 from family and friends. But most of the gifts were $20 or $50—some from people we knew, some from strangers.

Janna became enthused about the whole idea and began to believe that this could actually become a reality. One day she asked me, "Do you think this will work for getting my driver's permit?" I assured her that an affirmation would work. She tried it and she got her permit. By June 1st we joyfully received $3,750! We were thrilled! However, while this was wonderful, I still had no idea where I was going to get the last $250. I still had until June 5th to somehow raise the remaining money. On June 3rd the phone rang. It was a woman from one of the service organizations in our town. "I know I'm past the deadline; is it too late?" she asked.

"No," I replied.

"Well, we would really like to help Janna, but we can only give her $250."

In all, Janna had two organizations and 23 people who sponsored her and made her dream a reality. She wrote to each one of those 25 sponsors several times throughout the year, telling them about her experiences. When she returned, she gave a speech at two organizations. Janna was a foreign exchange student in Viersen, Germany, from September to May, and it was a wonderful experience for her. It broadened her perspective and gave her a new appreciation for the world and its people. She was able to see beyond the narrow Southern California life that she grew up in. Since then she has traveled throughout Europe, worked one summer in Spain and another in Germany. She graduated from college with honors, worked two years with VISTA at an AIDS Project in Vermont and is presently pursuing her master's degree in public health administration.

The year after Janna's Germany trip, I found the love of my life, again by using affirmations. We met at a Self-Esteem Seminar, married, and attended a Couples Seminar. At that seminar we created affirmations together, one of which was to travel. In the past seven years we have lived in several different states, including Alaska, spent three years in Saudi Arabia and are presently living in the Orient.

Like Janna, my horizons have broadened and my life is so much more exciting and wonderful because I learned to ask, affirm and take action for the things I want.

Claudette Hunter

A Life-Changing Experience

I have learned to use the word impossible with the greatest caution.

Wernher von Braun

A couple of years ago, I went through an experience that impacted my belief system to such an extent that it forever altered the way I view the world. At the time, I was involved in a human potential organization called LifeSpring. Fifty other individuals and I were going through a three-month training named The Leadership Program. My epiphany began at one of our weekly meetings when the individuals running the program came to us with a challenge. They said they wanted us to feed breakfast to 1,000 homeless people in downtown Los Angeles. Furthermore, we were also to acquire clothing that we were to give away. And most important of all, we were not to spend a single dime of our own money.

Now, since none of us were in the catering business or had ever come close to doing anything like this, my first reaction was, "Jeeze, this is going to really be a stretch to pull off." However, then they added, "By the way, we want you guys to do all of this on Saturday morning." They were telling us this on Thursday night, so I quickly upgraded my prognosis to I-M-P-O-S-S-I-B-L-E! I don't think I was alone.

Looking around the room, I saw 50 faces that were blanker than a freshly washed chalkboard. The fact was, none of us had a single clue as to how to even begin to pull something like this off. It was at this point that something amazing happened. Since none of us wanted to admit that we couldn't handle their challenge, we all said, with perfectly straight faces, "Okay. Yeah, sure we can do this, no problem."

Then one person said, "Okay, we need to break up into teams. We need one team to get the food and another to work on getting equipment to cook it with." Then somebody else said, "I have a truck; we could use it to pick up the equipment."

"Great!" We all chirped.

Then somebody else piped up with, "We need a team to be in charge of getting the entertainment and the donated clothing together." Before I knew it, I was in charge of the communication team.

By 2:00 A.M., we had made a list of every task we could think of that needed to be done, delegated it to the appropriate team, and then headed off for home to try to get some sleep. I remember thinking as I laid my head down on my pillow, "My God, I have no idea how we're going to do this, not even a clue . . . but we're going to give it our best shot!"

At 6:00 A.M. my alarm went off, and a few minutes later my two teammates showed up. The three of us, along with the rest of the team, had exactly 24 hours to see if we could turn the feeding of 1,000 homeless people into a reality.

We pulled out the phone book and began calling everybody on our list who we thought could help us. My first call was to Von's corporate headquarters. After explaining what we were doing, I was told that we had to submit our request for food in writing and that it would take two weeks for it to be processed. I patiently explained that we didn't have two weeks and that we needed the food that same day, preferably before nightfall. The regional manager said she would get back to me within an hour.

I called Western Bagel, pleaded my case, and to my delight, the owner said, "Okay." Suddenly, we had ourselves 1,200 bagels! Next, while I was on the phone with Zacky Farms trying to get us some chicken and some more eggs, my "call waiting" went off. It was one of the guys calling to say that he had stopped by Hansen's Juices and they had a truckload of fresh squeezed carrot, watermelon and other assorted juices they would be willing to donate—a definite home run that brought high-fives all around.

The Von's regional manager called back and said she had procured all kinds of food for us, including 600 loaves of bread! Ten minutes later someone else called to tell me they had arranged for 500 burritos to be donated. In fact, it seemed like every 10 minutes someone from the team was calling up, telling me that they got someone to donate X amount of something! "Wow," I thought. "Could we really be pulling it off?"

Finally, at midnight, after 18 straight hours of work, I found myself at a Winchell's Donuts picking up 800 donuts and carefully packing them in one side of my hatchback, so I'd have room for the 1,200 bagels I was scheduled to pick up at 5:00 A.M.

After a few hours of much needed rest, I hopped into my car, whipped by Western Bagel and picked up the bagels (my car now smelled like a bakery), and headed for downtown Los Angeles. It was Saturday morning and I was pumped up. As I pulled into the parking lot at around 5:45 A.M., I could see team members setting up large industrial barbecues, inflating helium balloons and positioning the Porta-Potties. (We thought of everything.)

I quickly hopped out of my car and began unloading the bags of bagels and boxes of donuts. By 7:00 A.M., a line had started to form outside the parking lot gate. As word began to spread throughout the poverty-stricken neighborhood about our hot breakfast program, the line began to grow until it extended down the street and around an entire city block.

By 7:45 A.M., men, women and even small children were beginning to come through the food lines, their plates piled high with hot barbecued chicken, scrambled eggs, burritos, bagels, donuts and many other goodies. Behind them were the many neatly folded piles of clothing that by day's end would be all snapped up. As the loud speakers from the DJ booth blasted out the stirring words of *We Are the World,* I looked over the sea of contented faces of all colors and ages, happily devouring their plates of food. By the time we ran out of food at 11:00 A.M., we had fed a total of 1,140 homeless people.

Afterwards, my teammates and the homeless people were dancing to the music in a joyous celebration that just seemed to happen naturally. During the dancing, two homeless men came up to me and said the breakfast was the nicest thing anyone had ever done for them, and that it was the first time they had ever attended a meal program where a fight had not broken out. As he squeezed my hand, I felt a lump in my throat. We had done it. We had fed over 1,000 homeless people with less than 48 hours notice. It was a personal experience that made a deep impression on me. Now when people tell me that they would like to do something but think it would be impossible, I think to myself, "Yeah, I know what you mean. I used to think that way myself . . ."

Michael Jeffreys

The Impossible Just Takes a Little Longer

I cannot discover that anyone knows enough to say definitely what is and what is not possible.

Henry Ford

At the age of 20, I was happier than I had ever been before in my life. I was active physically: I was a competitive water-skier and snow-skier, and played golf, tennis, racquetball, basketball and volleyball. I even bowled on a league. I ran nearly every day. I had just started a new tennis court construction company, so my financial future looked exciting and bright. I was engaged to the most beautiful woman in the world. Then the tragedy occurred—or at least some called it that:

I awoke with a sudden jolt to the sound of twisting metal and breaking glass. As quickly as it all started, it was quiet again. Opening my eyes, my whole world was darkness. As my senses began to return, I could feel the warmth of blood covering my face. Then the pain. It was excruciating and overwhelming. I could hear voices calling my name as I slipped away again into unconsciousness.

Leaving my family in California on a beautiful Christmas evening, I had headed for Utah with a friend of mine. I was going there to spend the rest of the holidays with my fiancee, Dallas. We were to finish our upcoming wedding plans—our marriage was to be in five short weeks. I drove for the first eight hours of the trip, then, being somewhat tired and my friend having rested during that time, I climbed from the driver's seat into the passenger seat. I fastened my seat belt, and my friend drove away into the dark. After driving for another hour and a half, he fell asleep at the wheel. The car hit a cement abutment, went up and over the top of it, and rolled down the side of the road a number of times.

When the car finally came to a stop, I was gone. I had been ejected from the vehicle and had broken my neck on the desert floor. I was paralyzed from the chest down. Once I was taken by ambulance to a hospital in Las Vegas, Nevada, the doctor announced that I was now a quadriplegic. I lost the use of my feet and legs. I lost the use of my stomach muscles and two out of my three major chest muscles. I lost the use of my right triceps. I lost most of the use and strength in my shoulders and arms. And I lost the complete use of my hands.

This is where my new life began.

The doctors said I would have to dream new dreams and think new thoughts. They said because of my new physical condition, I would never work again—I was pretty excited about that one, though, because only 93 percent of those in my condition don't work. They told me that I would never drive again; that for the rest of my life I would be completely dependent on others to eat, get dressed or even to get from place to place. They said that I should never expect to get married because . . . who would want me? They concluded that I would never again play in any kind of athletic sport or competitive activity. For the first time in my young life, I was really afraid. I was afraid that what they said might really be true.

While lying in that hospital bed in Las Vegas, I wondered where all my hopes and dreams had gone. I wondered if I would ever be made whole again. I wondered if I would work, get married, have a family and enjoy any of the activities of life that had previously brought me such joy.

During this critical time of natural doubts and fears, when my whole world seemed so dark, my mother came to my bedside and whispered in my ear, "Art, while the difficult takes time . . . the impossible just takes a little longer." Suddenly a once darkened room began to fill with the light of hope and faith that tomorrow would be better.

Since hearing those words 11 years ago, I am now president of my own company. I am a professional speaker and a published author—*Some Miracles Take Time.* I travel more than 200,000 miles a year sharing the message of The Impossible Just Takes a Little Longer™ to Fortune 500 companies, national associations, sales organizations and youth groups, with some audiences exceeding 10,000 people. In 1992, I was named the Young Entrepreneur of the Year by the Small Business Administration for a six-state region. In 1994, *Success* magazine honored me as one of the Great Comebacks of the Year. These are dreams that have come true for me in my life. These dreams came true not in spite of my circumstances . . . but, perhaps, because of them.

Since that day I have learned to drive. I go where I want to go and I do what I want to do. I am completely independent and I take care of myself. Since that day, I have had feeling return to my body and have gained back some of the use and function of my right triceps.

I got married to that same beautiful and wonderful girl a year and a half after that fateful day. In 1992, Dallas, my wife, was named Mrs. Utah and was third runner-up to Mrs. USA! We have two children—a three-year-old daughter named McKenzie Raeanne and a one-month-old son named Dalton Arthur—the joys of our lives.

I have also returned to the world of sports. I have learned to swim, scuba dive and parasail—as far as I know I am the first quadriplegic of record to parasail. I have learned to snow ski. I have also learned to play full-contact rugby. I figure they can't hurt me any worse! I also race wheelchairs in 10Ks and marathons. On July 10, 1993, I became the first quadriplegic in the world to race 32 miles in seven days between Salt Lake City and St. George, Utah—probably not one of the brightest things I have ever done, but certainly one of the most difficult.

Why have I done all of these things? Because a long time ago I chose to listen to the voice of my mother and to my heart rather than to the concourse of dissenting voices around me, which included medical professionals. I decided that my current circumstances did not mean I had to let go of my dreams. I found a reason to hope again. I learned that dreams are never destroyed by circumstances; dreams are born in the heart and mind, and only there can they ever die. Because while the difficult takes time, the impossible just takes a little longer.

Art E. Berg

The Day I Met Daniel

The dedicated life is the life worth living.

Annie Dillard

Every man has his own destiny; the only imperative is to follow it, to accept it, no matter where it leads him.

Henry Miller

Trust in the Lord with all thine heart, and lean not unto thine own understanding. In all thy ways acknowledge Him, and He shall direct thy paths.

Prov. 3:5-6

It was an unusually cold day for the month of May. Spring had arrived and everything was alive with color. But a cold front from the north had brought winter's chill back to Indiana.

I sat with two friends in the picture window of a quaint restaurant just off the corner of the town square. The food and the company were both especially good that day. As we talked, my attention was drawn outside, across the street. There, walking into town, was a man who appeared to be carrying all his worldly goods on his back. He was carrying a well-worn sign that read, "I will work for food."

My heart sank. I brought him to the attention of my friends and noticed that others around us had stopped eating to focus on him. Heads moved in a mixture of sadness and disbelief. We continued with our meal, but his image lingered in my mind.

We finished our meal and went our separate ways. I had errands to do and quickly set out to accomplish them. I glanced toward the town square, looking somewhat half-heartedly for the strange visitor. I was fearful, knowing that seeing him again would call for some response.

I drove through town and saw nothing of him. I made some purchases at a store and got back in my car. Deep within me, the spirit of God kept speaking to me: "Don't go back to the office until you've at least driven once more around the square."

And so, with some hesitancy, I headed back into town. As I turned the square's third corner, I saw him. He was standing on the steps of the stone-front church, going through his sack. I stopped and looked, feeling both compelled to speak to him yet wanting to drive on. The empty parking space on the corner seemed to be a sign from God: an invitation to park. I pulled in, got out and approached the town's newest visitor.

"Looking for the pastor?" I asked.

"Not really," he replied. "Just resting."

"Have you eaten today?"

"Oh, I ate something early this morning."

"Would you like to have lunch with me?"

"Do you have some work I could do for you?"

"No work," I replied. "I commute here to work from the city, but I would like to take you to lunch."

"Sure," he replied with a smile. As he began to gather his things, I asked some surface questions.

"Where you headed?"

"St. Louis."

"Where are you from?"

"Oh, all over; mostly Florida."

"How long you been walking?"

"Fourteen years," came the reply.

I knew I had met someone unusual.

We sat across from each other in the same restaurant I had left only minutes earlier. His hair was long and straight, and he had a neatly trimmed dark beard. His skin was deeply tanned, and his face was weathered slightly beyond his 38 years. His eyes were dark yet clear, and he spoke with an eloquence and articulation that was startling. He removed his jacket to reveal a bright red T-shirt that said, "Jesus is The Never Ending Story."

Then Daniel's story began to unfold. He had seen rough times early in life. He'd made some wrong choices and reaped the consequences. Fourteen years earlier, while backpacking across the country, he had stopped on the beach in Daytona. He tried to hire on with some men who were putting up a large tent and some equipment. A concert, he thought. He was hired, but the tent would house not a concert but revival services, and in those services he saw life more clearly. He gave his life over to God.

"Nothing's been the same since," he said. "I felt the Lord telling me to keep walking, and so I did, some 14 years now."

"Ever think of stopping?" I asked.

"Oh, once in a while, when it seems to get the best of me. But God has given me this calling. I give out Bibles. That's what's in my sack. I work to buy food and Bibles, and I give them out when His Spirit leads."

I sat amazed. My homeless friend was not homeless. He

was on a mission and lived this way by choice. The question burned inside for a moment and then I asked: "What's it like?"

"What?"

"To walk into a town carrying all your things on your back and to show your sign?"

"Oh, it was humiliating at first. People would stare and make comments. Once someone tossed a piece of half-eaten bread and made a gesture that certainly didn't make me feel welcome. But then it became humbling to realize that God was using me to touch lives and change people's concepts of other folks like me."

My concept was changing, too.

We finished our dessert and gathered his things. Just outside the door he paused. He turned to me and said, " 'Come ye blessed of my Father and inherit the kingdom I've prepared for you. For when I was hungry you gave me food, when I was thirsty you gave me drink, a stranger and you took me in.' "

I felt as if we were on holy ground.

"Could you use another Bible?" I asked. He said he preferred a certain translation. It traveled well and was not too heavy. It was also his personal favorite.

"I've read through it 14 times," he said.

"I'm not sure we've got one of those, but let's stop by our church and see."

I was able to find my new friend a Bible that would do well, and he seemed very grateful.

"Where you headed from here?" I asked.

"Well, I found this little map on the back of this amusement park coupon."

"Are you hoping to hire on there for a while?"

"No, I just figure I should go there. I figure someone under that star right there needs a Bible, so that's where I'm going next."

He smiled, and the warmth of his spirit radiated the sincerity of his mission. I drove him back to the town square where we'd met two hours earlier, and as we drove, it started raining. We parked and unloaded his things.

"Would you sign my autograph book?" he asked. "I like to keep messages from folks I meet."

I wrote in his little book that his commitment to his calling had touched my life. I encouraged him to stay strong. And I left him with a verse of scripture, Jeremiah 29:11. "I know the plans I have for you," declared the Lord, "plans to prosper you and not to harm you. Plans to give you a future and a hope."

"Thanks, man," he said. "I know we just met and we're really just strangers, but I love you."

"I know," I said. "I love you, too."

"The Lord is good."

"Yes, He is. How long has it been since someone hugged you?" I asked.

"A long time," he replied.

And so on the busy street corner in the drizzling rain, my new friend and I embraced, and I felt deep inside that I had been changed.

He put his things on his back, smiled his winning smile and said, "See you in the New Jerusalem."

"I'll be there!" was my reply.

He began his journey again. He headed away with his sign dangling from his bedroll and pack of Bibles. He stopped, turned and said, "When you see something that makes you think of me, will you pray for me?"

"You bet," I shouted back.

"God bless."

"God bless."

And that was the last I saw of him.

Late that evening as I left my office, the wind blew strong. The cold front had settled hard upon the town. I bundled up and hurried to my car. As I sat back and reached for the emergency brake, I saw them—a pair of well-worn brown work gloves neatly laid over the length of the handle. I picked them up and thought of my friend and wondered if his hands would stay warm that night without them. I remembered his words: "If you see something that makes you think of me, will you pray for me?"

Today his gloves lie on my desk in my office. They help me to see the world and its people in a new way, and they help me remember those two hours with my unique friend and to pray for his ministry.

"See you in the New Jerusalem," he said.

Yes, Daniel, I know I will.

Richard Ryan

8

ECLECTIC WISDOM

Wisdom comes more from living than from studying.

God's Jobs

Danny Sutton, eight years old, wrote this for his third-grade Sunday school teacher, who asked her students to explain God:

One of God's main jobs is making people. He makes these to put in the place of the ones who die so there will be enough people to take care of things here on earth. He doesn't make grownups, he just makes babies. I think because they are smaller and easier to make. That way he doesn't have to take up his valuable time teaching them to walk and talk. He can just leave that up to the mothers and fathers. I think it works out pretty good.

God's second most important job is listening to prayers. An awful lot of this goes on, 'cause some people, like preachers and things, pray other times besides bedtimes, and Grandpa and Grandma pray every time they eat, except for snacks. God doesn't have time to listen to the radio or watch TV on account of this. 'Cause God hears everything, there must be a terrible lot of noise in his ears unless he has thought of a way to turn it down.

God sees and hears everything and is everywhere, which keeps him pretty busy. So you shouldn't go wasting his time asking for things that aren't important, or go over parents' heads and ask for something they said you couldn't have. It doesn't work anyway.

Dan Sutton, Christ Church
St. Michael's, Maryland
Submitted by Vanessa Hewko

The Wisdom of One Word

A single conversation across the table with a wise man is worth a month's study of books.
Chinese Proverb

Isn't it amazing how one person, sharing one idea, at the right time and place can change the course of your life's history? This is certainly what happened in my life. When I was 14, I was hitchhiking from Houston, Texas, through El Paso on my way to California. I was following my dream, journeying with the sun. I was a high school drop-out with learning disabilities and was set on surfing the biggest waves in the world, first in California and then in Hawaii, where I would later live.

Upon reaching downtown El Paso, I met an old man, a bum, on the street corner. He saw me walking, stopped me and questioned me as I passed by. He asked me if I was running away from home, I suppose because I looked so young. I told him, "Not exactly, sir," since my father had given me a ride to the freeway in Houston and given me his blessings while saying, "It is important to follow your dream and what is in your heart, Son."

The bum then asked me if he could buy me a cup of coffee. I told him, "No, sir, but a soda would be great." We walked to a corner malt shop and sat down on a couple of swiveling stools while we enjoyed our drinks.

After conversing for a few minutes, the friendly bum told me to follow him. He told me that he had something grand to show me and share with me. We walked a couple of blocks until we came upon the downtown El Paso Public Library. We walked up its front steps and stopped at a small information stand. Here the bum spoke to a smiling old lady, and asked her if she would be kind enough to watch my things for a moment while he and I entered the library. I left my belongings with this grand-motherly figure and entered into this magnificent hall of learning.

The bum first led me to a table and asked me to sit down and wait for a moment while he looked for something special amongst the shelves. A few moments later, he returned with a couple of old books under his arms and set them on the table. He then sat down beside me and spoke. He started with a few statements that were very special and that changed my life. He said, "There are two things that I want to teach you, young man, and they are these:

"Number one is to never judge a book by its cover, for a cover can fool you." He followed with, "I'll bet you think I'm a bum, don't you, young man?"

I said, "Well, uh, yes, I guess so, sir."

"Well, young man, I've got a little surprise for you. I am one of the wealthiest men in the world. I have probably everything any man could ever want. I originally come from the Northeast and have all the things that money can buy. But a year ago, my wife passed away, bless her soul, and since then I have been deeply reflecting upon life. I realized there were certain things I had not yet experienced in life, one of which was what it would be like to live like a bum on the streets. I made a commitment to myself to do exactly that for one year. For the past year, I have been going from city to city doing just that. So, you see, don't ever judge a book by its cover, for a cover can fool you.

"Number two is to learn how to read, my boy. For there is only one thing that people can't take away from you, and that is your wisdom." At that moment, he reached forward, grabbed my right hand in his and put them upon the books he'd pulled from the shelves. They were the writings of Plato and Aristotle—immortal classics from ancient times.

The bum then led me back past the smiling old woman near the entrance, down the steps and back on the streets near where we first met. His parting request was for me to never forget what he taught me.

I haven't.

Fr. John F. Demartini

The Secret of Life

As the Lord God was creating the world
he called upon his archangels.
The Lord asked his archangels to help
him decide where to put the Secret of Life.

"Bury it in the ground," one angel replied.
"Put it on the bottom of the sea," said another.
"Hide it in the mountains," another suggested.

The Lord replied, "If I see to do any of those
only a few will find the Secret of Life.
The Secret of Life must be accessible to
EVERYONE!"

One angel replied, "I know: put it in each
man's heart.
Nobody will think to look there."
"Yes!" said the Lord. "Within each man's heart."
And so it was—
The SECRET OF LIFE lies within all of us.

Author Unknown

The Secrets of Heaven and Hell

The old monk sat by the side of the road. With his eyes closed, his legs crossed and his hands folded in his lap, he sat. In deep meditation, he sat.

Suddenly his *zazen* was interrupted by the harsh and demanding voice of a samurai warrior. "Old man! Teach me about heaven and hell!"

At first, as though he had not heard, there was no perceptible response from the monk. But gradually he began to open his eyes, the faintest hint of a smile playing around the corners of his mouth as the samurai stood there, waiting impatiently, growing more and more agitated with each passing second.

"You wish to know the secrets of heaven and hell?" replied the monk at last. "You who are so unkempt. You whose hands and feet are covered with dirt. You whose hair is uncombed, whose breath is foul, whose sword is all rusty and neglected. You who are ugly and whose mother dresses you funny. You would ask me of heaven and hell?"

The samurai uttered a vile curse. He drew his sword and raised it high above his head. His face turned to crimson, and the veins on his neck stood out in bold relief as he prepared to sever the monk's head from its shoulders.

"That is hell," said the old monk gently, just as the sword began its descent.

In that fraction of a second, the samurai was overcome with amazement, awe, compassion and love for this gentle being who had dared to risk his very life to give him such a teaching. He stopped his sword in mid-flight and his eyes filled with grateful tears.

"And that," said the monk, "is heaven."

Fr. John W. Groff Jr.

What Courage Looks Like

I know what courage looks like. I saw it on a flight I took six years ago, and only now can I speak of it without tears filling my eyes at the memory.

When our L1011 left the Orlando airport that Friday morning, we were a chipper, high-energy group. The early-morning flight hosted mainly professional people going to Atlanta for a day or two of business. As I looked around, I saw lots of designer suits, CEO-caliber haircuts, leather briefcases and all the trimmings of seasoned business travelers. I settled back for some light reading and the brief flight ahead.

Immediately upon takeoff, it was clear that something was amiss. The aircraft was bumping up and down and jerking left to right. All the experienced travelers, including me, looked around with knowing grins. Our communal looks acknowledged to one another that we had experienced minor problems and disturbances before. If you fly much, you see these things and learn to act blasé about them.

We did not remain blasé for long. Minutes after we were airborne, our plane began dipping wildly and one wing lunged downward. The plane climbed higher but that didn't help. It didn't. The pilot soon made a grave announcement.

"We are having some difficulties," he said. "At this time, it appears we have no nose-wheel steering. Our indicators show that our hydraulic system has failed. We will be returning to the Orlando airport at this time. Because of the lack of hydraulics, we are not sure our landing gear will lock, so the flight attendants will prepare you for a bumpy landing. Also, if you look out the windows, you will see that we are dumping fuel from the airplane. We want to have as little on board as possible in the event of a rough touchdown."

In other words, we were about to crash. No sight has ever been so sobering as seeing that fuel, hundreds of gallons of it, streaming past my window out of the plane's tanks. The flight attendants helped people get into position and comforted those who were already hysterical.

As I looked at the faces of my fellow business travelers, I was stunned at the changes I saw in their faces. Many looked visibly frightened now. Even the most stoic looked grim and ashen. Yes, their faces actually looked gray in color, something I'd never seen before. There was not one exception. *No one faces death without fear,* I thought. Everyone lost composure in one way or another.

I began searching the crowd for one person who felt the peace and calm that true courage or great faith gives people in these events. I saw no one.

Then a couple of rows to my left, I heard a still, calm voice, a woman's voice, speaking in an absolutely normal conversational tone. There was no tremor or tension. It was a lovely, even tone. I had to find the source of this voice.

All around, people cried. Many wailed and screamed. A few of the men held onto their composure by gripping armrests and clenching teeth, but their fear was written all over them.

Although my faith kept me from hysteria, I could not

have spoken so calmly, so sweetly at this moment as the assuring voice I heard. Finally, I saw her.

In the midst of all the chaos, a mother was talking, just talking, to her child. The woman, in her mid-30s and unremarkable looking in any other way, was staring full into the face of her daughter, who looked to be four years old. The child listened closely, sensing the importance of her mother's words. The mother's gaze held the child so fixed and intent that she seemed untouched by the sounds of grief and fear around her.

A picture flashed into my mind of another little girl who had recently survived a terrible plane crash. Speculation had it that she had lived because her mother had strapped her own body over the little girl's in order to protect her. The mother did not survive. The newspapers had been tracking how the little girl had been treated by psychologists for weeks afterward to ward off feelings of guilt and unworthiness that often haunt survivors. The child was told over and over again that it had not been her fault that her mommy had gone away. I hoped this situation would not end the same way.

I strained to hear what this mother was saying to her child. I was compelled to hear. I needed to hear.

Finally, I leaned over and by some miracle could hear this soft, sure voice with the tone of assurance. Over and over again, the mother said, "I love you so much. Do you know for sure that I love you more than anything?"

"Yes, Mommy," the little girl said.

"And remember, no matter what happens, that I love you always. And that you are a good girl. Sometimes things happen that are not your fault. You are still a good girl and my love will always be with you."

Then the mother put her body over her daughter's, strapped the seat belt over both of them and prepared to crash.

For no earthly reason, our landing gear held and our touchdown was not the tragedy it seemed destined to be. It was over in seconds.

The voice I heard that day never wavered, never acknowledged doubt, and maintained an evenness that seemed emotionally and physically impossible. Not one of us hardened business people could have spoken without a tremoring voice. Only the greatest courage, undergirded by even greater love, could have borne that mother up and lifted her above the chaos around her.

That mom showed me what a real hero looks like. And for those few minutes, I heard the voice of courage.

Casey Hawley

Golden Rules for Living

If you open it, close it.
If you turn it on, turn it off.
If you unlock it, lock it up.
If you break it, admit it.
If you can't fix it, call in someone who can.
If you borrow it, return it.
If you value it, take care of it.
If you make a mess, clean it up.
If you move it, put it back.
If it belongs to someone else and you want to use it, get
   permission.
If you don't know how to operate it, leave it alone.
If it's none of your business, don't ask questions.
If it ain't broke, don't fix it.
If it will brighten someone's day, say it.
If it will tarnish someone's reputation, keep it to yourself.

Author Unknown

Angel with a Red Hat

I was so scared but I would not admit it, as I sat in the coffee shop across from the Mayo Clinic. Tomorrow I would be a patient there, undergoing spinal surgery. The risk was high, but my faith was strong. Just weeks before, I sat through my father's funeral. My guiding light had been sent back to heaven—"O heavenly Father, in my time of trial, send me an angel."

As I looked up, preparing to leave, I saw an elderly lady walking very slowly to the register. I stood behind her, admiring her flair for fashion—a bright paisley dress of red and purple, a scarf, a brooch and a brilliant scarlet hat. "Excuse me, madam. I just must say what a beautiful woman you are. You've made my day."

She clasped my hand and spoke these words: "My sweet child, bless you, for you see, I have an artificial arm and a plate in the other, and my leg is not my own. It takes me quite some time to get dressed. I try to do my best, but as years go by, people don't seem to think it matters. You've made me feel so special today. May the Lord watch over and bless you, for you must be one of his little angels." When she walked away from me that day, I uttered not a word, for she had touched my soul in such a way that she could only have been the angel.

Tami Fox

It's Never Too Late

Several years ago, while attending a communications course, I experienced a most unusual process. The instructor asked us to list anything in our past that we felt ashamed of, guilty about, incomplete about or that we regretted. The next week he invited participants to read their lists aloud. This seemed like a very private process, but there's always some brave soul in the crowd who will volunteer. As people read their lists, mine grew longer. After three weeks, I had 101 items. The instructor then suggested that we find ways to make amends, apologize to people or take some action to right any wrongdoing. I seriously wondered how this could ever improve my communications, and had visions of alienating just about everyone in my life.

The next week, the man next to me raised his hand and volunteered this story:

> *While making my list, I remembered an incident from high school. I grew up in a small town in Iowa. There was a sheriff in town that none of us kids liked. One night, my two buddies and I decided to play a trick on Sheriff Brown. After drinking a few beers, we found a can of red paint, climbed the tall water tank in the middle of town, and wrote on the tank, in bright red*

letters: Sheriff Brown is an s.o.b. The next day, the town arose to see our glorious sign. Within two hours, Sheriff Brown had the three of us in his office. My friends confessed and I lied, denying the truth. No one ever found out.

Nearly 20 years later, Sheriff Brown's name appears on my list. I didn't even know if he was still alive. Last weekend, I dialed Information in my hometown back in Iowa. Sure enough, there was a Roger Brown still listed. I dialed his number. After a few rings, I heard: "Hello?" I said: "Sheriff Brown?" Pause. "Yup." "Well, this is Jimmy Calkins. And I want you to know that I did it." Pause. "I knew it!" he yelled back. We had a good laugh and a lively discussion. His closing words were: "Jimmy, I always felt badly for you because your buddies got it off their chests, and I knew you were carrying it around all these years. I want to thank you for calling me . . . for your sake."

Jimmy inspired me to clear up all 101 items on my list. It took me almost two years, but it became the springboard and true inspiration for my career as a conflict mediator. No matter how difficult the conflict, crisis or situation, I always remember that it's never too late to clear up the past and begin resolution.

Marilyn Manning

The Station

Tucked away in our subconscious is an idyllic vision. We see ourselves on a long trip that spans the continent. We are traveling by train. Out the windows, we drink in the passing scene of cars on nearby highways, of children waving at a crossing, of cattle grazing on a distant hillside, of smoke pouring from a power plant, of row upon row of corn and wheat, of flatlands and valleys, of mountains and rolling hillsides, of city skylines and village halls.

But uppermost in our minds is the final destination. On a certain day at a certain hour, we will pull into the station. Bands will be playing and flags waving. Once we get there, so many wonderful dreams will come true and the pieces of our lives will fit together like a completed jigsaw puzzle. How restlessly we pace the aisles, damning the minutes for loitering—waiting, waiting, waiting for the station.

"When we reach the station, that will be it!" we cry. "When I'm 18." "When I buy a new 450SL Mercedes Benz!" "When I put the last kid through college." "When I have paid off the mortgage!" "When I get a promotion." "When I reach the age of retirement, I shall live happily ever after!"

Sooner or later, we must realize there is no station, no one place to arrive at once and for all. The true joy of life is the trip. The station is only a dream. It constantly outdistances us.

"Relish the moment" is a good motto, especially when coupled with Psalm 118:24: "This is the day which the Lord hath made; we will rejoice and be glad in it." It isn't the burdens of today that drive men mad. It is the regrets over yesterday and the fear of tomorrow. Regret and fear are twin thieves who rob us of today.

So stop pacing the aisles and counting the miles. Instead, climb more mountains, eat more ice cream, go barefoot more often, swim more rivers, watch more sunsets, laugh more, cry less. Life must be lived as we go along. The station will come soon enough.

Robert J. Hastings

More Chicken Soup?

Many of the stories and poems you have read in this book were submitted by readers such as yourself after they read the first two volumes of *Chicken Soup for the Soul.* So we invite you, too, to share a story, poem or article that you feel belongs in a future volume of *Chicken Soup for the Soul.* This may be a story you clip out of the local newspaper, a magazine, or a church or company newsletter. It might be something you receive on the fax network, that favorite quotation you have on the refrigerator door, a poem you have written or a personal experience that has touched you deeply.

We are planning to publish a new *Chicken Soup for the Soul* book every year. We are also planning special collections of *Chicken Soup for the Soul* for cancer survivors, people in recovery, teachers, parents, couples, salespeople, Christians, Jews, women, teenagers, athletes, pet lovers and business people, as well as a treasury of Christmas stories and a special volume of humorous stories entitled *Chicken Soup for the Laughing Soul.*

Just send a copy of your favorite stories and other pieces to us at this address:

Jack Canfield and Mark Victor Hansen
The Canfield Training Group
P.O. Box 30880 • Santa Barbara, CA 93130
Fax: 805-563-2945

We will be sure that both you and the author are credited for your submission. Thank you for your contribution.

Lectures, seminars and workshops: You can also contact us at the above address for speaking engagements or for information about our newsletters, other self-help books, audiotapes, workshops and training programs.

Soup Kitchens for the Soul

One of the most exciting developments with the *Chicken Soup for the Soul* book was the impact it had on readers who were welfare recipients, homeless or incarcerated in state prisons. Here is just one excerpt from a letter we received from a prisoner in the Billerica House of Corrections in Massachusetts:

> *I received a copy of* Chicken Soup *when I attended a 10-week course on alternatives to violence. Since reading this book, my whole perspective as an inmate dealing with other inmates has dramatically changed. I no longer feel violent or have hatred toward anyone. My soul has been blessed with these wonderful stories. I simply can't thank you enough.*
>
> *Sincerely,*
> *Phil S.*

A teenage girl writes:

> *I have just finished reading your book,* Chicken Soup for the Soul. *I feel that I have the power to do anything, after reading it.*
>
> *You see, I had given up on a lot of my dreams, to travel around the world, to go to college, to marry and to have children, but after reading this book, I feel I have the power to do everything and anything. Thanks!!*
>
> *Erica Lynn P. (age 14)*

As a result, we have established the Soup Kitchens for the Soul Project. We have already donated over 15,000 copies of *Chicken Soup for the Soul* and *A 2nd Helping of Chicken Soup for the Soul* to men and women in prisons, halfway houses, homeless shelters, battered-women's shelters, literacy programs, inner-city schools, AIDS hospices, hospitals, churches and other organizations that serve adults and teenagers in need.

We welcome and invite your participation in this project in the following ways. For every $12.95 you contribute, we will send a copy of two *Chicken Soup* books to a prison, county jail, shelter, hospice or other nonprofit agency. We also invite you to submit the names of worthy programs that you think should receive copies of the books.

The program will be administered by the Foundation for Self-Esteem in Culver City, California. Please make your check payable to The Foundation for Self-Esteem and send it to:

Soup Kitchens for the Soul
The Foundation for Self-Esteem
6035 Bristol Parkway
Culver City, CA 90230
or
call 310-568-1505 and make your contribution
by credit card

We will acknowledge receipt of your contribution and let you know where the books you paid for were sent.

Give the Gift of Life

It is our fervent hope that, through these stories, our readers find their lives re-energized by a heightened understanding of how they can make a meaningful difference in the lives of others.

One of the most direct and literal ways to translate your caring and concern into immediate action is to donate blood to the American Red Cross national blood program. Every four seconds, someone in this nation turns to this time-honored organization for the life-saving gift of blood. However, with blood collections continuing to decline over the last several years, the American Red Cross faces a daily challenge to meet America's blood needs. Please call now to schedule a blood donation at the site nearest you by calling 1-800-GIVE-LIFE.

For over 100 years, the American Red Cross has served this nation through a wide variety of community services including disaster relief, health and safety education, and service to the Armed Forces. We hope you will also explore opportunities to support these other important services through donations of time and/or money by contacting your local American Red Cross chapter.

Mark Victor Hansen and Jack Canfield have selected the American Red Cross as their charity of choice, and have actively supported it by offering their time, expertise and energy to help this venerable institution fulfill its mission of service to the public. In addition, they generously contributed thousands of their books to Red Cross staff as a motivational tool and are donating a significant share of the proceeds from *A 3rd Serving of Chicken Soup for the Soul* to the charity. So call now and schedule to give blood—the gift of life. You may be saving the life of someone you love.

Who Is Jack Canfield?

Jack Canfield is one of America's leading experts in the development of human potential and personal effectiveness. He is both a dynamic and entertaining speaker and a highly sought-after trainer, with a wonderful ability to inform and inspire audiences toward increased levels of self-esteem and peak performance.

He is the author and narrator of several best-selling audio and video cassette programs, including *Chicken Soup for the Soul—Live, Self-Esteem and Peak Performance, How to Build High Self-Esteem* and *Self-Esteem in the Classroom.* He is regularly seen on television shows such as *Good Morning America, 20/20, Eye to Eye* and *NBC Nightly News.* He has co-authored 10 books, including *Chicken Soup for the Soul, A 2nd Helping of Chicken Soup for the Soul, Chicken Soup for the Soul Cookbook, Dare to Win* and *The Aladdin Factor* (all with Mark Victor Hansen), and *100 Ways to Build Self-Concept in the Classroom* (with Harold C. Wells).

Jack addresses over 100 groups each year. His clients include professional associations, school districts, government agencies, churches, sales organizations and corporations. His corporate clients have included the American Management Association, AT&T, Campbell Soup, Clairol, Domino's Pizza, G.E., ITT Hartford Insurance, Johnson & Johnson, NCR, New England Telephone, Re/Max, Scott Paper, Sunkist, Supercuts, TRW and Virgin Records. Jack is also on the faculties of two schools for entrepreneurs—Income Builders International and the Life Success Academy.

Jack conducts an annual eight-day Training of Trainers Program in the areas of self-esteem and peak performance. It attracts educators, counselors, parenting trainers, corporate trainers, professional speakers, ministers and others interested in developing their speaking and seminar-leading skills.

For further information about Jack's books, tapes and trainings, or to schedule him for a presentation, please contact:

The Canfield Training Group
P.O. Box 30880
Santa Barbara , CA 93130
Call toll free 800-237-8336, or fax 805-563-2945

Who Is Mark Victor Hansen?

Mark Victor Hansen is a professional speaker who, in the last 20 years, has talked to over 1 million people in 32 countries, making over 4,000 presentations in the areas of sales excellence and strategies, and personal empowerment and development.

Mark has spent a lifetime dedicated to his mission of making a profound and positive difference in people's lives. Throughout his career, he has inspired hundreds of thousands of people to create more powerful and purposeful futures for themselves while stimulating the sale of billions of dollars worth of goods and services.

Mark has written numerous books, including *Future Diary, How to Achieve Total Prosperity, The Miracle of Tithing* and *Dare to Win* (with Jack Canfield), all best-sellers.

As well as speaking and writing, Mark has produced a complete library of personal empowerment cassette and video programs that have enabled his listeners to recognize and use their innate abilities in their business and personal lives. His message has also made him a popular television and radio personality, with appearances on ABC, NBC, CBS, CNN and HBO.

Mark has also appeared on the cover of numerous magazines, including *Success* and *Changes. Success* magazine reported his achievements on the cover of their August 1991 issue.

Mark is a big man with a big heart and a big spirit, an inspiration to all who seek to better themselves.

You can contact Mark by writing 711 W. 17th Street #D2, Costa Mesa, CA 92627, or by calling 714-759-9304 (from outside of California call 800-433-2314).

Contributors

Many of the stories in this book were taken from books and magazines we have read. These sources are acknowledged in the Permissions section. Some of the stories and poems were contributed by friends of ours, who, like us, are professional speakers. If you would like to contact them for information on their books, tapes and seminars, you can reach them at the addresses and phone numbers provided below.

Many of the stories were also contributed by readers like yourself, who, after reading the first two volumes of *Chicken Soup for the Soul*, were inspired to submit a story out of their life's experience. We have included information about them as well.

Richard R. ("Dick") Abrahamson, Ph.D., is Professor of Literature for Children and Adolescents in the College of Education at the University of Houston. An author of more than 100 articles on children's books and reading motivation, Dr. Abrahamson is the winner of the Education Press Association Award for Excellence in Educational Journalism. He is a frequent consultant to school districts and keynote speaker at conferences dealing with literacy and reading motivation. He can be reached at the Department of Curriculum and Instruction, University of Houston, Houston, TX 77204-5872.

M. Adams was born in Russia and immigrated to Canada, along with her parents and most of her family, in 1924. She is the mother of seven—one son and six daughters. Her late husband served in both World Wars. She believes in helping others and has done volunteer work at a Veterans Hospital. She lives in Manitoba, where she enjoys the love and support of her family.

Thea Alexander is the author of *2150 A.D.* and *Macro Philosophy*, which have changed millions of lives, as has her seven-title *Macro Study Series.* Honored in *Marquis Who's Who* for her work toward a better world, Thea has lectured internationally, authored a newspaper column and conducted two TV interview series. Educated (Phi Beta Kappa) as a counselor, she invented a new, succinct technique (requiring two to six hours) of assisting people in reaching their potential, called Personal Evolution Tutoring, which she both uses and teaches others to use. She can be reached by writing to P.O. Box 26880, Tempe, AZ 85285-6880 or by calling 602-991-7077, or by fax at 602-991-0766.

Robert G. Allen, author of the colossal No. 1 *New York Times* best-seller, *Nothing Down,* and *Creating Wealth,* is one of America's most influential investment advisors. Today, thousands of millionaires attribute their success to Mr. Allen's powerful ideas. He is a popular television and radio guest appearing on such programs as *Good Morning America* and *Larry King.* He has been written about in *The Wall Street Journal,* the *Los Angeles Times, Barron's* and *Reader's Digest,* to name just a few. He lives in San Diego with his wife, Daryl, and their three children.

Beth Ashley is a columnist and feature writer for the *Independent Journal* in Marin County, California, and is the author of *Marin,* a book about the area. Her column deals with her job, her family and the complexities of life in the 1990s. Her features are often profiles of the many interesting and accomplished individuals who live where she works, across the Golden Gate Bridge from San Francisco. A 21-year veteran of the *Independent Journal,* Ashley has also worked in Paris, Berlin, Moscow and Beijing. You can contact her at 348 Bretano Way, Greenbrae, CA 94904, (phone 415-461-2383); or at her place of work, Independent Journal, Box 6150, Novato, CA 94958 (phone 415-382-7281).

Art E. Berg is president of Invictus Communications, Inc. and resides in Highland, Utah. He is a professional speaker, traveling 200,000 miles per year, and has been heard by more than one million people. Art has written two books, *Some Miracles Take Time* and *Finding Peace in Troubled Waters.* For further information about Art Berg, write Invictus Communications, Inc., P.O. Box 246, Highland, UT 84003 (fax 800-400-0084; e-mail: 74117.332@compuserve.com or call 800-ART-BERG).

Fr. Brian Cavanaugh, TOR, began collecting quotations, anecdotes and stories as a form of journal-writing therapy. Over the years he has compiled more than 40 handwritten journals. Drawing upon this collection, he writes *Apple Seeds,* a monthly quote letter of motivation and inspiration. These journals have also resulted in four books published by Paulist Press: *The Sower's Seeds: One Hundred Inspiring Stories for Preaching, Teaching and Public Speaking; More Sower's Seeds: Second Planting; Fresh Packet of Sower's Seeds: Third Planting* and *Sower's Seeds Aplenty: Fourth Planting.* Fr. Brian is a storytelling motivational/inspirational lecturer. Fr. Brian can be contacted at Franciscan University, Steubenville, OH 43952.

Alan Cohen brings a profoundly endearing energy to spiritual awakening. Author of 10 popular inspirational books, including the classic *The Dragon Doesn't Live Here Anymore* and his recent best-seller, *I Had It All the Time,* Alan offers powerful insights on applying spiritual principles to practical living. Alan's syndicated column, *From the Heart,* appears in new thought magazines internationally. Described by *Celestine Prophecy* author James Redfield as "the most eloquent spokesman of the heart," Alan embodies a rare combination of wisdom, humor, intimacy and vision.

James E. Conner, Ed.D., is president of Possibilities Unlimited. After a lively career as teacher, principal, college professor and college president, curriculum specialist, Senior Associate for Education with the U.S. Chamber of Commerce, columnist for a national educational journal, and governor's speech writer, he is currently freelance and ghost-writing. His chief areas of interest are ways that American schools can achieve real breakthroughs in learning achievement, and enriching readers with articles and stories about triumphs of the human spirit. He can be contacted at 4505 Leaf Court, Raleigh, NC 27612. Call 919-782-0069.

Valerie Cox is the author of *Valerie's Verse,* a collection of original, humorous and inspirational poems, prose and limericks. She is currently working on a second book, *Hugs and Other Works of Heart.* Valerie and her husband, Rich, conduct marketing and business training seminars. She also enjoys song-leading with two nursing home ministry teams. Valerie can be reached at 31849 Pacific Hwy. South, Suite 210, Federal Way, WA 98003 or call 206-781-7317.

Kathi M. Curry has a degree in Recreation Administration from Chico State in Chico, California. She will be fulfilling her lifelong dream on April 15, 1996, by being a part of the 100th run of The Boston Marathon. Kathi has relocated from Hawaii to Pleasant Hill, California.

Beth Dalton is a third-grade teacher in Cookeville, Tennessee. She has a husband, two sons (Ryan, age 15, and Billy, age 11) and one special angel, Tanner. Beth received a B.S. in business from Tennessee Tech University in 1982 and went back to school in 1990 to get her master's and certification in K-3 education. She has been lucky to be a teacher at the new Cane Creek Elementary School that opened August of 1995. Beth can be reached at 1150 Winterhill, Cookeville, TN 38501.

Fr. John Demartini is a researcher, writer and philosopher whose studies have made him a leading expert on personal development, philosophy and health. He has an inherent ability to trailblaze, motivate and enthuse his audiences with gentle, fun, informative lectures that mingle entertaining stories with transformational wisdom and insights. Fr. Demartini works as an adviser to people from all walks of life, from Wall Street financiers and health professionals to politicians, Hollywood stars and sports personalities.

Stan Frager is a professional motivational speaker who has given wonderful talks to high school students, parents and corporations. He is the author of *The Champion Within You.* He can be reached at Frager Associates, 3906 Dupont Square South, Louisville, KY 40207 or by calling 502-893-6654.

Robert Gass, Ed.D., synthesizes a diverse background in humanistic psychology, business, social activism, music, work with the terminally ill and spiritual study. He is the creator of the well-known Opening the Heart workshops. Over 100,000 people have participated in seminars with Robert on leadership, healing, personal effectiveness, relationships and spirituality. As an organizational consultant, Robert has worked at the most senior levels in Fortune 500 corporations, as well as with government agencies such as the EPA, and non-profit and activist groups. A recording artist, composer, instrumentalist and singer, he has released 20 albums of transformational music with his group On Wings of Song. Robert shares a rewarding and loving family life with his wife, Judith, and their three children in Boulder, Colorado.

Lynne C. Gaul volunteers full-time as chauffeur, coach, financial advisor, engineer, nurse and CEO for the Gaul family (alias "Mom"). She grew up in Curwensville, Pennsylvania, earned a bachelor's degree in English Communications at Indiana University of Pennsylvania, and currently enjoys life with her husband, Tom, and two boys, Joshua and Stephen, in Lancaster, Ohio.

Barbara A. Glanz is an internationally known author, speaker and consultant specializing in the areas of creative communication, building customer loyalty and regenerating the spirit in the workplace. She is president of Barbara Glanz Communications and author of *The Creative Communicator—399 Tools to Communicate Commitment without Boring People to Death!* and *Building Customer Loyalty—How YOU Can Help Keep Customers Returning.* Her latest book is *C.A.R.E. Packages for the Workplace—Dozens of Little Things You Can Do to Regenerate Spirit at Work,* published by McGraw-Hill. For more information, write to her at 4047 Howard Avenue, Western Springs, IL 60558, or call her at 708-245-8594, or fax 708-246-5123.

Patty Hansen has her priorities straight—being Mom is number one. As the other half of the "Mark/Patty Team," she divides her time between being chief financial officer and troubleshooter at M.V. Hansen & Associates, Inc., and full-time driver, caretaker and homework assistant to their two daughters, Elisabeth and Melanie. She also loves to squeeze in some time to garden, raise chickens and play on the beach. She is currently at work on her first book. She can be reached at 711 W. 17th Street. #D2, Costa Mesa, CA 92627. Call 714-759-9304 or from outside California, 800-433-2314.

Casey Hawley leads seminars on Powerful Business Writing for Georgia Pacific, Equifax and other top companies. She is also one of the nation's top writers of winning sales proposals, business plans and other highly visible documents. Her Marietta, Georgia, company has just launched a moving and powerful seminar, Friendship, Change and Triumph. The seminar touches people with its heartfelt stories, humor and encouragement as it explores the asset of friendship throughout a corporate career. Casey reveals eye-opening research about the link between friendship and coping with change, absenteeism, corporate climate and productivity. You can call her at 770-419-7260.

Cindy Dee Holms has a double master's degree in education and is a professional speaker, trainer and consultant who has given dynamic AIDS education workshops to thousands of students, teachers and parents. Fifteen years ago, in addition to working as a biology teacher, school counselor and mother of two, Cindy began assisting her physician husband in patient health care. She began presenting programs on disease prevention with a particular commitment to the pediatric AIDS cause. Cindy currently works for the Delaware

County Intermediate Unit in Media, Pennsylvania, where she is an AIDS specialist and coordinator of drug and alcohol education. She has recently written an uplifting children's story about AIDS entitled "Red Balloons Go to Heaven." She can be reached at 2709 Stoney Creek Road, Broomall, PA 19008.

Janice Hunt has been an educational psychologist in California and Hawaii for the past 20 years. Her artistic endeavors, which include watercolors and drawings, have brought her national recognition. Inspired by her son, Court, and his friend, Wesley, "Don't Worry, It'll Be Alright" is her first published writing. Janice can be reached at Orange Unified School District. Call 714-997-6314.

D. Trinidad Hunt is an international trainer, keynote speaker, author and educator. Over the last three years, she has trained over 40,000 children via a humorous self-esteem program that she wrote and co-produced with entertainer Frank Delima for the Hawaii state school system. Her newest book is *Operator's Manual for Planet Earth* (Hyperion Press). Her award-winning book, *Learning to Learn: Maximizing Your Performance Potential*, as well as her other books and tapes are available by calling 800-707-3526, or fax 808-239-2482.

Claudette Hunter attended her first self-esteem seminar 10 years ago. The principles she learned changed her life. She worked with Jack Canfield for five years, assisting at his seminars. By asking, affirming and taking action, she also found the "love of her life" and is on a worldwide adventure with her husband, Jim. Currently she facilitates Canfield's STAR Workshops in Saudi Arabia, her home the last three years. Her next goal is STAR in Japan.

Michael Jeffreys is a motivational speaker and the author of four books, including *Selling with Magic, Speaking with Magic* and his latest, *America's Greatest Speakers Reveal Their Secrets*. In it, he interviewed the top 24 motivational speakers in the country, including Anthony Robbins, Zig Ziglar, Wayne Dyer, Barbara De Angelis, Brian Tracy, Denis Waitley, Jack Canfield and Mark Victor Hansen. Michael can be reached at Powerful Magic Publishing, 1516 Purdue Avenue #7, Los Angeles, CA 90025, or by calling 310-473-6291.

Rud Kendall was born in Winnipeg, Manitoba. Rud spent many years trucking throughout Canada's rugged northern territories. He also worked as an oilfield roughneck, a miner, a pipeliner and on various heavy construction projects, as well as serving in the Royal Canadian Navy as a boatswain's mate. After working as a newspaper reporter in Dawson Creek, B.C. (Mile 0 of the famous Alaska Highway), he became a freelance writer. Today he is the owner of a small communications company in Langley, B.C.

Casey Kokoska lives in Rosenberg, Texas. Although she is only 16, she has written several stories. Her pastimes are writing and performing. She has won several awards and a scholarship for her prose interpretations at speech and debating contests. She hopes to major in theater and is writing her first novel. Her goal is to become a best-selling writer and an actress.

Kathy Lamancusa is a dynamic professional speaker, author and television personality. She travels nationally and internationally each year, creatively touching the lives of her audiences. Her topics include family lifestyle, creativity and creative skills. Over 1 million copies of her books and videos have been sold throughout the world. Kathy has a column in several national and international consumer magazines. Her show, *Kathy Lamancusa's at Home with Flowers*, appears on PBS stations around the country. You can contact her at Lamancusa Live! Kathy Lamancusa, P.O. Box 2717CHX, North Canton, OH 44720, or call 216-494-7224, or fax 216-494-2918.

Michelle Lawrence is a corporate publicist, specializing in media relations. She works with a variety of clients and public relations agencies in Southern California and throughout the country. Michelle happily resides with her advertising executive/poet husband, Ron, and their two wonderful children, Almierose and Dylan, in Bel Air, California.

Patricia Lorenz is an inspirational writer, columnist, writing teacher and speaker. Of her articles and stories, 400 have appeared in over 70 publications, including *Reader's Digest, Guideposts, Working Mother* and *Single-Parent Family*. She is the author of the book *Stuff That Matters for Single Parents*, published by Servant Publications in Ann Arbor, Michigan. You can write to her at 7547 S. Pennsylvania Avenue, Oak Creek, WI 53154.

Julie A. Manhan is a native of Reno, Nevada, and is the theology department chairperson, campus minister and retreat director at St. Vincent de Paul High School in Petaluma, California. She is a graduate of Seattle University. Though she has taught all levels, from pre-school though college, working with teenagers is her first love. Her stories are an integral part of her teaching and retreat ministry. She can be reached at 707-763-1032.

Marilyn Manning, Ph.D., CSP, international speaker, trainer and conflict mediator, is the author of five books, including *The NAFE Guide to Starting Your Own Business* (1995) and *Leadership Skills for Women* (in six languages, over 30,000 copies sold). Dr. Manning speaks on managing conflict and change, team rebuilding, using stress positively, and the seven laws of leadership. She has run her own consulting firm for 16 years and is past president of the National Speakers Association, Northern California. She can be reached at 945 Mountain View Avenue, Mountain View, CA 94040, or by calling 415-965-3663; fax 415-965-3668; e-mail: DRMMANNING@aol.com.

Elaine McDonald, a former journalist and a mother of two, is now an attorney in Des Moines, Iowa. She can be reached at 4932 Ashley Park Drive, West Des Moines, IA 50265.

Robert J. McMullen Jr. is a retired Presbyterian minister. After duty as a pilot in World War II with missions over Germany, he served churches in West Virginia, suburban Washington, D.C., Atlanta and Charlotte. He and his wife, Becky, have three children, one of whom has cerebral palsy. That has been a liberal education! In addition to occasional preaching and teaching, he has written for *Guideposts* and his local newspaper. He may be reached at 5150 Sharon Road, Charlotte, NC 28210, or by calling 704-553-0603.

David Naster is a nationally known comedian. His numerous major television appearances and national tours reflect his uncanny ability to share his humor with people of all ages and flavors. David travels throughout the world sharing his Your Sense of Humor Will Get You Through It keynote. Writing children's stories is David's latest passion and is soon to turn into a published dream. Please feel free to contact him at 12317 W. 79th Place, Lenexa, KS 66215, or call 913-438-4722.

Omar Periu is a successful public speaker, trainer, business owner, sales executive, lyricist, recording star and performer. A member of the National Speakers Association, Omar became a self-made millionaire at the age of 31. He has trained hundreds of thousands of salespeople, sales managers, entrepreneurs, executives and business owners in how to succeed in today's business and sales environments. Omar was assisted early in his career, and as such his main purpose in life is to help others achieve greatness. You can reach him by writing Tom Hopkins International, Inc., PO Box 1969, Scottsdale, AZ 85252, or by calling 602-949-1590.

Kathleen Podolsky is a photographer whose works have been exhibited in the U.S. and abroad. Worldwide travel with her physician-writer husband has exposed her to different cultures, customs and traditions and has given her a keen understanding of diverse peoples. Many of Kathleen's experiences have been documented on film as well as in short stories.

Barbara Rogoff is a writer and co-creator of Beyond Survival into Triumph, a workshop for adult survivors of abuse. Barbara and her partner, Dr. Patricia Bell, have been invited to train other therapists in using their experiential techniques at the World Congress of Logotherapists in Dallas. Barbara is currently developing a prison ministry that incorporates some of these methods to help inmates find hope and move into personal freedom. Barbara lives in Stilwell, Kansas, with her husband and best friend of 19 years, Gary. She can be reached at The Unity Church of Overland Park in Kansas; phone 913-649-6825 extension 3033.

David Roth is a singer, songwriter, recording artist (five albums), conference presenter and emcee, humorist, playwright *(The Grapes of Wroth)* and workshop facilitator (Singing for Shy People). His song "Rising in Love" was performed at the 100th anniversary of Carnegie Hall, the same season he first sang the national anthem for the NBA's Chicago Bulls. The story of Manuel Garcia was reported by William Janz in the *Milwaukee Sentinel*, and the song can be found on David's first recording, *Rising in Love*. He can be reached by writing 18952 40th Place NE, Seattle, WA 98155, or by calling 800-484-2367 extension 3283.

Richard Ryan is a pastor, recording artist, actor and inspirational writer. An award-winning vocalist and director of the regionally acclaimed vocal ensemble *ONE VOICE,* he travels frequently in solo and group concert ministry. His solo recordings *Love Found a Way* and *Promises* and the ensemble's *ONE VOICE in Praise* have received nationwide attention. His story, "The Day I Met Daniel," was the first-prize winner in *The Christian Reader* magazine's 1995 Writing Contest. He and his wife, Cathy, have three children and live in New Albany, Indiana. For recordings or concert information, write him at the Old Capitol United Methodist Church, 141 Heidelberg Road West, Corydon, IN 47112, or call 812-738-4736.

Dan Schaeffer is Andrew, Christi and Katie's dad. He has been married to their mother, Annette, for the "13 best years of my life." He is also pastor of Foothills Evangelical Free Church in Rancho Santa Margarita, California. He is the author of *Dancing with a Shadow, Making Sense of the Silence of God* and most recently, *The Bush Won't Burn for Me, and I'm All Out of Matches.*

Frank Slazak learned some important lessons in life by losing a dream. In 1985, Frank had an opportunity to compete in NASA's Teacher in Space program. Despite his best efforts, he was not chosen in the final process. A teacher named Christa McAuliffe was chosen. On January 28, 1986, the Challenger exploded just 73 seconds after liftoff, killing all seven members on board. Frank Slazak won because he lost. Today, Frank has the privilege of speaking to audiences throughout the world about the lessons that can be derived from such an experience. His emotional presentations focus on the triumphs of the human spirit, the power of faith and the hero that is found in each of us. Frank has become known as the speaker that "speaks from the heart."

Peter Spelke is an adventurer, a truth seeker and an inspirational speaker. Aside from his business pursuits, Pete volunteers his time feeding the homeless and working with inmates in the federal prison system. He can be reached at 115 Deep Valley Drive, Stamford, CT 06903.

Jana Stanfield's music has been described as "sonic soup for the soul." With songs like "I'm Not Lost, I'm Exploring," "U.B.U., I.M.E." and "What Is Mine Will Find Me," her five "heavy-mental" albums express her positive outlook. Her lyrics have been sung by Reba McEntire, Andy Williams and others. As a performer, she has shared stages with Deepak Chopra, Wayne Dyer, Bernie Siegel and Les Brown. From concert halls to kindergartens to conventions, she fills her keynote concerts with songs that speak volumes about this adventure called "life." Jana Stanfield can be reached at P.O. Box 60146, Nashville, TN 37206, or by calling 615-226-4764.

Dr. Roger William Thomas has been the preaching minister of First Christian Church since the fall of 1993. Roger is a native of McLean County, Illinois. He is a graduate of Lincoln Christian College and Seminary. His Doctorate of Ministry degree is from Northern Baptist Theological Seminary. Roger has served as preacher, campus minister and Bible college teacher in Illinois, Missouri and Oklahoma. He is also the author of six books and hundreds of magazine and journal articles on a variety of topics related to the Christian faith and scripture.

Renee R. Vroman lives in Vancouver, Washington, with her husband of 26 years and is the proud mother of three sons, Jay, Trent and Trevor. After helping put her husband and sons through college, she took the plunge herself and is currently a senior (in more ways than one!) at Washington State University, Vancouver, majoring in psychology. "The Gift" is her first published work. She may be reached at 13901 NE 7th Circle, Vancouver, WA 98684, or by calling 360-256-6984.

Angie K. Ward-Kucer is a senior operator with the Sarpy County E-911 Center and resides in Papillion, Nebraska, with her husband, John Andrew. "The Coolest Dad in the Universe" is her first story and was written as a tribute to her late father, Thomas Wesley Ward Sr., so that other fathers may learn from his simple acts of love and realize that even as their children become adults, they still need their daddy. She can be reached at 514 S. Monroe Street, Papillion, NE 68046, or by calling 402-331-7687.

Bettie B. Youngs is a former Iowa farm girl and is now a California resident and worldly citizen. Her passions revolve around her mission of increasing our sense of the important role parents and families have in laying the foundation for the value, purpose and meaning we assign to our lives. Bettie is a professional speaker, a consultant to parents, schools and organizations, and the author of 12 books published in 24 countries. Bettie may be contacted at 3060 Racetrack View Drive, Del Mar, CA 92014, or by calling 619-481-6360.

Permissions *(continued from page iv)*

A Secret Promise Kept. Reprinted by permission of *The Middlesex News.* ©1993 Brian Keefe.

A Sandpiper to Bring You Joy. Reprinted with permission from the June, 1980 *Reader's Digest.* ©1979 The Reader's Digest Association, Inc. Originally appeared in *Our Family,* October 1979.

The Most Caring Child. Reprinted from *The Best of Bits & Pieces* by permission of The Economics Press, Inc. ©1994 The Economics Press, Inc.

Information Please. Reprinted with permission from the June, 1966 *Reader's Digest.* ©1966 by The Reader's Digest Association, Inc.

Two Nickels and Five Pennies. Reprinted from *The Best of Bits & Pieces* by permission of The Economics Press, Inc. ©1994 The Economics Press, Inc.

The Ice Cream Girl. Reprinted by permission of Marion Schoeberlein. ©1995 Marion Schoeberlein.

How Magic Helped a Blind Girl See and *A Life-Changing Experience.* Reprinted by permission of Michael Jeffreys. ©1995 Michael Jeffreys.

The Horai Box. Reprinted by permission of Kathleen Podolsky. ©1990 Kathleen Podolsky.

Manuel Garcia. Reprinted by permission of David Roth. ©1986 David Roth.

A Taste of Freedom. Reprinted by permission of Barbara Rogoff. ©1994 Barbara Rogoff.

Compassion Is in the Eyes. Reprinted from *The Sower's Seeds* by permission of Paulist Press. ©1994 Brian Cavanaugh.

Warm in Your Heart. Reprinted by permission of Mastermedia Book Publishing. ©1995 Scott Gross.

An Act of Kindness. Reprinted from *The Best of Bits & Pieces* by permission of The Economics Press, Inc. ©1994 The Economics Press, Inc.

Two Families. Reprinted by permission of *Guideposts Magazine.* ©1983 by Guideposts, Carmel, NY 10572.

Guests in the Night. Reprinted by permission of Robert Gass. ©1995 Robert Gass.

An Afternoon in the Park. Reprinted by permission of Julie A. Manhan. ©1995 Julie A. Manhan.

The Little Boy and the Old Man. Reprinted by permission of HarperCollins Publishers from *A Light in the Attic.* ©1981 by Evil Eye Music, Inc.

Teddy Bear. Written by Dale Royal, Tommy Hill, Red Sovine and J. William Denny. ©1976 Cedarwood Publishing. Used by Permission. All Rights Reserved.

Paco, Come Home. Reprinted by permission of Alan Cohen. ©1995 Alan Cohen.

Tommy's Essay. Reprinted by permission of Jane Lindstrom. ©1975 Jane Lindstrom.

Almie Rose. Reprinted by permission of Michelle Lawrence. ©1995 Michelle Lawrence.

Why I Wear a Plastic Dinosaur. Reprinted from *Pursuit Magazine* by permission of Dan Schaeffer. ©1993 Dan Schaeffer.

The Coolest Dad in the Universe. Reprinted by permission of Angie K. Ward-Kucer. ©1995 Angie K. Ward-Kucer.

Workin' Man. Reprinted by permission of International Union of Operating Engineers.

No Charge. Reprinted by permission of M. Adams. ©1995 M. Adams.

Recognize Your Winners. From TEAMTHINK by Donald E. Martin. Used by permission of Dutton Signet, a division of Penguin Books USA Inc.

Courage of the Heart. Reprinted by permission of Patty Hansen. ©1995 Patty Hansen.

What It Means to Be Adopted. Reprinted from *The Best of Bits & Pieces* by permission of The Economics Press. ©1994 The Economics Press.

Class Reunion. Reprinted by permission of Lynne C. Gaul. ©1995 Lynne C. Gaul.

The Gift. Reprinted by permission of Renee R. Vroman. ©1995 Renee Vroman.

To Beth's First-Grade Teacher. Reprinted by permission of Dick Abrahamson. ©1984 Dick Abrahamson.

Mr. Washington. Reprinted from *Mentors, Masters and Mrs. MacGregor* by permission of Health Communications, Inc. ©1995 Jane Bluestein.

Faith, Hope and Love. Reprinted by permission of Peter Spelke. ©1995 Peter Spelke.

The Shoes. Reprinted by permission of the National Education Association by Paul E. Mawhinney, head, Division of Education and Psychology, Southeast Missouri State College, Cape Girardeau, Missouri. ©1966, *NEA Journal.*

Bonehead. Reprinted by permission of Larry Terherst. ©1995 Larry Terherst.

Footprints on My Heart. Reprinted by permission of Laura D. Norton. ©1995 Laura D. Norton.

The Golden Crane. Reprinted from *Mature Outlook* by permission of Patricia Lorenz. ©1994 Patricia Lorenz.

If I Had Only Known. By Craig Morris and Jana Stanfield. ©1991, Alabama Band Music (a division of Wildcountry, Inc.)/Jana Stantunes. Used by permission. All rights reserved.

A Trucker's Last Letter. Reprinted by permission of Rud Kendall. ©1983 Rud Kendall.

For the Love of a Child. Reprinted by permission of Thea Alexander. ©1995 Thea Alexander.

The Last Dance. Reprinted by permission of Rick Nelles. ©1995 Rick Nelles.

My Daddy. Reprinted by permission of Kelly J. Watkins. ©1995 Kelly J. Watkins.

Where Do the Sparrows Go When They Die? Reprinted by permission of Casey Kokoska. ©1995 Casey Kokoska.

The Courage Not to Fight. Reprinted with permission from *Guideposts Magazine.* ©1991 by *Guideposts,* Carmel, NY 10512.

Please Dress Me in Red. Reprinted by permission of Cindy Dee Holms. ©1995 Cindy Dee Holms.

Don't Worry, It'll Be Alright. Reprinted by permission of Janice Hunt. ©1995 Janice Hunt.

The Eternal Optimist. Reprinted by permission of Beth Dalton. ©1995 Beth Dalton.

To Remember Me. Reprinted by permission of Andre Test. ©Robert N. Test.

Keep Your Fork. Reprinted by permission of Roger William Thomas. ©1994 Roger William Thomas.

There Are No Wheelchairs in Heaven. Reprinted by permission of D. Trinidad Hunt. ©1995 D. Trinidad Hunt.

The Cookie Thief. Reprinted by permission of Valerie Cox. ©1993 Valerie Cox.

The True Story of Arbutus and Sea Gull. Reprinted from *The Boston Globe.*

Lady, Are You Rich? Reprinted from *The Bigness of the Fellow Within* by Dr. B. J. Palmer, by permission of Palmer College of Chiropractic.

The Flower in Her Hair. Reprinted by permission of Bettie B. Youngs. ©1995 Bettie B. Youngs.

Avalanche. Reprinted by permission of Robert G. Allen. ©1995 Robert G. Allen.

You Very Good; You Very Fast. Reprinted by permission of Kathi M. Curry. ©1995 Kathi M. Curry.

The Accident. Reprinted by permission of Robert J. McMullen Jr. ©1995 Robert J. McMullen Jr.

From the Mouth of a Small Boy. Reprinted by permission of Elaine McDonald. ©1995 Elaine McDonald.

I Won Because I Lost. Reprinted by permission of Frank Slazak. ©1995 Frank Slazak.

Whiners. Reprinted from *Wouldn't Take Nothing for My Journey Now* by permission of Random House. ©1993 Maya Angelou.

Great Value in Disaster. Reprinted from *The Sower's Seeds* by permission of Paulist Press. ©1994 Brian Cavanaugh.

Good News. Reprinted from *The Best of Bits & Pieces* by permission of The Economics Press. ©1994 The Economics Press.

When We're Alone, We Can Dance. Reprinted by permission of Beth Ashley. ©1987 Beth Ashley.

Johnny. Reprinted by permission of Barbara A. Glanz. ©1995 Barbara A. Glanz.

TEXT EXCERPT AS SUBMITTED from *I Can't Accept Not Trying* by MICHAEL JORDAN and PHOTOGRAPHS BY SANDRO MILLER. ©1994 by Rare Air, Ltd. Text ©1994 by Michael Jordan. Reprinted by permission of HarperCollins Publishers, Inc.

The Passionate Pursuit of Possibility. Reprinted by permission of James E. Conner. ©1984 James E. Conner.

Player of the Game. Reprinted with permission from the February, 1995 *Reader's Digest.* ©1995 by The Reader's Digest Association, Inc.

We Never Told Him He Couldn't Do It. Reprinted by permission of Kathy Lamancusa. ©1995 Kathy Lamancusa.

A Lesson in Heart. Reprinted by permission of Stan Frager. ©1995 Stan Frager.

Fourteen Steps. First published in the *Ensign* Magazine of The Church of Jesus Christ of Latter-day Saints. Used by permission.

My Body Was Turning to Stone. Reprinted with permission of *McCall's* Magazine. ©1995 by Gruner & Jahr USA Publishing.

The Beauty Remains; the Pain Passes. Reprinted from *The Best of Bits & Pieces* by permission of The Economics Press. ©1994 The Economics Press.

The Miracle Bridge. Reprinted from *A Fresh Packet of Sower's Seeds* by permission of Paulist Press. ©1994 Brian Cavanaugh.

True Height. Reprinted by permission of David Naster. ©1995 David Naster.

Opportunity. Reprinted by permission of Omar Periu. ©1995 Omar Periu.

Crusader Could Close Her Eyes to Trouble No More. Reprinted from *The Virginia Pilot & Ledger-Star.* ©1995 *The Virginian Pilot & Ledger-Star.*

Ask, Affirm, Take Action. Reprinted by permission of Claudette Hunter. ©1995 Claudette Hunter.

The Impossible Just Takes a Little Longer. Reprinted by permission of Art E. Berg. ©1995 Art E. Berg.

The Day I Met Daniel. Reprinted by permission of Rev. Richard Ryan from *The Christian Reader.* ©1995 Rev. Richard Ryan.

God's Jobs. Reprinted from Christ Church, St. Michaels, Maryland.

The Wisdom of One Word. Reprinted by permission of John F. Demartini. ©1995 John F. Demartini.

The Secrets of Heaven and Hell. Reprinted by permission of Fr. John W. Groff Jr. An excerpt from "A Proper Hell." Published in the July/September 1994 issue of *Christian*New Age Quarterly,* P.O. Box 276, Clifton, NJ 07011-0276.

What Courage Looks Like. Reprinted by permission of Casey Hawley. ©1995 Casey Hawley.

Angel with a Red Hat. Reprinted by permission of Tami Fox. ©1995 Tami Fox.

It's Never Too Late. Reprinted by permission of Marilyn Manning, Ph.D. ©1995 Marilyn Manning, Ph.D.

The Station. Reprinted by permission from *The Station and Other Gems of Joy* by Robert J. Hastings.

Share the Magic of Chicken Soup

Chicken Soup for the Soul™
101 Stories to Open the Heart and Rekindle the Spirit

The #1 *New York Times* bestseller and ABBY award-winning inspirational book that has touched the lives of millions. Whether you buy it for yourself or as a gift to others, you're sure to enrich the lives of everyone around you with this affordable treasure.

Code 262X: Paperback $12.95
Code 2913: Hardcover $24.00
Code 3812: Large print $16.95

A 2nd Helping of Chicken Soup for the Soul™
101 More Stories to Open the Heart and Rekindle the Spirit

This rare sequel accomplishes the impossible—it is as tasty as the original, and still fat-free. If you enjoyed the first *Chicken Soup for the Soul* be warned: it was merely the first course in an uplifting grand buffet. These stories will leave you satisfied and full of self-esteem, love and compassion.

Code 3316: Paperback $12.95
Code 3324: Hardcover $24.00
Code 3820: Large print $16.95

A 3rd Serving of Chicken Soup for the Soul™
101 More Stories to Open the Heart and Rekindle the Spirit

The latest addition to the *Chicken Soup for the Soul* series is guaranteed to put a smile in your heart. Learn through others the important lessons of love, parenting, forgiveness, hope and perseverance. This tasty literary stew will stay with you long after you've put the book down.

Code 3790: Paperback $12.95
Code 3804: Hardcover $24.00
Code 4002: Large print. $16.95

Available at your favorite bookstore or call
1-800-441-5569 for Visa or MasterCard orders. Prices do not include shipping and handling. Your response code is **HCI**.

Extra Helpings of Chicken Soup

Chicken Soup for the Soul™ Cookbook
Stories and Recipes from the Heart

Here authors Jack Canfield and Mark Victor Hansen have teamed up with award-winning cookbook author Diana von Welanetz Wentworth and dished up a delightful collection of stories accompanied by mouthwatering recipes.

Code 3545: Paperback $16.95
Code 3634: Hardcover $29.95

Sopa de pollo para el alma
(Spanish Language Version)
Relatos que conmueven el corazón y ponen fuego en el espíritu

The national bestseller and 1995 ABBY Award winner *Chicken Soup for the Soul* is now available in a lovingly prepared Spanish language edition. The stories found in *Sopa de pollo para el alma* are as rich as mole sauce and as robust and invigorating as café Cubano.

Code 3537: Paperback $12.95

Chicken Soup for the Surviving Soul
101 Stories to Comfort Cancer Patients and Their Loved Ones

For years, the uplifting stories in the *Chicken Soup for the Soul* series have empowered individuals who have serious illnesses. Now Jack Canfield and Mark Victor Hansen have joined with Patty Aubery and Nancy Mitchell for a special batch of *Chicken Soup* devoted to stories of people beating cancer and finding renewed meaning in their lives.

Code 4029: Paperback $12.95
Code 4037: Hardcover $24.00

Available at your favorite bookstore or call 1-800-441-5569 for Visa or MasterCard orders. Prices do not include shipping and handling. Your response code is HCI.